Business and Industry

EDITORS

William R. Childs
Scott B. Martin
Wanda Stitt-Gohdes

VOLUME 2

BUSINESS CYCLE
to COPYRIGHT

MARSHALL CAVENDISH

NEW YORK · TORONTO · LONDON · SYDNEY

Marshall Cavendish
99 White Plains Road
Tarrytown, New York 10591-9001

www.marshallcavendish.com

Library of Congress Cataloging-in-Publication Data

Business and industry / editors, William R. Childs, Scott B. Martin, Wanda Stitt-Gohdes.
    p. cm.
  Includes bibliographical reference and index.
  Contents: v. 1. Accounting and bookkeeping to Burnett, Leo--v. 2. Business Cycle to Copyright--
v. 3. Corporate Governance to Entrepreneurship--v. 4. Environmentalism to Graham,
Katherine--v.5. Great Depression to Internship--v. 6. Inventory to Merrill Lynch--
v. 7. Microeconomics to Philip Morris Companies--v. 8. Price Controls to Sarnoff, David--
v. 9. Savings and Investment Options to Telecommuting--v. 10. Temporary Workers to Yamaha--
v. 11. Index volume
   ISBN 0-7614-7430-7 (set)--ISBN 0-7614-7432-3 (v. 2)
     1. Business--Encyclopedias. 2. Industries--Encyclopedias. I. Childs, William R., 1951-II. Martin,
Scott B., 1961-III. Stitt-Gohdes, Wanda.

HF1001 .B796 2003
338'.003--dc21   2002035156

Printed in Italy

06 05 04 03 5 4 3 2 1

MARSHALL CAVENDISH
Editorial Director   Paul Bernabeo
Production Manager   Alan Tsai

Produced by The Moschovitis Group, Inc.

THE MOSCHOVITIS GROUP
President, Publishing Division   Valerie Tomaselli
Executive Editor   Hilary W. Poole
Associate Editor   Sonja Matanovic
Design and Layout   Annemarie Redmond
Illustrator   Richard Garratt
Assistant Illustrator   Zahiyya Abdul-Karim
Photo Research   Gillian Speeth
Production Associates   K. Nura Abdul-Karim, Rashida Allen
Editorial Assistants   Christina Campbell, Nicole Cohen, Jessica Rosin
Copyediting   Carole Campbell
Proofreading   Paul Scaramazza
Indexing   AEIOU, Inc.

Alphabetical Table of Contents

PHOTO CREDITS

Business Cycles

Business cycles involve patterns of expansion and contraction in employment, production, and price levels that occur in an economy over time. Consider the biggest dip in U.S. economic history, the Great Depression. Between 1929 and 1932, stock prices as measured by the Dow Jones Industrial Average fell about 89 percent and did not recover their value for many years. Unemployment soared from 7.7 million in 1937 to 10.4 million in 1938, an increase in the unemployment rate from 14 to 19 percent in one year, and this was eight years after the stock market crash. Bank failures climbed from 167 in 1920 to more than 4,000 in 1933. Indeed, the country lost about one-half of all commercial banks to bankruptcy during the Depression. Industrial production also declined sharply. Factories produced at about one-half of their capacity, and investment in new equipment collapsed from $16 billion to less than $1 billion.

Business cycles affect the economies of all nations. Since World War II, the United States has experienced nine business cycle contractions and expansions. Fluctuations in business activity are repetitive, and cycles in the United States affect other economies as well—from Japan, Great Britain, Germany, and Brazil to Canada, Indonesia, South Korea, and Italy.

Debates on Business Cycles

Business cycles have many names and competing explanations for their occurrence: observed patterns include Kitchin's 40-month cycle, Juglar's 8-year cycle, or Kondratieff's 50-year waves. Some experts explain cycles by looking at the fluctuations of inventories; others identify changes in the level of investment in capital technology as the cause. In general, economists rely on two broad schools of thought when trying to understand fluctuations in the business cycle: the classical school and the Keynesian school.

Classical thinkers assume the economy obeys the laws of supply and demand. Markets work to bring themselves into balance. Price fluctuations reflect real changes in the economy and, if allowed to operate freely, provide enough information to savers and investors so that saving and investment decisions promote stability. According to this school of thought, business cycles are

See also:
Great Depression;
Gross Domestic Product;
Keynes, John Maynard;
Macroeconomics;
Unemployment.

In March 1939, during the Great Depression, people wait in line to receive food from a relief program in San Antonio, Texas.

self-correcting unless misguided government economic policies make matters worse.

The classical formulation holds that economies tend toward long-run stability in employment, prices, and output, because what is manufactured generates sufficient income to be taken off the market. Supply creates its own demand. Gluts and shortage are temporary and actually perform usef signaling functions in a decentralized, sel regulating system that continuously adjus itself. Ineffective tax hikes and disruptive tir kering with monetary policy exacerbate th fluctuations in business cycles. The Depressio

U.S. Business Cycles 1854 to 2001					
Business cycle dates		**Duration in months**			
Trough	Peak	Recession	Expansion	Cycle	
		Trough from previous peak	Trough to peak	Trough from previous trough	Peak from previous peak
December 1854	June 1857	–	30	–	–
December 1858	October 1860	18	22	48	40
June 1861	April 1865	8	46	30	54
December 1867	June 1869	32	18	78	50
December 1870	October 1873	18	34	36	52
March 1879	March 1882	65	36	99	101
May 1885	March 1887	38	22	74	60
April 1888	July 1890	13	27	35	40
May 1891	January 1893	10	20	37	30
June 1894	December 1895	17	18	37	35
June 1897	June 1899	18	24	36	42
December 1900	September 1902	18	21	42	39
August 1904	May 1907	23	33	44	56
June 1908	January 1910	13	19	46	32
January 1912	January 1913	24	12	43	36
December 1914	August 1918	23	44	35	67
March 1919	January 1920	7	10	51	17
July 1921	May 1923	18	22	28	40
July 1924	October 1926	14	27	36	41
November 1927	August 1929	13	21	40	34
March 1933	May 1937	43	50	64	93
June 1938	February 1945	13	80	63	93
October 1945	November 1948	8	37	88	45
October 1949	July 1953	11	45	48	56
May 1954	August 1957	10	39	55	49
April 1958	April 1960	8	24	47	32
February 1961	December 1969	10	106	34	116
November 1970	November 1973	11	36	117	47
March 1975	January 1980	16	58	52	74
July 1980	July 1981	6	12	64	18
November 1982	July 1990	16	92	28	108
March 1991	March 2001	8	120	100	128

The duration of the peaks and valleys of business cycles.

Note: Figures printed in red are wartime expansions (Civil War, World War I and II, Korean War, and Vietnam War), the postwar contractions, and the full cycles that include the wartime expansions.
Sources: National Bureau of Economic Research and the U.S. Department of Commerce, *Survey of Current Business,* Washington, D.C., Government Printing Office, 2002.

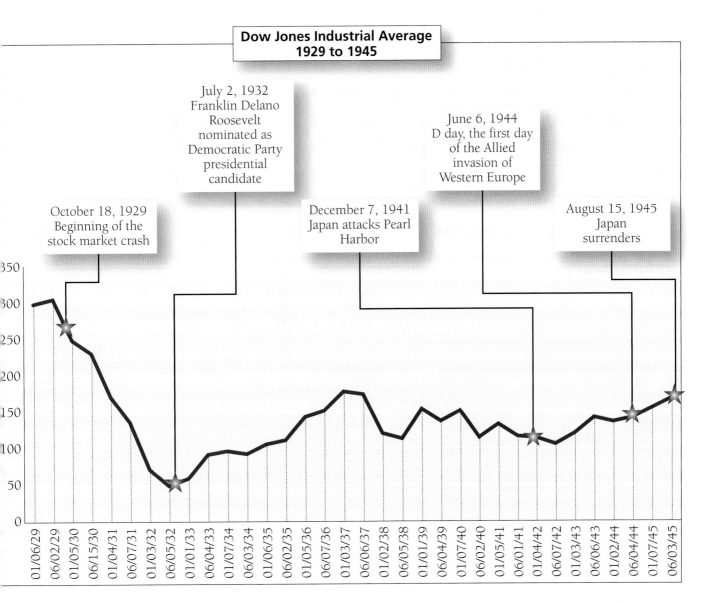

**Dow Jones Industrial Average
1929 to 1945**

July 2, 1932
Franklin Delano Roosevelt nominated as Democratic Party presidential candidate

June 6, 1944
D day, the first day of the Allied invasion of Western Europe

October 18, 1929
Beginning of the stock market crash

December 7, 1941
Japan attacks Pearl Harbor

August 15, 1945
Japan surrenders

according to the classical school, was made much worse by the bad timing of tax increases, cuts in the money supply, and enormous increases in tariffs.

By contrast, British economist John Maynard Keynes claimed that capitalism was chronically ill. The illness predisposed the economy toward instability in prices, output, and employment. The sickness of capitalism was attributable in part to the disconnected nature of the plans of savers and investors. Mismatches in savings and investment decisions could become a source of long-term disruption for the real economy of goods and services and for production, distribution, and consumption. Acknowledging some of the self-correcting market tendencies described by the classical school, followers of Keynes believed that some sort of governmental

demand-management policies were required to keep capitalism healthy. According to this line of thinking, an optimal combination of monetary and fiscal policy would promote stability in the labor and financial markets during periodic imbalances. To make good savings and investment decisions, individuals and businesses needed help and assistance from the public sector.

Stocks and Cycles

An important question emerges in the course of this argument between the classical and Keynesian schools. What is the relationship between stock market fluctuations and the real economy of jobholders who make consumption decisions and savers who make investment decisions? Studies indicate stock prices do affect consumption and investment

Experts often look to the stock market when analyzing business cycles. This chart shows the activity of the Dow Jones Industrial Average during the Great Depression and World War II.

As stock values continued to slide during the recession that began in 2001, trader Robert Schwartz signals a trade in the Nasdaq 100 stock index futures pit at the Chicago Mercantile Exchange.

decisions, but only slightly. A 10 percent sustained increase in stock market values in one year is associated with a 4 percent increase in consumption spending during the next three years. The connection between investment spending and stock values is even weaker.

Apparently, however, stock market bubbles matter much more. When the prices of shares outstrip the underlying value of the issuer, as happened in the 1990s, it can cause serious problems in the real economy. Stock market bubbles are the product of unbridled optimism (reflected in the popular misconception that recessions are a thing of the past in the new economy), frenzied speculation (the dot-com craze), or just plain "irrational exuberance," as Federal Reserve chairman Alan Greenspan asserted. Falling stock prices can wreak havoc as workers are laid off, consumption plans postponed, and investment projects cancelled. The intoxicating euphoria of the run-up is replaced by the hangover of gloom and doom.

Can stock market prices predict changes in the business cycle? The answer is uncertain. Insofar as stock price indexes like the New York Stock Exchange Index or the Standard and Poor's 500 Index accurately measure the mood of the investment community, they may be said to show some kind of connection between stock market and business cycle fluctuations. However, the precise connection is unclear. Most of the American recessions since 1945 were preceded by general decreases in

stock price measures. Yet stock market prices alone do not always predict recessions. Stock market indexes sometimes fall sharply without being followed by a business cycle downturn, as was the case in 1987 when a 508-point drop in the Dow Jones Industrial Average was not followed immediately by a downturn in the economy. Although the exact connection is unclear, the general level of stock prices is deemed important enough to be included in the government's top 10 leading economic indicators that, taken together, may predict future directions of business activity.

The economists' quarrel over the causes of business cycles has become increasingly important. Substantial differences result when the government does little or nothing, on the one hand, or adjusts taxes and spending levels to mitigate the effects of a recession, on the other. These policy choices matter a great deal. Business cycles in the United States, Japan, Venezuela, and the European Union are increasingly interconnected as globalization brings markets closer together. The United States committed itself to achieving full employment and stable prices in the Full Employment Act of 1946 and in its subsequent amendments; dealing with the business cycle is the law of the land. So, in addition to being the subject of debate between economists, the roller coaster ride of the business cycle is important to people concerned with their jobs or with how far their paychecks will take them during the ride.

Further Reading

Dow, Christopher. *Major Recessions: Britain and the World, 1920–1995.* Oxford: Oxford University Press, 1998.

Hall, Thomas, and J. David Ferguson. *The Great Depression: An International Disaster of Perverse Economic Policies.* Ann Arbor: University of Michigan Press, 2001.

McConnell, Campbell R., and Stanley L. Brue. *Economics: Principles, Problems, and Policies.* Boston: McGraw-Hill Irwin, 2002.

Tvede, Lars. *Business Cycles: The Business Cycle Problem from John Law to Chaos Theory.* Amsterdam: Harwood Academic Publishers, 1997.

Zarnowitz, Victor. *Business Cycles: Theory, History, Indicators, and Forecasting.* Chicago: University of Chicago Press, 1992.

—*Stephen Haessler*

Business Ethics

A product designer considers making public the fact that the company he works for has decided to manufacture a product that could have dangerous defects. A government purchasing manager considers awarding an important contract to a high bidder because he has made investments in that bidder's company. A chief executive officer (CEO), concerned about his corporation's decreased competitiveness, contemplates moving operations to a foreign county with cheaper labor, which would result in the layoff of thousands of his company's U.S. employees.

These situations all involve businesspeople making decisions about actions that have an ethical dimension. These individuals have moral choices to make, choices that involve business ethics. Ethics is a branch of philosophy that examines moral judgments and the principles underlying those judgments. Business ethics is a form of applied ethics: it considers how ethical principles influence business judgments and vice versa. On a more practical level, a code of business ethics helps businesspeople to distinguish right behavior from wrong and to practice doing right at the same time that they fulfill their functions in the world of business.

Present-day business decisions cannot be made without some consideration of their ethical dimensions. CEOs, mid-level managers, professional staff, and factory and plant workers are all confronted with choices every day; their decisions may affect an entire corporation, industry, or community. Despite media reports that tend to revel in the scandalous behavior inside the largest corporations, the image of business as completely unconcerned about and unconstrained by moral considerations is not true. The smooth functioning of business requires that shareholders and managers, employers and employees, sellers and buyers, and corporations and the communities in which they are based engage in relationships of trust with one another. Businesses suffer when those relationships of trust are damaged by questionable or unethical practices, as evidenced by the decline of the U.S. stock market in 2002, when investors were made wary—and poorer—by the shady business dealings and accounting practices of large corporations, including Enron, Tyco International, Ltd., and WorldCom.

Key Issues in Business Ethics

Business ethics is a vast field that examines business practices from a variety of perspectives. Often, it involves the application of philosophical theories like utilitarianism, which says that ethical actions are those that result in the greatest good for the greatest number of people. Another important principle used in business ethics is Kant's categorical imperative, which identifies ethical acts as those whose rules the

See also:
Business Law; Corporate Governance; Corporate Social Responsibility; Environmentalism; Multinational Corporation.

Areas of Business Affected by Ethics

Area affected	Examples
Employee–employer relations	Fair and just wages
	Hiring and promotion
	Workplace safety
	Monitoring of employees
Corporate relations with suppliers and customers	Fair contracts
	Honestly performed contracts
	Fair and reasonable pricing of goods
Corporate relations with society at large	Truthful advertising
	Impact on environment
	Impact on welfare of community
	Influence on political and international affairs

The philosopher Immanuel Kant's theory of the categorical imperative is the basis for many aspects of business ethics.

actor would want willed into universal law. It asks: What would happen if everyone did that? For instance, a manager who bribes foreign officials to secure tax breaks for his company might justify the act by arguing that bribery is the only way to do business in that country, and that bribery has allowed him to increase profits for the company's shareholders—a duty with which he has been entrusted as agent for those shareholders. However, a universal law that allowed everyone to use bribery to serve the special interests of his or her employer would significantly impede business; thus in this application of Kant's theory, bribery cannot be considered ethical behavior.

While these and other philosophical principles form the basis of many arguments about and discussions of business ethics, business ethicists investigate such a wide array of issues that it is impossible to formulate one theory that can be successfully applied to all situations. In one area, business ethics considers the rights and responsibilities of employers in relation to employees. Key questions include: What constitutes fair and just wages, hiring and promotion practices, and monitoring of employees? To what extent is an employer obliged to protect employees' health, safety, and right to privacy, and what responsibility do employers have to prevent sexual harassment or discrimination in the workplace? To what extent is an employee obliged to avoid conflicts of interest, remain loyal, and protect confidentiality? At what point are such duties superseded by an employee's obligations to consumers and society in general, as in the case of whistleblowers alerting the public to a company wrongdoing?

Business ethics also investigates the relationship between corporations and the suppliers and customers. Here, concern about fair contracts, waste or fraud in the performance of contracts, and the fair and reasonable pricing of goods come into play, as well as the morality of initiating and maintaining business relationships through gifts, entertainment, and bribery. Another key question in this area involves advertising. What constitutes deceptive advertising practices? To what extent are corporations and the advertising agencies they hire responsible for presenting a thorough and accurate portrayal of their products? What are the ethics of creating desire for goods that are unlikely to provide the popularity, beauty, wealth, and status that advertisements often imply?

Business ethicists also debate corporate practices that have sweeping consequences for society. To what extent should corporations be responsible for their effect on the environment and for the health and safety of individuals living near their plants and factories? Corporations have become powerful enough to determine the fates of entire communities in many cases, so should they be responsible for bettering those communities through charitable donations and business practices that help to reduce poverty, urban blight, and racial and gender discrimination? What are the ethical implications of corporate downsizing, involvement in political action committees, and investment in countries whose governments abuse civil and human rights?

Many of these questions are integral to the discussion of and debate about corporate social responsibility, a concept that emerged after World War II in response to the growing influence of corporations on American life. Proponents of corporate

Eight Guidelines for Managing Ethics in the Workplace

1. *Recognize that managing ethics is a process.* Ethics is a matter of values and associated behaviors. Values are discerned through the process of ongoing reflection. Therefore, ethics programs may seem more process-oriented than most management practices. Managers tend to be skeptical of process-oriented activities, and instead prefer processes focused on deliverables with measurements.... Ethics programs do produce deliverables, e.g., codes, policies and procedures, budget items, meeting minutes, authorization forms, newsletters, etc. However, the most important aspect of an ethics management program is the process of reflection and dialogue that produces these deliverables.

2. *The bottom line of an ethics program is accomplishing preferred behaviors in the workplace.* The best of ethical values and intentions are relatively meaningless unless they generate fair and just behaviors in the workplace. That's why practices that generate lists of ethical values, or codes of ethics, must also generate policies, procedures, and training that translate those values to appropriate behaviors.

3. *The best way to handle ethical dilemmas is to avoid their occurrence in the first place.* That's why practices such as developing codes of ethics and codes of conduct are so important. Their development sensitizes employees to ethical considerations and minimizes the chances of unethical behavior occurring in the first place.

4. *Make ethics decisions in groups, and make decisions public, as appropriate.* This usually produces better quality decisions by including diverse interests and perspectives, and increases the credibility of the decision process and outcome by reducing suspicion of unfair bias.

5. *Integrate ethics management with other management practices.* When developing the values statement during strategic planning, include ethical values preferred in the workplace. When developing personnel policies, reflect on what ethical values you'd like to be most prominent in the organization's culture and then design policies to produce these behaviors.

6. *Use cross-functional teams when developing and implementing the ethics management program.* It's vital that the organization's employees feel a sense of participation and ownership in the program if they are to adhere to its ethical values. Therefore, include employees in developing and operating the program.

7. *Value forgiveness.* An ethics management program may at first actually increase the number of ethical issues to be dealt with because people are more sensitive to their occurrence. Consequently, there may be more occasions to address people's unethical behavior. The most important ingredient for remaining ethical is trying to be ethical. Therefore, help people recognize and address their mistakes and then support them to continue to try to operate ethically.

8. *Note that trying to operate ethically and making a few mistakes is better than not trying at all.* All organizations are comprised of people and people are not perfect. However, when a mistake is made by any of these organizations, the organization has a long way to fall. In our increasingly critical society, these organizations are accused of being hypocritical and they are soon pilloried by social critics. Consequently, some leaders may fear sticking their necks out publicly to announce an ethics management program. This is extremely unfortunate. It's the trying that counts and brings peace of mind—not achieving an heroic status in society.

Source: Reprinted by permission from Carter McNamara, *The Complete Guide to Ethics Management,* The Free Management Library, http://www.mapnp.org/library/ (January 2, 2003).

social responsibility contend that corporations have a responsibility not just to their shareholders, but also to all who have a stake in the corporation's activities, including

The Foreign Corrupt Practices Act of 1977
(Excerpt)

It shall be unlawful for any domestic concern, or for any officer, director, employee, or agent of such domestic concern or any stockholder thereof acting on behalf of such domestic concern, to make use of the mails or any means or instrumentality of interstate commerce corruptly in furtherance of an offer, payment, promise to pay, or authorization of the payment of any money, or offer, gift, promise to give, or authorization of the giving of anything of value to—

(1) any foreign official for purposes of—

(A) (i) influencing any act or decision of such foreign official in his official capacity, (ii) inducing such foreign official to do or omit to do any act in violation of the lawful duty of such official, or (iii) securing any improper advantage; or

(B) inducing such foreign official to use his influence with a foreign government or instrumentality thereof to affect or influence any act or decision of such government or instrumentality,

in order to assist such domestic concern in obtaining or retaining business for or with, or directing business to, any person;

(2) any foreign political party or official thereof or any candidate for foreign political office for purposes of—

(A) (i) influencing any act or decision of such party, official, or candidate in its or his official capacity, (ii) inducing such party, official, or candidate to do or omit to do an act in violation of the lawful duty of such party, official, or candidate, or (iii) securing any improper advantage; or

(B) inducing such party, official, or candidate to use its or his influence with a foreign government or instrumentality thereof to affect or influence any act or decision of such government or instrumentality,

in order to assist such domestic concern in obtaining or retaining business for or with, or directing business to, any person.

The Foreign Corrupt Practices Act was passed in 1977 to regulate the behavior of U.S. companies doing business abroad.

employees, suppliers, consumers, and the communities they affect. Hence, business managers must shape their policies according to how they will affect not just profits but also their broad group of stakeholders, with each group given equal weight in the decision-making process. Where earlier theories of the corporation reflect Adam Smith's concept that businesses act as an "invisible hand" in society, providing social benefits via economic growth, the concept of corporate social responsibility charges businesses with providing social good in more tangible and purposeful ways.

The free-market or shareholder theory of the corporation holds that corporate managers have neither the obligation nor the necessary knowledge to provide social good. As agents entrusted by shareholders to maximize profits for the corporation, managers' ethical duties go no further than to shareholders and

to acting within the constraints of governmental regulations imposed upon them. Indeed, the government is responsible for the social good, not corporations, and the two should be kept separate in their functions, with the government regulating corporations in keeping with the ethical standards of society. Other arguments against the theory of corporate social responsibility contend that the theory raises more questions than it answers: Who gets to determine what kinds of social good corporations should provide? How much of a corporation's resources should be allocated to socially responsible projects? Is corporate social responsibility truly feasible in the real world, where companies spending resources to improve social well-being might lose their competitive edge and even go out of business?

Despite these arguments, the general trend has been for corporations to embrace he idea of corporate social responsibility, perhaps because the two sides of the debate are not so at odds with each other as they first appear. Many theorists argue that "doing good" is, in fact, the best way to ensure the long-term success of a company—and hence fulfill duties to shareholders. After all, with the media, government, and investment community more carefully scrutinizing corporate behavior, businesses engaging in unethical or questionable practices often face litigation, stricter and more expensive forms of governmental regulation, anxious, less productive employees, and skittish shareholders. For example, in 1996, Texaco Corporation was involved in high-profile discrimination litigation that triggered a boycott of the company, leading to a marked decrease in share value. Research has shown that companies that are considered socially responsible often enjoy healthy profits and long-term growth. Good ethics—or at least the appearance of good ethics—is increasingly understood to be good for business.

The Law and Ethical Gray Areas

Bad behavior in the business world is, unfortunately, inevitable. Often, market forces, particularly in times of recession, are cited as forcing company managers to encourage or engage in unethical practices (or to ignore company ethics codes or guidelines) to make a profit. As some individuals will always be ready to cross ethical lines, the task of the legal system, as an embodiment of society's moral standards, is to make engaging in such damaging behavior unprofitable for businesses. In the United States, a vast network of state and federal regulations sets standards for corporate behavior in finance, contracts, employee and employer rights and obligations, workplace safety, product safety, and the environment. Ethics laws are constantly evolving: for example, the corporate accounting scandals of 2001 led directly to enactment of the Sarbanes–Oxley Act, which went into effect in July 2002 and was aimed at reining in some of the worst accounting abuses.

One important function that the law serves is to create a level playing field on which companies can compete. By requiring that all companies in a particular industry play by the same rules, less socially responsible companies do not achieve a competitive advantage over those that, for example, implement pollution controls or workplace safety programs and rules.

Yet the law must also protect and facilitate commerce. Often, state and federal regulations have as much practical as moral justification: for instance, most would agree that bribery and fraud are unethical, but such practices are also not in the best interests of the U.S. economy, so the law strictly prohibits them. In other contexts, it is less clear to what extent U.S. law should intervene to set ethical standards. Strict U.S. regulations and standards, plus increased litigation that often favors individuals over corporations, are criticized for requiring so much of companies that they have difficulty competing.

For instance, corporations are expected to adhere to high standards in relation to their effect on the environment, a heated issue that is often treated as its own area of business ethics. Critics argue that environmental regulations imposed on business and industry are unnecessarily costly to implement, thus encouraging companies to move operations to countries with lower standards. Others claim that more incentives could be provided to corporations to encourage them to go beyond the minimum required by law. Another ethical question arises when corporations devote resources to lobbying against environmental and other forms of regulation: How much influence should corporations be allowed to have on our legislative bodies?

Although these concerns are important, more often the law sets the minimum moral standard for corporations to meet, which, critics contend, often leaves too much room for companies to act in ethically questionable ways. For example, the Federal Trade Commission's prohibition of deceptive advertising goes a long way to prevent advertisements that contain lies; ethicists, however, question the more subtle forms of deception that businesses and advertisers sometimes practice. Laws can be difficult to enforce, or may even conflict with existing laws and ethical considerations. For instance, though law and public policy generally protect consumers against unsafe products, no universal standard exists for determining the line between safe and unsafe. When is an inherently dangerous product safe enough to be considered marketable? Should different standards be applied in the case of goods that are needed desperately and quickly, for example, new medications that treat deadly illnesses?

Along the same lines, workplace safety laws require that employers report workplace hazards to employees, but sometimes what constitutes a reportable hazard is unclear. This has become a particular concern because workplace safety laws often conflict with laws protecting employees' privacy rights: In the case of employees who have tested positive for drug use or AIDS, which employee right takes precedence, the right to a safe workplace or the right to privacy? How does the long-standing "employment at will" doctrine, which protects employers' rights to hire, fire, and promote at their discretion, conflict with antidiscrimination and sexual harassment policies? Often, these murky waters can be navigated only on a case-by-case basis through litigation, as the U.S. legal and judicial systems struggle to delineate clearer ethical frameworks that respond to social concerns while still protecting commerce.

The Case of Multinationals

The rise of multinational corporations has introduced a host of new and complicated ethical issues that are separate from the ones raised by corporations with operations confined to a single country. Multinational companies typically have a base in a home country at the same time that they establish factories or plants in a host country—often an impoverished nation that offers cheaper labor, tax breaks, inexpensive land, and ready access to natural resources. While multinationals are credited with helping to improve and expand impoverished nations' economies, critics argue that they often do more harm than good by engaging in bribery, exploiting poor countries' land and mineral resources, taking advantage of lax or

L. Dennis Kozlowski, former chief of Tyco International, leaves a New York courthouse on June 4, 2002, after his arraignment on charges of tax evasion.

nonexistent pollution controls, violating worker and human rights, and generally aggravating the poverty and instability of host countries. They have even been charged with worsening labor conditions in their home countries. For instance, labor conditions in the U.S. garment industry changed dramatically after many of its companies became multinationals: the relatively few factories that remained on U.S. soil were forced to revert to sweat-shop conditions to remain competitive with overseas factories.

The stakes get higher when the host country's government is considered corrupt or is a notorious violator of human rights. For instance, before apartheid was abolished in South Africa in 1993, U.S. corporations with South African operations were criticized for helping to support that country's oppressive regime. Although many of these corporations claimed that they served as a powerful instrument of social change in that country, the public outcry against them resulted in large-scale U.S. disinvestment.

A key question in the case of multinationals is the ethics of doing in host countries what is considered unethical or illegal in the home country. Adhering strictly to the moral and legal standards of home countries is not possible or even desirable in many instances. For example, imagine if a U.S. law required U.S. corporations to pay foreign factory workers the same wage as U.S. workers. In addition to the obvious economic disadvantages this law would present for U.S. corporations, such a law would also encourage skilled labor to seek employment at the U.S. companies, thus decreasing the pool of skilled labor for host countries' businesses. At the same time, many ethicists agree that simply "doing what the Romans do" in host countries is, more often than not, morally wrong. Many impoverished nations may desire to enact or even have existing laws that address bribery, pollution, and labor exploitation, but such nations may simply lack the means to create or enforce such regulations. Certainly, multinationals should not have

---

Major Provisions of the Sarbanes–Oxley Act of 2002

- Chief executive and financial officers are required to certify periodic financial reports and are subject to criminal penalties based on the certifications.
- In most cases, companies are prohibited from extending personal loans to executives.
- Protections for whistle-blowers are enhanced.
- The statute of limitations for securities fraud is extended.
- New criminal securities fraud statute enacted.
- Maximum penalties for willful violations of the securities laws are increased to fines of up to $5 million and imprisonment of up to 20 years.
- Maximum term of imprisonment for mail and wire fraud, and for destroying documents in a federal investigation or bankruptcy, is set at 20 years.
- Maximum term of imprisonment for any accountant who fails to maintain audit work papers for five years is set at 10 years.
- Criminal penalties for intentional interference with an official proceeding are enhanced.

---

the burden of correcting all the social problems of a host country, but the general consensus is that these powerful corporations should not take advantage of or further perpetuate any country's problems in the pursuit of profit.

Many governments of host countries—assisted by U.S. legislation like the Foreign Corrupt Practices Act, which prohibits U.S. companies from engaging in bribery or other acts of coercion in foreign business dealings—have made some headway in establishing ethical and legal standards for multinationals. The real need is for the international community to agree on laws that would regulate multinational companies—a task complicated by the challenge of enforcing those laws effectively.

The Sarbanes–Oxley Act was passed in 2002 to address some of the worst excesses of late-twentieth-century corporate behavior.

Further Reading

Hawken, Paul. *The Ecology of Commerce: A Declaration of Sustainability.* New York: HarperBusiness, 1993.
Madsen, Peter, and Jay M. Shafritz, eds. *Essentials of Business Ethics.* New York: Meridian, 1990.
Snoeyenbos, Milton, Robert Almeder, and James Humber, eds. *Business Ethics.* 3rd ed. New York: Prometheus Books, 2001.
Wekesser, Carol, ed. *Ethics: Current Controversies.* San Diego, Calif.: Greenhaven Press, 1995.

—*Andrea Troyer*

See also:
Arbitration; Contracts and
Contract Law; Regulation of
Business and Industry.

Business Law

News stories about business and the law are common. Multibillion-dollar mergers of corporations, accounting scandals, the bribing of business and government officials to obtain contracts, and large jury verdicts awarded against companies for defective goods have captured headlines and public attention in recent years. Although many individuals think of business law only in terms of high-profile cases, business law actually shapes almost all commercial transactions and relationships.

Although economic activities are regulated by law, these laws are ineffective without a legal system—institutions like courts and law enforcement agencies—to enforce them. No business transaction can be entered into with confidence without a legal system to govern the rights and duties of the parties.

The law both limits and facilitates business transactions. Some rules—principles of contract law, for example—promote the sale, purchase, and exchange of goods and services. Many businesses would not acquire new

In 2000 an unidentified man displays Bridgestone-Firestone tires to congressional investigators during testimony about possible defects; 6.5 million tires were recalled in the United States alone.

equipment or construct new buildings without assurance that their ownership rights are protected by the law. Intellectual property law, for example, the rules relating to patents, trademarks, and copyrights, encourage business to invest in research and development. Other laws, those regulating environmental pollution or safeguarding pension funds, for example, restrain business practices and protect employees.

Contracts

Contracts are crucial to business. Every business, whether large or small, must enter into contracts with its employees, its suppliers, and its customers to conduct business operations. Contract law provides the certainty, stability, and predictability required for the smooth and efficient performance of essential economic transactions. For example, a shirt manufacturer in Los Angeles must know that it can rely on the promise of a store in Boston to pay for a thousand specially made shirts.

A contract is a set of promises that the courts will enforce. It is formed by two or more parties who agree to perform or to refrain from performing some act now or in the future. Usually the party who breaches a contract must pay monetary damages for failing to perform; in certain cases, the party may be required to perform the promised act.

For persons to enter into a valid and enforceable contract, several requirements must be met: mutual assent, consideration, legality of object, and capacity. Mutual assent requires that the parties to a contract must manifest by words or conduct that they have agreed to enter into a contract. The usual method of showing mutual assent is by offer and acceptance.

An offer does not have to be in any specific form. However, it must show an intent to enter into a contract. The offer must be communicated by the person making the offer (the offeror) to another (the offeree). It must also be definite and certain. An acceptance is a positive and unequivocal expression of an offeree's intent to enter into a contract on the terms set out in the offer.

Consideration requires that each party to a contract must intentionally exchange a legal benefit or incur a legal detriment as an inducement to the other party to make a return exchange. In many cases, the promises exchanged by each party are the consideration. For consideration to exist, the parties must really intend to exchange one thing for another.

Legality of object requires that the purpose of a contract must not be criminal or against public policy. For example, contracts to sell heroin or to restrain trade are void because their objective is illegal.

Capacity requires that the parties must have the legal ability to enter into a contract. Persons judicially declared incompetent lack contractual capacity. Others, including minors and intoxicated persons, have limited contractual capacity.

Although occasionally a contract must be in writing to be enforceable, in most cases an oral contract is binding and enforceable. If these four essentials are present, the promise is contractual and legally binding.

Torts

Tort is a broad area of law imposing liability for intentional and unintentional conduct. It affects individuals, businesses, and governments. A tort is a private or civil wrong or injury, other than breach of contract. Tort law involves compensation when others injure another's property, person, or reputation. Injuries to the property of others may involve crimes as well as torts, but the law of torts itself is civil rather than criminal.

Tort law imposes liability for injuries caused by auto accidents and airline crashes, by dangerous conditions on land, by fraud or defamation, by defective products, or by medical or legal malpractice. Potential tort liability is a fundamental consideration in prudent personal and business planning and is a major reason for insurance. The perceived risk of tort liability often determines what goods or services businesses provide, the form those goods or services take, and the design and maintenance of buildings and equipment used in manufacturing, wholesaling, retailing, and service operations.

Torts may be divided into three main categories: intentional torts, negligence (the most important), and strict liability. Intentional torts involve deliberate actions that cause injury. Examples include assault and battery, intentional infliction of emotional distress, invasion of privacy, false imprisonment, malicious prosecution, trespass, defamation, trade disparagement, interference with contractual relations, and fraud. Negligence involves injury following a failure to use reasonable care. Strict liability entails imposing legal responsibility for injury even though a liable party neither intentionally nor negligently causes the injury.

In the United States, more lawsuits allege negligence than any other kind of claim. Four separate elements make up the tort of negligence. First is the duty of care owed by one party (the defendant) to another party (the plaintiff). Second, the defendant must fail to exercise reasonable care that results in a breach of a duty of care owed to the plaintiff.

Stella Liebeck sued McDonald's for injuries she received when she spilled a cup of hot coffee on her lap; a jury awarded her $2.7 million in damages.

Third, the defendant's failure to exercise reasonable care must have actually caused the injury or damage. Fourth, the plaintiff must have suffered actual injury or damage.

In business, negligence may occur when employees cause injury to customers or others, when those invited to a business are injured because the business fails to protect them, when products are not carefully made, when services, for example, legal and accounting services, are not carefully provided, and in many other situations. Potential tort liability often determines what goods or services businesses provide, the form those goods or services take, and the design and maintenance of equipment and buildings used in business operations.

Negotiable Instruments

The vast number of commercial transactions that occur would not be possible without negotiable instruments. A negotiable instrument is a signed document that contains an unconditional promise to pay an exact sum of money on demand or at an exact future date to a given person or order or bearer. The checks a person writes to pay for groceries and other items are negotiable instruments.

Uniform Commercial Code
Article 3: Negotiable Instruments
(Excerpt)

(a) Except as provided in subsections (c) and (d), "negotiable instrument" means an unconditional promise or order to pay a fixed amount of money, with or without interest or other charges described in the promise or order, if it:

(1) is payable to bearer or to order at the time it is issued or first comes into possession of a holder;

(2) is payable on demand or at a definite time; and

(3) does not state any other undertaking or instruction by the person promising or ordering payment to do any act in addition to the payment of money, but the promise or order may contain (i) an undertaking or power to give, maintain, or protect collateral to secure payment, (ii) an authorization or power to the holder to confess judgment or realize on or dispose of collateral, or (iii) a waiver of the benefit of any law intended for the advantage or protection of an obligor.

(b) "Instrument" means a negotiable instrument.

(c) An order that meets all of the requirements of subsection (a), except paragraph (1), and otherwise falls within the definition of "check" in subsection (f) is a negotiable instrument and a check.

(d) A promise or order other than a check is not an instrument if, at the time it is issued or first comes into possession of a holder, it contains a conspicuous statement, however expressed, to the effect that the promise or order is not negotiable or is not an instrument governed by this Article.

(e) An instrument is a "note" if it is a promise and is a "draft" if it is an order. If an instrument falls within the definition of both "note" and "draft," a person entitled to enforce the instrument may treat it as either.

(f) "Check" means (i) a draft, other than a documentary draft, payable on demand and drawn on a bank or (ii) a cashier's check or teller's check. An instrument may be a check even though it is described on its face by another term, such as "money order."

(g) "Cashier's check" means a draft with respect to which the drawer and drawee are the same bank or branches of the same bank.

(h) "Teller's check" means a draft drawn by a bank (i) on another bank, or (ii) payable at or through a bank.

(i) "Traveler's check" means an instrument that (i) is payable on demand, (ii) is drawn on or payable at or through a bank, (iii) is designated by the term "traveler's check" or by a substantially similar term, and (iv) requires, as a condition to payment, a countersignature by a person whose specimen signature appears on the instrument.

(j) "Certificate of deposit" means an instrument containing an acknowledgment by a bank that a sum of money has been received by the bank and a promise by the bank to repay the sum of money. A certificate of deposit is a note of the bank.

Article 3 of the Uniform Commercial Code defines the different kinds of negotiable instrument.

nother example of a negotiable instrument a promissory note or, in simple terms, a written "IOU." A third kind of negotiable instrument is a certificate of deposit (CD) or the receipt of money by a bank that it promises to repay with interest.

The use of negotiable instruments has increased to such an extent that payments made with these instruments, particularly checks, are many times greater than payments made with cash. Negotiable instruments are close to cash for payment purposes, but are not equivalent because they may be forged, drawn on insufficient funds, materially altered, or subject to a stop payment order. Thus, a major objective of the law of negotiable instruments is to reduce these risks by increasing the safety, soundness, and operating efficiency of the payment system.

Operation of the payment system is facilitated by negotiable instruments because they serve as substitutes for money or as extensions of credit. Negotiability is a legal concept that requires an instrument like a check to be easily transferable without danger of being uncollectible. An instrument is considered negotiable if it complies with certain requirements contained in Article 3 of the Uniform Commercial Code (UCC). The UCC is a set of uniform laws, passed by all states except Louisiana (which has passed parts of the UCC), that govern commercial transactions (including the sale of goods, bank deposits and collections, negotiable instruments, investment securities, bills of lading, and secured transactions).

According to the UCC, negotiability is a matter of form. An instrument must contain within its "four corners" all the information necessary to decide whether it is negotiable. To be negotiable, an instrument must be in writing; be signed; contain a promise or order to pay; be unconditional; be for a fixed amount; be for money; contain no other undertaking; be payable on demand or at a definite time; and be payable to order (or bearer).

Principal and Agent

Agency is a relationship of trust in which one party, an agent, agrees to act on behalf of and under the control of another, known as the principal. The principal is the person for whom an action is to be taken and the agent is the person who is to act. Most employees, including managers, clerks, truck drivers, salespersons, or factory workers, are agents of the employer. By using agents, one person (the principal) may enter into any number of transactions as though she had personally carried them out, thus multiplying and expanding her business activities. Practically every kind of contract or business transaction can be created or conducted through an agent.

Agents may perform a wide variety of tasks for their principals. They may buy or sell property, pay or collect money, drive motor vehicles or operate machinery, manage people and assets, and perform any task a person could do without an agent.

Agency is based upon the premise that a person who acts through another, acts himself. That is, the acts of the agent are treated in law as the acts of the principal. Either of the parties to the agency relationship may be a person, a partnership, or a corporation. In fact, a partnership involves an agency relationship existing among the co-owners of the business, that is, the partners. A corporation, the dominant form for modern business, is an artificial person that acts only through agents.

Unless the parties otherwise agree, agency law imposes various duties upon both principal and agent. Among these duties are those of loyalty and obedience owed by an agent to a principal and the duties of compensation, indemnity, and protection owed by a principal to an agent. The agent has a duty to obey all reasonable instructions from the principal regarding the manner of performing the agency. The agent must also keep and render accurate accounts of money or property received or disbursed on the principal's behalf. Under the duty of loyalty, the agent is required to act solely for the benefit of the principal regarding all matters within the scope of the agency. The principal is obligated to pay compensation to the agent for work done on the principal's behalf. The principal is

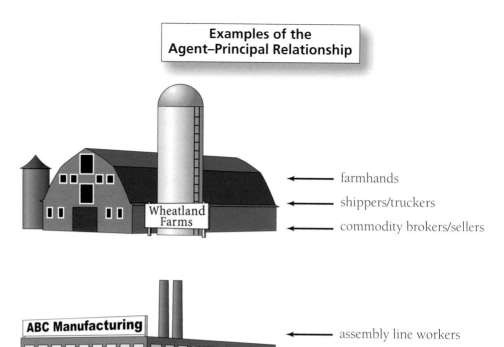

**Examples of the
Agent–Principal Relationship**

←— farmhands
←— shippers/truckers
←— commodity brokers/sellers

Wheatland Farms

ABC Manufacturing

←— assembly line workers
←— managers
←— lawyers
←— accountants

Business law regulates agents, or those who act on behalf of others. In these examples, the employees and contractors of the farm and the factory act as agents for their firms.

also required to indemnify or reimburse the agent for expenses incurred on the principal's behalf. Also, the principal owes a general duty to use reasonable care to prevent agents from being injured during their performance of the agency.

Intellectual Property

Businesses depend on technology to create and improve products and processes for success. Essential to the development and growth of technology is the legal protection of intellectual property, which includes trade secrets, trade symbols, copyrights, and patents. A business would be far less willing to invest resources in research and development if resulting discoveries, inventions, and processes were not protected by patents and trademarks. Also, a firm would not be secure in allocating time and money to marketing its products and services without laws that protect its trade names and symbols. Without copyright protection, the computer software, music, motion picture, and publishing industries would have no protection against piracy.

A trade secret is commercially valuable information that is guarded from disclosure

and is not general knowledge. A famou[s] example of a trade secret is the formula f[or] Coca-Cola. A trade secret is protected by la[w] only if its owner makes reasonable efforts t[o] preserve its secrecy. Measures that ar[e] deemed reasonable vary from case to case b[ut] may include keeping secret information in [a] locked area, restricting employee access, [or] obtaining confidentiality agreements fro[m] those to whom the trade secret is revealed.

Four kinds of trade symbols exis[t:] trademark, service mark, certification mar[k,] and collective mark. A trademark is a dis[-] tinctive mark, word, letter, number, desig[n,] picture, or combination thereof used t[o] identify and distinguish goods made or sol[d] from those of others. Examples include th[e] Kodak logo and the Campbell's Soup labe[l.] A service mark is used to identify and dis[-] tinguish one person's services from those [of] others. Examples include Howard Johnson['s] orange roof or McDonald's golden arches. [A] certification mark is used in connectio[n] with goods or services to certify their ori[-] gin, composition, quality, means of manu[-] facture, or other characteristics. The mar[k] "Good Housekeeping Seal of Approval" i[s] an example of a certification mark. A collective mark is a distinctive mark used to indicate either that the producer is a member of a trade union or association or that the goods or services are produced by members of a collective group.

A copyright is the exclusive right to reproduce and distribute a creative work. The federal Copyright Act protects only original works of authorship fixed in any tangible medium of expression. Works protected under the copyright law include literary works, musical works, dramatic works, pantomime and choreographic works, pictorial, graphic, and sculptural works, motion pictures, sound recordings, architectural works, and computer software. In no case does copyright protection extend to an idea, procedure, process, system, concept, method of operation, principle, or discovery.

A patent is a legal instrument granting an inventor exclusive rights to his or her invention for a definite period of time. Receipt of a patent enables an inventor to exclude others from making the invention, using it, selling or offering to sell it, or importing it into the United States. To qualify for a patent, an invention must be novel and nonobvious. A patent holder can prevent infringement of a patent by filing a lawsuit in any federal district court.

Intellectual property law has been profoundly affected by the technological advances of the late twentieth century. Indeed, the legal area undergoing the most change because of new business practices is cyberlaw—legal issues involving e-commerce, the Internet, and computers. The growth and development of technology depends upon the legal protection afforded by intellectual property law. The electronic copying and distribution of intellectual property like music and films present both opportunities and challenges to the corporate world.

Business activities influence the development of the law, while at the same time, the law clearly shapes the conduct of business. For instance, statutes and court decisions involving new legal areas, like securities regulation, antitrust, and consumer protection,

Laurence Lessig: The Paul Revere of the World Wide Web

The Internet has presented a number of challenges to traditional business law. Attorney and professor Lawrence Lessig has been at or near the center of most of the key cyberlaw cases of the digital age. Lessig has said that his goal is to help prevent corporate interests from grinding digital progress to a halt, and he has been dubbed "a James Madison of our time" and "the Paul Revere of the Web."

Lessig's philosophies have not always put him on the winning side of cyberlaw debates. He argued in favor of file-swapping service Napster in its suit against major record labels and music publishers; Napster lost badly in court. He also took the side of hackers who posted DVD-cracking code on the Web, a move that might have allowed people to make unauthorized private copies of movies; that was a losing battle, too.

Lessig also argued before the U.S. Supreme court in an effort to repeal the so-called "Sonny Bono Law" that extended copyright monopolies on some artistic and creative works. Lessig and others argued that the law violates the spirit of the U.S. founding fathers, who intended that copyrights should be of limited duration. According to Lessig, the limitation of copyright is crucial to continuing innovation and is an important way to limit the power of corporations to turn cyberlaw to their advantage. The Supreme Court disagreed, and they upheld the copyright extention law in 2003.

Nearly as important as his involvement in legal disputes are Lessig's writings. His 1999 book, *Code and Other Laws of Cyberspace,* has helped define the most pressing issues of cyberlaw. The chief warning of *Code and Other Laws of Cyberspace* is that unchecked capitalism could kill the free Internet. According to Lessig's argument, code—the instructions that underlie computer programs—can be written in such a way as to control how the Internet is used without the need of new laws or rulings from the courts. In effect, Lessig says, "Code is law."

—*Kevin Featherly*

have been written in response to evolving business activities. Business and law engage in an interactive process, each shaping the development of the other.

Further Reading

Beatty, Jeffrey F., and Susan S. Samuelson. *Business Law for a New Century.* 2nd ed. Cincinnati, Ohio: West Publishing, 2002.

Reed, O. L., P. Shedd, J. Morehead, and R. Corley. *The Legal and Regulatory Environment of Business.* 12th ed. New York: McGraw-Hill Irwin, 2002.

Scaletta, Phillip, and George Cameron. *Foundations of Business Law and Regulation.* 5th ed. Cincinnati, Ohio: West Publishing, 2002.

—*Carl Pacini*

Business Plan

A business plan is a formal document designed to attract investment in or capital resources to a start-up business or an established business that wants to expand. Such a document takes a reader from a general idea (or business concept), to a perceived opportunity, to the presentation of a plan for the practical operation of a business. A business plan summarizes potential limitations and obstacles and proposed strategies for overcoming them. It forecasts costs, profits, and overall values. In many ways, a business plan is to an entrepreneur what a term paper is to a student: a research paper that presents and defends a new concept.

Business plans vary greatly depending upon the authors and their businesses. For example, Lamar Muse and Herb Keller of Southwest Airlines wrote a business plan for a low-fare airline that concentrated on a narrow market (Texas) with a special emphasis on customer service. Of course, Southwest Airlines has grown beyond its original business plan to service areas outside its initial market. However, the other two foundations of its initial business plan—low fares and customer service—remain core principles of the airline today.

Elements of a Business Plan

Like a term paper, a business plan begins with an introduction. Frequently titled "Executive Summary," this section is commonly described as one of the two most important components of a business plan (the other, "Financials," comes at the end). The executive summary is intended to capture a reader's attention by presenting clearly and concisely the product or service being offered, the market, and the operational strategy behind a business. Its general purpose is always the same: to attract the attention of the audience and to make readers want to continue reading.

Most business plans follow the executive summary with a "Company Description." This section offers general information about the business without including overwhelming amounts of detail. Commonly provided details include (but are not limited to) the company's name, location, product(s) or service(s), mission statement, legal status, and ownership.

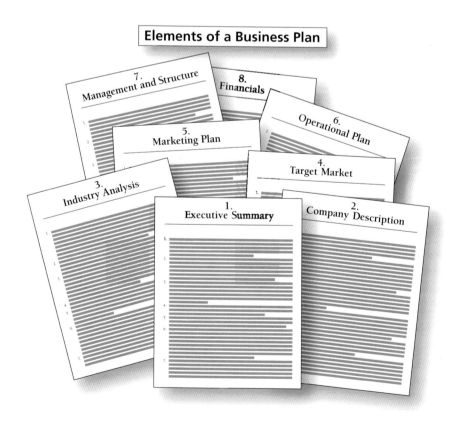

Elements of a Business Plan

7. Management and Structure
8. Financials
6. Operational Plan
5. Marketing Plan
4. Target Market
3. Industry Analysis
1. Executive Summary
2. Company Description

he mission statement describes, in a sentnce or two, what a business does and ow its employees execute their business. business's legal status may be, for example, a partnership, a corporation, or a non-profit organization.

The next section, "Industry Analysis," escribes other businesses that provide milar products or services and other businesses that supply critical resources. This nformation is typically followed by a brief mmary of industry trends and examples f how the business concept being presented addresses a market opportunity. upporting information in this section may nclude industry growth rates, size and arket share of likely competitors, short-rm obstacles to entering into the market, nd long-term opportunities described by e business plan.

The "Target Market" section identifies e group of customers (or client base) of e business. In its simplest form, this secton addresses and briefly quantifies the arket's demand. An investor always vants to know that a product or service to e offered will not change fundamentally ithin a few weeks or months of its initial ffering. Short-term reactive changes in a roduct or service might show an entre-reneur's poor understanding of the mar-et, the product, or the service. This ection must demonstrate a clear under-tanding of the target market and explain ow the product or service will fill a need n that market.

The next section of a business plan is usually the "Marketing Plan." Based upon narket surveys and forecasts of trends vithin the industry, the marketing plan lemonstrates that a quantifiable, long-erm opportunity exists and that the ootential benefits of investment in this pportunity outweigh all of the associated osts. Details in the marketing plan should lescribe the market opportunity (some-imes referred to as the "strategic posi-ion"), a sales strategy, and the limitations sometimes referred to as "risk assess-nent") associated with the business.

Reasons for Creating a Business Plan

- Tests feasibility of business idea.
- Becomes business's resume for lenders and outside investors and for attracting employees.
- Creates a timetable for operations.
- Serves as a modeling tool that helps evaluate variable factors affecting the business.
- Establishes a vehicle for tracking business progress.
- Provides benchmarks against which to adjust operations to achieve business goals.
- Is the starting point for future planning.

The "Operational Plan," which may later serve as the outline for a procedures manual, summarizes how the entrepreneur intends to conduct a functioning business. It describes resources and assets that are critical to the success of the business; it tells when those resources and assets will be needed; and it explains how the proposed company will distinguish itself from the competition. Frequently, this section also addresses production and cost-effectiveness. What kind of labor force will be required? How will the business measure cost, productivity, quality, efficiency, and capacity?

The operational plan should flow smoothly into the section describing the

Web Resources for Business Plans

www.sba.gov/starting/indexbusplans.html is part of the Small Business Administration Web site. It provides a step-by-step guide to writing a business plan and a detailed outline of what a business plan should include.

www.bplans.com provides electronic resources to help write a business plan as well as sample plans.

www.businessplans.org, home page of the Center for Business Planning, provides a variety of resources for writing a successful business plan.

web.mit.edu/entforum/www/Business_Plans/bplans.html, established by the MIT Enterprise Forum, provides an extensive bibliography of business plan resources.

www.businessplanarchive.org is an archival collection of business plans and related material from the dot-com era.

www.bizplanit.com is the home page of a consulting firm that provides advisory services for writing business plans.

www.business-plan.com is the home page of a publisher of business books and business plan software.

www.cbsc.org/ibp is a Canadian-sponsored, interactive aid for writing business plans.

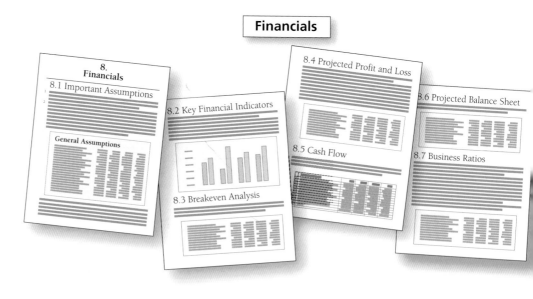

Financials

8.
Financials
8.1 Important Assumptions

General Assumptions

8.2 Key Financial Indicators

8.3 Breakeven Analysis

8.4 Projected Profit and Loss

8.5 Cash Flow

8.6 Projected Balance Sheet

8.7 Business Ratios

"Management and Structure" of the business. Through short biographical sketches, this section should introduce those employees who are most important to the business and explain why their presence is critical to its success. A brief overview of any advisory bodies, for example, board of directors, consultants, or committees, is commonly given. Organizational charts that show a business's reporting structure (telling who reports to whom within the organization) are also commonly provided in this section.

Business and financial professionals agree that the two most important sections of a business plan are the first and last: the "Executive Summary" and "Financials." The financial section of a business plan must quantify the vision presented in the "Executive Summary." The figures presented in this section include the anticipated profits, the anticipated costs, and the anticipated value of the business as a whole. Typically, a business plan forecasts these figures for three to five years. Investors can and do hold an entrepreneur to the numbers presented in the financial section—a fact that makes careful research throughout all preceding sections critical to the success of a business plan and indeed to the success of the business as a whole.

A well-researched and well-written business plan is essential to the creation of a new business or the expansion of an existing business. In many cases, a start-up business or an expansion requires additional capital or investment that goes beyond what is readily available. A business plan presents the business case for capital investment in a perceived opportunity. Should an automobile manufacturer, for example, invest in the development of alternative-fuel vehicles or should it strive to make future models with greater fuel efficiency? A business plan can provide quantifiable answers to such questions for entrepreneurs and investors alike.

Further Reading

Coke, Al. *Seven Steps to a Successful Business Plan.* New York: American Management Association, 2001.

Eglash, Joanne. *How to Write a .Com Business Plan: The Internet Entrepreneur's Guide to Everything You Need to Know about Business Plans and Financing Options.* New York: McGraw-Hill, 2001.

Pinson, Linda. *Anatomy of a Business Plan: A Step-by-Step Guide to Building a Business and Securing Your Company's Future.* 5th ed. Chicago: Dearborn Trade Publishing, 2001.

Record, Matthew. *Preparing a Winning Business Plan: How to Plan to Succeed and Secure Financial Backing.* 3rd ed. Oxford: How To Books, 2000.

Shepherd, Dean A., and Evan J. Douglas. *Attracting Equity Investors: Positioning, Preparing, and Presenting the Business Plan.* Thousand Oaks, Calif.: Sage Publications, 1999.

—John Western

Business-to-Business Sales

When people think of sales transactions, they usually think of consumer sales. However, before products ever arrive at a store, a series of business-to-business sales transactions have likely taken place. Indeed, many business-to-business transactions are made to create products and services that are never seen by the average consumer.

Supply Chains and Webs

Business-to-business sales encompass any sales transactions between two or more businesses. The object of sale can be a product, such as a truckload of steel to an automaker, or it can be a service, such as when an information technology firm agrees to help a business establish and maintain a computer network in exchange for a fee. Every industry and every business participating in an industry engage in a series of ongoing business-to-business transactions and relationships that are often called the supply chain and, in some cases, may more accurately be characterized as a supply network or web.

For example, the supply chain in a manufacturing environment may include many companies, all linked through business-to-business sales transactions, either on a one-time basis or as part of an ongoing business relationship. The supply chain may start with companies that mine raw materials for steel and carry forward through other companies that refine the steel to yet others that manufacture and assemble components, before finally reaching the companies responsible for assembly of the final product. However, the chain

See also:
Distribution Channels;
E-Business; Health Care
Services Industry;
Manufacturing Industry.

As part of a supply chain that begins with raw materials and ends with finished cars, auto manufacturers assemble parts and materials purchased from business-to-business vendors.

does not end there. Companies producing the final product may have business-to-business sales transactions with distributors and wholesalers that sell the product to final purchasers.

That is just a brief example of the direct participants in the supply chain. Indirect participants interact with direct participants at each stage of the process, and more business-to-business sales transactions are made at each of these points of interaction. Indirect participants may be law firms, accounting firms, consulting companies, market research firms, and transportation or logistics companies that provide services to each participant in the supply chain and play a crucial role in their ability to bring products to market. Even the utility companies that supply the electricity to companies at each stage are participants in this web of business-to-business sales transactions.

Somewhat different business-to-business relationships can be found in the health care field. When visiting a hospital, a person may get the impression that it is a self-contained entity that provides an array of services largely on its own. Look close and a web of business-to-business relationships is revealed; often those relationships link the hospital to multiple supply chains with each intersection of the web made possible by a business-to-business sale. Some of the business-to-business sales relationships relate to supply chain activities similar to those described for an industrial setting. Hospitals purchase medical equipment and other supplies that are created from raw materials and eventually sold to the hospital by the final supplier. Hospitals also might subcontract services like laundry and food service vendors, legal assistance, billing, or contracted specialty services like diagnostic imaging and anesthesia services.

Market Channel Strategies

Just as many kinds of businesses participate in business-to-business sales, a variety of methods, often referred to as market channel strategies, are used to pursue and transact sales. Some common approaches include face-to-face sales visits, telemarketing, distributors, and trade shows.

Many of these techniques involve the use of third-party service, the contracts for which represent at least one, and often many, business-to-business sale. For example, a trade show is a large event at which companies exhibit their products or services for a large group of attending customers to see and discuss. Trade shows are typically sponsored by a third-party organization, for example, a trade association or a publisher, and all exhibitors pay a fee per square foot of exhibit space. They also pay shippers to move and set up their exhibits and may pay for a variety of other services, including Internet service and hotel rooms. Attendees often pay fees to attend, stay in hotels, and purchase airline tickets. All these transactions represent kinds of business-to-business sales made in response to efforts of the exhibiting companies to develop business-to-business sales leads.

When businesses develop a plan for bringing their products or services to market, they must weigh the advantages and

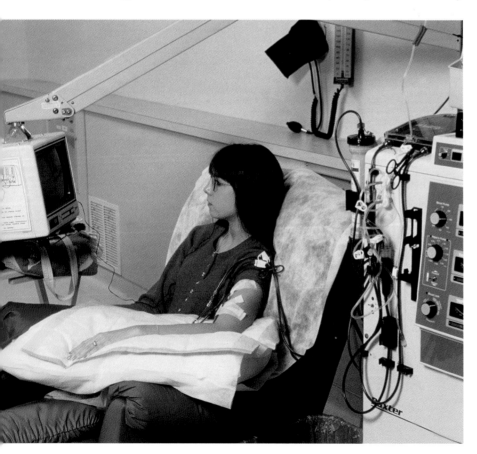

A young woman undergoes kidney dialysis with equipment purchased by the hospital from a medical technology vendor.

isadvantages of various approaches by considering many factors, some of which might include the kind of product or service to be sold, the cost of the particular sales approach, and the amount of staff time required.

For example, whether to sell directly to other businesses or through distributors is a key decision for many companies. Establishing a sales force and selling directly can be very costly; such a sales strategy is easier to manage when there is a limited group of larger customers (for example, small companies that sell primarily to a few large manufacturers). Direct sales offers the opportunity to develop closer relationships with customers and a better understanding of their needs, which may lead to product improvements and the development of more marketable products.

On the other hand, in highly fragmented markets with many potential customers, selling through distributors may be the most manageable approach. Once solid relationships are developed, the distributors may assist in promotion. Distributors can be particularly helpful in the sale of more complex products.

Trends in Market Channels

Market channel strategies do not have to be mutually exclusive. Businesses often pursue multiple strategies, yet must be careful not to create disruptive channel conflict in the process. For example, a key trend affecting business-to-business sales in recent years has been e-business development. E-business can serve to create business-to-business sales opportunities and strengthen existing relationships between sellers and buyers. Yet, new e-business sales channels may be a source of channel conflict that can damage business-to-business sales relationships. Businesses planning to sell through distributors and directly via e-business must strike a careful balance to avoid disenfranchising the distributors on whom they depend for a large portion of their sales. A company may choose to limit channel conflict by pursuing a new and distinct set of customers through e-business or to market

Publishers and vendors meet annually at the Frankfurt Book Fair, an important international trade show for the publishing industry.

only certain products through e-business channels. Others limit disruptive channel conflict by creating cooperative e-business strategies with their distributors.

Establishing and maintaining the optimal mix of sales methods requires continual assessment, adjustment, and planning.

Market Channel Strategies: Examples

- Direct face-to-face sales visits.
- Business-to-business telemarketing sales.
- Selling through distributors.
- Selling directly via Internet e-commerce techniques.
- Marketing products through trade journals.
- Exhibiting and making contacts at trade shows.

Other key trends have also magnified the need for companies to rethink and revamp their market channel strategies; in particular, the increasing globalization of many industries is having a profound impact on where businesses purchase goods and to whom they can sell.

Procurement

Advances in supply chain management, often with the help of new e-business tools (and sometimes with tried and true electronic data interchange methods that predate the Internet), have changed business-to-business sales: such sales are no longer necessarily a function of the active seller pursuing passive buyers. Many corporate purchasers have found that the supply chain has become more like a ball of yarn, with business transactions leading in many directions with little apparent sense.

In an effort to make supply chains more rational, predictable, and responsive, some companies with sufficient purchasing power have sought to narrow the range of suppliers to more select groups able and willing to comply with, in some cases, stringent requirements for price, quality, and timely delivery. The leverage exerted on suppliers, or sellers, through supply chain management techniques has in many instances created a new set of business-to-business sales relationships in which purchasers have redefined the sales channel.

These attempts to remake the sales channel into more of a procurement channel can be seen in both the health care and industrial supply chains described above. For example, automotive manufacturers have traditionally exerted considerable leverage on their suppliers. This leverage has advanced from a focus on price requirements, to requiring specific quality standards, to expecting suppliers to take greater responsibility for recalls and warranty costs and even to supply their products using specific e-business platforms. (An example of this can be found at www.covisint.com the automotive purchasing exchange developed by major automakers to facilitate their supply chain management strategies.)

Conversely, purchasers of health care services are trying to reverse a long-standing inability to control costs and hold health care providers (sellers, such as hospitals and insurers) accountable for quality care by applying the principles of supply chain management. Many businesses have banded together in cooperative health care purchasing coalitions to create the purchasing leverage they need to negotiate on price and accountability requirements (examples of health care purchasing coalitions are listed on the Web site of the National Business Coalition on Health at www.nbch.org/coalition.htm, which itself serves as a coalition and a membership organization for other coalitions).

The automotive and health care industries are just two (herein simplified) examples of the complex network of business-to-business sales relationships and how they are evolving. The same or similar concepts generally apply in many other industries with variations depending on the kind and complexity of products, number of industry participants, and rate with which they have embraced e-business and supply chain management tools and moved into more global markets.

Further Reading

Hines, Peter, Richard Lanming, Daniel Jones, Paul Cousins, Nick Rich, eds. *Value Stream Management: Strategy and Excellence in the Supply Chain.* Harlow, U.K.: Financial Times/Prentice Hall, 2000.

Morris, Michael H., Leyland F. Pitt, Earl D. Honeycutt, Jr., eds. *Business-to-Business Marketing: A Strategic Approach.* 3rd ed. Thousand Oaks, Calif.: Sage Publications, 2001.

—*Peter Alle*

Capital

Capital is money or wealth that is put at risk in order to fund a business enterprise. It is the long-term financing used by a business. The combination of financing sources for a business, therefore, is called the capital structure. The process of placing capital at risk, also known as investing, is an important part of the process of wealth creation in a market economy.

Debt Capital and Equity Capital

Capital used to finance the purchase of assets may take the form of equity capital or debt capital. Equity capital is capital supplied by the actual owners of the business, while capital in the form of debt is supplied by entities that may or may not have an actual ownership interest in the firm. These two forms of capital differ in several important ways. First, when earnings are to be distributed, the claims of the suppliers of debt capital are paid first. Only after the suppliers of debt capital are paid can the suppliers of equity capital, the owners of the firm, receive any portion of the firm's earnings.

The second difference between debt and equity capital involves control of the firm. In general, the suppliers of debt capital do not have any control of the day-to-day activities of the firm. They may place some specific limitations on the actions of the firm but, unless the firm defaults on the debt, the suppliers of equity capital and their agents (the management) control the firm and make the decisions.

See also:
Debt; Venture Capital.

Stock prices are displayed in the offices of Nasdaq, a primary capital market.

Debt Capital vs. Equity Capital				
	Supplier	**Order of distribution**	**Control of firm**	**Repayment**
Equity capital	Owners of business	Paid after all lenders	Yes	No fixed payment
Debt capital	Borrowed from other sources	Paid first	Usually no	Fixed payments of principal and interest

The final significant difference between debt and equity capital involves the compensation that the suppliers of the capital receive. In exchange for debt capital, the owners of a business promise to make fixed payments of principal and interest over the life of a loan agreement. Because the payments to the suppliers of debt capital are fixed, the financial securities that represent ownership of these debt claims against the earnings of the firm are called fixed income securities. In contrast, the suppliers of equity capital do not receive a fixed payment. They are the residual claimants against the firm's earnings; that is, they will receive whatever is left after the firm pays its debt obligations.

Raising Capital

Firms can raise capital by selling their financial liabilities in financial markets. Financial markets where firms raise long-term capital—funds that do not have to be repaid for more than one year—are known as capital markets. Capital markets allocate capital, and other scarce resources, to those firms that have the greatest ability to pay for its use. In other words, markets reward those firms that have the most promising investment opportunities by supplying them with capital to fund their projects.

When firms initially raise capital they do so in the primary capital markets. In the primary capital markets, firms sell their securities to the public. In these transactions, the firm receives capital funding in exchange for claims against the firm's future earnings. These claims are in the form of financial securities, or stocks.

In secondary capital markets, investors buy and sell securities among themselves. These transactions do not directly affect the firm that issued the securities. If the price of a firm's stock increases in trading today, the firm will not receive any additional capital; however, the investors who purchased the securities will see an increase in the value of their holdings.

Secondary markets provide liquidity to investors by allowing them to alter their holdings over time, and, by doing so, secondary markets increase the willingness of investors to provide capital to firms that are seeking funding. The capital that is raised by firms in the primary market is used to fund projects or purchase assets that the firm hopes will increase its earnings in the future. This increase in earnings, through subsequent payments of interest and principal in the case of debt capital and dividends and share price increases in the case of equity capital, provides the incentive for the suppliers of capital to purchase the financial liabilities of the firm.

Further Reading

Berle, Gustav. *Raising Start-up Capital for Your Company*. New York: Wiley, 1990.

Brealy, Richard A., Stewart C. Myers, and Alan J. Marcus. *Fundamentals of Corporate Finance*. New York: McGraw-Hill Irwin, 2001.

Husick, Gail Clayton, and J. Michael Arrington. *The Initial Public Offering: A Practical Guide for Executives*. New York: Bowne & Co., 1998.

Livingston, Miles. *Money and Capital Markets*. Miami, Fla.: Kolb, 1993.

Ross, Stephen A., Randolph W. Westerfield, and Jeffrey Jaffe. *Corporate Finance*. 6th ed. Boston, Mass.: McGraw-Hill/Irwin, 2002.

—*Shelton Week*

Capital Gains

Investors purchase risky assets in hope of increasing their wealth. This potential increase in wealth can come in different forms, one of which is capital gain. Capital gains are the reward investors receive when the value of assets increases over the period of investment. Because investment is considered a good activity, capital gains are taxed at a lower rate than current income. This favorable tax treatment encourages investors to substitute investment for current consumption, thus resulting in greater output and employment across the economy.

Capital gains occur for a variety of reasons. Sometimes the demand for an item increases over time because of changes in market conditions. For example, a residential lot in a neighborhood on the outskirts of town may be worth $1,000 today. However, as time passes and more amenities are added nearby, the lot may become more attractive to potential residents. Therefore, if the lot were purchased today for $1,000 and sold five years later for $5,000, the capital gain would be equal to the difference between the purchase price and the selling price, or $4,000. In percentage terms the capital gain would be 400 percent.

Another source of capital gains is the retention and investment of earnings by businesses. When a firm is successful, it generates earnings from its operation that can be paid out to the owners of the firm. If the firm has opportunities to invest these earnings and earn more than the owners would be able to earn on investments of comparable risk, the firm may invest the earnings instead of paying them out to the owners of the business. The goal of the business in investing the earnings is to increase the value of the common stock that represents ownership of the firm. For example, a firm with a current stock price of $10 per share may decide to retain and invest all of its earnings for the next five years. As a result of the investment, the stock price may increase to $15 at the end of five years. Therefore, anyone who purchases the stock today for $10 and sells the stock five years from today for $15 would earn a capital gain of $5 per share, or 50 percent.

Investment can result in increased output and well-being for society. Consider an investment in a new factory: The factory will employ individuals, who will have increased income to spend on goods and services. Additional goods will be produced in the factory. Both employment and the quantity of goods available for society to consume will increase. These are considered good economic outcomes.

For this reason, the tax system in the United States encourages investment by

See also:
Savings and Investment
Options; Taxation.

Building Lot 1 bought in 2002 could increase in value over the course of five years because of the addition of amenities like schools and shopping. If the land is sold, the increased value would be considered a capital gain.

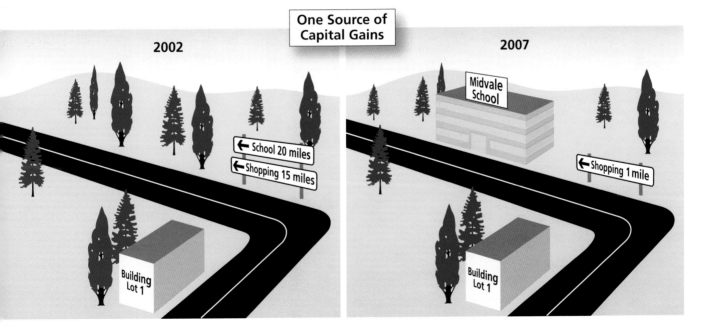

One Source of Capital Gains

2002

School 20 miles
Shopping 15 miles

Building Lot 1

2007

Midvale School

Shopping 1 mile

Building Lot 1

	Capital Gains	
Year One	Deferring Capital Gains Tax	Not Deferring Capital Gains Tax
Investment	$1,000.00	$1,000.00
Earnings (10%)	+ 100.00	+ 100.00
Taxes (20%)	- 0.00	- 20.00
Year-end Total	$1,100.00	$1,080.00
Year Two		
Investment	$1,100.00	$1,080.00
Earnings (10%)	+ 110.00	+ 108.00
Pre-Tax Subtotal	$1,210.00	$1,188.00
Taxes (20%)	- 242.00	- 237.60
Year-end Total	$968.00	$950.40

This chart shows the financial benefits of deferring tax on capital gains.

The U.S. tax system is structured to encourage businesspeople to invest their earnings, for example, in a new factory like this electronics assembly shop in New York City.

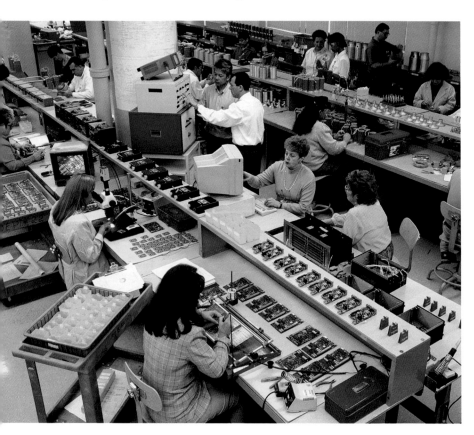

taxing capital gains at a lower rate than current income. Normally, a minimum investment period is required for the increase in value to be treated as a capital gain instead of current income. This period is usually one year. Capital gains realized in less than one year are known as short-term capital gains and are taxed as current income, while those gains from investment periods greater than one year are known as long-term capital gains and are taxed at the lower rate. In terms of the earlier example of business earnings, if the earnings had been paid to the owners of the firm, the earnings would have been taxed as current income. If the earnings were retained and the firm invested them in new projects, the value of the firm would increase. The owners of the firm could then sell their shares and receive a long-term capital gain.

In addition to the lower tax rate, investors are attracted to investments that offer returns in the form of capital gains because they offer the chance to defer taxes. In contrast to current income, which is taxed when it is earned, capital gains are not taxed until they are realized by the investor. A capital gain is realized when an asset is sold. Consider the earlier example of a stock purchase where the initial price was $10 and the price at the end of a five-year investment period was $15. Assume the value of the stock increased at a rate of $1 per year. At the end of each year, the investor may recognize an increase of $1 in the value of the stock. However, the investor does not have to pay taxes on this gain because it has not been realized or locked in. The gain is realized when the stock is sold. Therefore, the $5 capital gain is realized and is taxed at the end of year five when the stock is sold.

The deferral of taxes is justified on economic grounds because of the continued risk faced by the investor and the cost associated with estimating the values of assets that are not frequently traded. Most investments entail some degree of risk, the chance that the investor will receive something other than the amount expected at the end of the investment period. By waiting until the end of the investment period to collect the tax, the exact amount of the gain is known.

Further Reading

Burman, Leonard. *The Labyrinth of Capital Gains Tax Policy: A Guide for the Perplexed.* Washington, D.C.: Brookings Institution Press, 1999.
Scholes, Myron S., and Mark A. Wolfson. *Taxes and Business Strategy: A Planning Approach.* Englewood Cliffs, N.J.: Prentice Hall, 1992.

—*Shelton Weeks*

Capitalism

Capitalism is an economic and social system based on private ownership of the means of production and on the distribution of goods and services through the coming together of supply and demand in the competitive free market.

The abstract concept of capitalism is made concrete in specific historical and cultural situations. Accordingly, a number of models of capitalism have evolved, all of which are characterized by a mixture of private, state, and communal modes of ownership, and by various kinds of modifications of the market. Therefore, no one definitive model of capitalism exists; capitalism is frequently best defined against noncapitalist models, like agrarianism or communism.

Historical Origins

Merchants, trade, and markets have always existed, but capitalism as a coherent system has its roots in early modern Europe, where it gradually emerged as the successor to the feudalism of the Middle Ages.

Historians and sociologists have commonly associated the transition from feudalism to capitalism with a succession of important events and processes. First, Europeans conquered the New World in the late fifteenth and early sixteenth centuries, gaining access to abundant resources and expanded markets. The humanist ideas of the Renaissance created a new emphasis on individualism in European thought, while the sixteenth-century Protestant Reformation intensified the spirit of individualism. The Reformation also freed economic activity from the strictures of the Roman Catholic church and contributed to the breakup of European Christendom into modern nation-states.

The seventeenth- and eighteenth-century revolution in scientific thought, exemplified by the work of the English mathematician and physicist Isaac Newton, laid the foundations for the technological innovations that multiplied human productivity. Finally, the eighteenth-century Enlightenment undermined traditional sources of authority and created an intellectual climate sympathetic to the development of a coherent capitalist philosophy.

A Capitalist Philosophy

From the sixteenth to the eighteenth centuries, the mercantilist system made merchant corporations the agents of the state and made national wealth accumulation the central objective of economic policy. During the Enlightenment, mercantilism was subject to rigorous intellectual criticism, first by the French physiocrats, who argued for free markets in agriculture and opposed the French state's efforts to encourage industry, and then by the Scottish moral philosopher Adam Smith.

In *The Wealth of Nations* (1776), Smith argued for a system of political economy in which theoretically unlimited growth would be achieved by the invisible hand of the free market and the division of labor into increasingly specialized tasks. Individual consumers and entrepreneurs thereby replaced the state as the focus of economic activity. Smith's design rested on a number of core philosophical assumptions about human nature. First, it presupposed individualism and self-interest as predominant human traits. Second, it conceived of humans

See also:
Communism; Globalization; Marx, Karl; Mercantilism; Price Controls; Smith, Adam; *Wealth of Nations, The.*

An engraving of Adam Smith from 1790.

as social creatures who engage in exchange for mutual advantage. Third, it assumed that people are motivated by a spirit of competition. According to Smith, therefore, a free-market economy would be superior to other models of political economy because it worked with the grain of human nature.

The Capitalist Century

Capitalism, both as an idea and as an economic system, had its heyday during the Industrial Revolution in nineteenth-century Britain. The techniques of industrialism greatly facilitated the specialization of labor and generated unprecedented rates of economic growth. Meanwhile, European imperialism, combined with improvement in transport and communications, spread industrial capitalism around the globe.

The immense economic growth came a great social cost. The process of urbanization resulted in slums with massively inadequate sanitation that led to disease; the inequality of bargaining power between workers and employers led to exploitation and poverty. The capitalist economy was also prone to recurrent crises as periods of expansion were followed by recessions and bouts of high unemployment. Several responses were made to the profound social problems of industrialism. Reformers and philanthropists, usually motivated by Christian principles, or by an aristocratic sense of social responsibility, demanded legislation that addressed issues like child labor and excessive working hours.

Meanwhile, socialist philosophers and political activists began to develop anticapitalist ideas and organizations, and workers began to organize in trade unions to improve pay and workplace conditions. Public health problems led to direct government intervention in the areas of sanitation and housing, and as the demand for skilled workers grew, the state also became directly involved in the provision of public education. Consequently, by the end of the nineteenth century, the world's first industrial capitalist state had significantly modified the theoretical model developed by Smith, though Britain continued to champion international free trade.

However, from the perspective of the United States and Germany as emerging countries, the British advocacy of free trade merely reflected Britain's interests as the world's leading industrial capitalist power. Alexander Hamilton in the United States and Friedrich List in Germany both advocated systems of protective tariffs behind which their young countries could industrialize and challenge the economic predominance of Britain.

In the United States, toward the end of the nineteenth century, dominant corporations organized themselves into trusts and used their political influence to protect themselves from potential competitors. During

Peace through Trade: The Corn Laws Controversy

Throughout the nineteenth century, advances in capitalist theory and practice were mutually reinforcing. In 1817 the English economist David Ricardo made a compelling case for extending the principle of economic specialization to international trade. His arguments had an important effect on what came to be known as the Corn Laws controversy.

In 1815 landowners, working through the Tory Party in the British Parliament, secured the passage of tariffs on cheap agricultural imports of maize (corn) and grain. This protected the landowners' interests but also inflated food prices, resulting in worker demands for higher wages, which in turn reduced the profits of the emerging class of industrial capitalists. Consequently, the Anti-Corn Law League was formed in Manchester in 1839, under the leadership of manufacturers Richard Cobden and John Bright. The league, and the growing political influence of the industrialists, secured the repeal of the Corn Laws in 1846. Over the course of its campaigns, the leadership of the league also advanced a theory of peace through free trade, according to which international economic interdependence would make war undesirable or even impossible.

The arguments concerning the Corn Laws remain relevant. The free trade versus protectionism debate continues in the era of globalization.

An illustration of an Anti-Corn Law meeting in 1844.

In this cartoon from 1873 entitled "The American Juggernaut," financiers and politicians ride a large train—the nineteenth-century symbol of corporate power—that crushes American workers.

what became known as the Progressive Era, his corporate influence was challenged both by advocates of liberal capitalism and by radical populist movements. The result was government regulation and the development of antitrust laws. For the most part, however, government attempts to regulate the economy did not seriously inhibit free market activity, and the U.S. economy continued to expand.

Capitalism in Crisis

In the first half of the twentieth century, capitalism faced a succession of deep crises: world war, communist revolution, and economic depression. World War I (1914–1918) had three major consequences for capitalism. First, it shattered the nineteenth-century confidence that the spread of free trade would ensure international peace. Second, the demands of modern technological warfare led to increased government intervention to harness the economy for the war effort. Third, the United States emerged from the war economically strengthened, and New York replaced London as the center of world finance.

In October 1917, the Bolsheviks seized power in Russia and put a halt to the country's incipient capitalist economy. Led by Vladimir Lenin, they created the Soviet Union as the world's first communist state, in which the economy was taken over by the government. Under Joseph Stalin's leadership after 1928, the Soviets embarked upon a rapid program of centrally planned industrialization and agricultural collectivization.

The Great Depression (1929–1939) posed four major threats to the future of the capitalist system. First, it undermined public confidence in the system itself. Second, leading capitalist economies responded to the Depression with protective tariffs, doing further damage to the international trading system on which capitalism relied. Third, the Soviet Union, being insulated from the world economy, avoided the Depression, thus increasing the international prestige and credibility of communism. Fourth, the collapse of the German economy paved the way for the rise of the Nazi Party, which promoted nationalist and anticapitalist policies of economic management.

The economic crisis of the 1930s induced major changes in Western capitalist economies. In the United States, the New Deal of President Franklin Delano Roosevelt, elected in 1932, reformed the American financial system to prevent further speculative excesses of the

A slum in Newcastle, England, circa 1880; the abominable living conditions of urban workers inspired progressive reform movements both in England and the United States.

and theoreticians like Keynes emerged as the new orthodoxy in capitalist economics.

Welfare Capitalism

By surviving these crises, capitalism proved itself adaptable and durable. In North America, Western Europe, and Scandinavia, the first three decades after World War II were an era of Keynesian consensus during which mainstream parties of the Left and the Right adopted policies of macroeconomic demand management. The Keynesian model was internationalized at the Bretton Woods conference in 1944, which put in place a new architecture of global finance. The Bretton Woods agreement stabilized exchange rates by pegging them to the U.S. dollar and founded the World Bank to fund development projects and the International Monetary Fund to stabilize the international economy by avoiding or managing currency crises. The agreement also gave rise to a new regime of international free trade, the General Agreement on Tariffs and Trade (GATT), which was designed to prevent a return to the rivalrous protectionism of the 1930s.

In Western Europe and Scandinavia, governments established cradle-to-grave welfare states and mixed economies, in which some strategic industries were taken into public ownership. The government also established a range of models of corporatism, under which national economic policy was negotiated between representatives of governments, employers' organizations, and trade unions. These efforts seemed to overcome earlier instabilities of the capitalist system, and governments were freed to pursue social projects like educational reform, public housing, and initiatives to reduce economic inequality. In the United States, postwar welfare provision was less generous and comprehensive than in Europe but underwent significant expansion in the Great Society program of President Lyndon Johnson (1963–1968) with programs like Medicare and Medicaid.

The Noncapitalist Postwar World

The communist sphere expanded significantly after World War II with the Soviet occupation of Eastern Europe and the 1949 revolution in

kind that led to the stock market crash of 1929. Roosevelt also established a series of national job-creation agencies, including the Civilian Conservation Corps and the Public Works Administration. This period also saw the introduction of unemployment insurance and of Social Security, and it marks the origin of the American welfare system.

The theoretical basis for government economic intervention came from the British economist John Maynard Keynes, who argued that governments could take an even more active role in insuring against sharp booms and busts in the economy by manipulating the money supply and adjusting taxes to increase or decrease investment activity. This "Keynesian revolution" challenged the prevailing economic orthodoxy and advocated controversial policies like deficit spending.

The Depression was followed by World War II (1939–1945), which did more than any previous war to expand government direction of the economy. Consequently, after the war, the ideas of politicians like Roosevelt

Capitalism

1776
In *The Wealth of Nations*, Adam Smith argues for the free market and the division of labor.

1800s
Industrialization is in full swing in Europe and the United States.

1890
The Sherman Antitrust Act strives to limit corporate power.

1918
At the conclusion of World War I, New York replaces London as the center of world finance.

1929
Wall Street crash begins the Great Depression.

1932
Franklin Delano Roosevelt elected president; the New Deal programs of his administration create jobs and increase government involvement in the economy.

1944
Bretton Woods conference stabilizes exchange rates and founds the World Bank and the International Monetary Fund.

1963–1968
Great Society program of the Lyndon B. Johnson administration.

1971
President Richard Nixon devalues the dollar, effectively ending the Bretton Woods exchange rate management system.

1980s
British prime minister Margaret Thatcher and U.S. president Ronald Reagan lead a "neoliberal" revolution in Britain and the United States.

1985–1991
Soviet president Mikhail Gorbachev introduces perestroika (economic liberalization) to the Soviet Union.

1993
North American Free Trade Agreement is signed by the United States, Canada, and Mexico.

1991
Breakup of Soviet Union.

1995
World Trade Organization is created to liberalize world trade.

China. Both Moscow and Beijing began to aid communist liberation movements in the colonial world and to exert significant influence over the political and economic organization of postcolonial states. The Soviet model of economic planning even inspired noncommunist leaders of former colonies, for instance, Jawaharlal Nehru in India.

Elsewhere in the developing world, governments of various political complexions

Two icons of late-twentieth-century capitalism, U.S. president Ronald Reagan and British prime minister Margaret Thatcher, meet at the White House in 1987.

The Neoliberal Revolution

The Keynesian era came to an end over the course of the 1970s. In 1971, with the U.S. economy suffering the strains of the war in Vietnam, President Richard Nixon effectively ended the Bretton Woods exchange rate management system when he devalued the dollar. With the outbreak of war in the Middle East in 1973, Western economies were hit by an Arab oil embargo, levied as a protest against the West's support of Israel. By mid-decade, Western capitalist economies were experiencing "stagflation"—the simultaneous increase in both unemployment and inflation—which undermined the theoretical credibility of Keynesian economics. Governments responded with unpopular and unsuccessful public spending cuts and attempts to control wages and prices; many leaders were replaced in subsequent elections.

Monetarist economists, notably Milton Friedman at the University of Chicago, identified inflation as the central economic problem and prescribed deflationary economic policies based on the restriction of the money supply. They also advocated privatization, deregulation, welfare cuts, and measures to curb trade union powers. These ideas formed the basis of the so-called neoliberal revolution, led by British prime minister Margaret Thatcher (1979–1990) and U.S. president Ronald

sought to accelerate their countries' development with policies of economic nationalism. This strategy, exemplified by the Institutional Party of the Revolution in Mexico, aimed to develop indigenous industries with policies of protectionism and import substitution, not unlike those pursued by Germany and the United States in the nineteenth century. At the same time, many countries, principally on the continent of Africa, remained agricultural economies with premodern forms of economic organization.

In post-communist Russia, a vendor sells communist paraphernalia on a Moscow street in 1993.

Reagan (1981–1989). The more left-wing governments of Australia and New Zealand introduced monetarist economic policies, signaling that neoliberal economic ideas had spread across the political spectrum.

Toward the end of the decade, even communist countries were introducing economic reforms, for example, the perestroika of Soviet general secretary Mikhail Gorbachev (1985–1991) and the Chinese government's market socialism, the liberalization of a socialist economy. At the same time, many developing countries renounced economic nationalism and aimed at development through international trade. Mexico, for example, signed the North American Free Trade Agreement (NAFTA) with the United States and Canada in 1993. African political leaders also began to emphasize trade over aid in their economic development strategies.

Contemporary Capitalism

When Soviet communism collapsed between 1989 and 1991, no viable alternative to capitalism came forward. There remained, however, a variety of capitalist models. The Anglo-Saxon model of the United States, Britain, Australia, and New Zealand emphasizes market incentives, privatization, and economic deregulation. By contrast, the European social market model is characterized by greater state intervention in the form of regulated labor markets, high government expenditure on education, detailed structures of employer–union cooperation, and fiscal incentives for training and for research and development. The Asian model features a close structural relationship between finance and industry and a degree of economic planning, of which the Japanese Ministry of International Trade and Industry (MITI) is the prime example.

During the 1990s the term *globalization* emerged to describe the process of world economic integration driven by a combination of free trade and the revolution in information technology. In 1995 a series of GATT negotiations culminated in the creation of the World Trade Organization, an intergovernmental organization whose primary goal is the progressive liberalization of world trade relations.

Critics of globalization, who span the political spectrum, contend that the new capital mobility has increased the power of multinational corporations at the expense of national governments, resulting in the erosion of labor and environmental standards. The debate in the twenty-first century between advocates and opponents of free trade resembles the original arguments about the nature and purpose of capitalism in the nineteenth century.

Thousands converged on Seattle in 1999 to stage protests against the World Trade Organization, which held its meeting that year at the Washington State Convention Center.

Further Reading

Barber, Benjamin. *Jihad versus McWorld.* New York: Ballantine Books, 1996.

Bhagwati, Jagdish. *Free Trade Today.* Princeton, N.J.: Princeton University Press, 2002.

Deane, Phyllis. *The State and the Economic System.* New York and London: Oxford University Press, 1989.

Turner, Adair. *Just Capital: The Liberal Economy.* New York: Macmillan, 2001.

—*Peter C. Grosvenor*

Carnegie, Andrew

1835–1919
U.S. Steel magnate and philanthropist

Andrew Carnegie was one of the most important industrial leaders in the United States of the late nineteenth century. His innovative management methods made Carnegie Steel (later United States Steel) the leading firm in the steel industry. He was also among the greatest of American philanthropists, giving away most of the fortune he amassed to schools, churches, libraries, and other institutions for the welfare of the public.

Andrew Carnegie was born on November 25, 1835, in Dunfermline, Scotland. His father was a skilled weaver whose income fell drastically as the market for woven cloth was taken over by factories with power-driven looms. In 1848 the Carnegie family immigrated to Allegheny, Pennsylvania, near Pittsburgh, where Mrs. Carnegie's sisters lived. Thirteen-year-old Andrew found work in a textile mill and later a job in a factory that made bobbins, the spools upon which thread is wound. He soon was given other part-time responsibilities at the mill, including writing letters and making out bills. He became interested in accounting and attended night school to learn bookkeeping.

Young Carnegie's first real opportunity came in 1849 when, through his aunt's husband, he got a job as a messenger boy for a telegraph office in Pittsburgh. He learned telegraphy and worked his way up into a position as a telegraph operator. When the Pennsylvania Railroad opened a line between Philadelphia and Pittsburgh in 1853, he became the personal telegrapher for Thomas A. Scott, the superintendent of the Western Division of the Pennsylvania Railroad. Under the sponsorship of Scott, young Carnegie rose quickly in the railroad organization. When Scott became vice president of the railroad in 1859, Carnegie was promoted to Scott's old position.

From 1859 to 1865, Carnegie worked with Scott and with the railroad's president, J. Edgar Thomson; during this time the Pennsylvania Railroad grew to be the largest private business in the United States. Thomson and Scott pioneered efficient management methods, characterized by statistical analysis and continual lowering of costs, that were widely imitated by other firms in the United States and Great Britain. In this environment Carnegie perfected the skills he later employed to make his own firm, Carnegie Steel, one of the most successful in the world.

During his years as a railroad executive, Carnegie began to invest in other companies.

A hand-colored photograph of Andrew Carnegie from 1896.

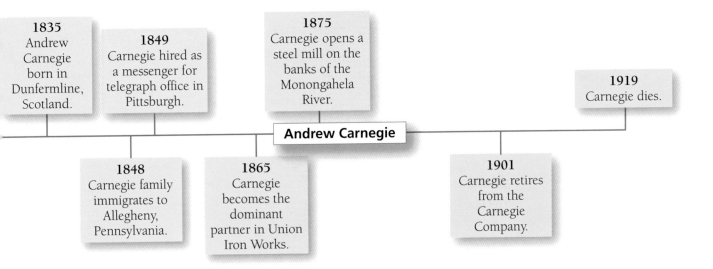

1835 Andrew Carnegie born in Dunfermline, Scotland.

1849 Carnegie hired as a messenger for telegraph office in Pittsburgh.

1875 Carnegie opens a steel mill on the banks of the Monongahela River.

1919 Carnegie dies.

Andrew Carnegie

1848 Carnegie family immigrates to Allegheny, Pennsylvania.

1865 Carnegie becomes the dominant partner in Union Iron Works.

1901 Carnegie retires from the Carnegie Company.

Within a few years his investments made him a wealthy man with substantial interests in several firms closely tied to the railroad business, including an iron works, a sleeping car firm, and a telegraph company. He worked with fellow investors Scott and Thomson to reorganize these businesses to make them more efficient.

Carnegie resigned from the railroad in 1865 but continued his association with Scott and Thomson. The three had been involved since 1862 with a company that built iron bridges. As railroad men, they were familiar with the frequent fires that destroyed wooden railroad bridges, and iron was becoming a popular bridge-building material. Their Keystone Bridge Company grew so rapidly during the post–Civil War railroad boom that it needed more financial capital than could be raised in the United States. Carnegie went to Europe to sell Keystone bonds. For the next few years he was involved mainly in raising capital for the companies in which he had an interest.

In 1865 Carnegie became the dominant partner in Union Iron Works, which supplied iron beams and plates to Keystone Bridge. He introduced the efficient management methods he had learned in the railroad industry to both firms. By assuring a reliable supply of iron components to Keystone Bridge, and by coordinating the operations of the two firms, Carnegie lowered the cost of making bridges. Controlling successive stages of the productive process in this way is now called vertical integration.

In 1872 Carnegie formed a partnership to build a steel mill on the banks of the Monongahela River, a few miles south of Pittsburgh. The major product of the new mill, which opened in 1875, was steel rails for railroad tracks. The mill's first order came from Carnegie's old employer, the Pennsylvania Railroad. However, Carnegie also supplied steel for the Brooklyn Bridge and, in 1885, acquired the nearby Homestead Works, which he converted to producing structural steel for buildings. As the need for railroad track declined, the company found new markets in the rapidly growing cities of the United States.

Andrew Carnegie amassed a fortune and gave most of it away; for example, between 1881 and 1917, the Carnegie Foundation built more than 2,500 libraries all around the world.

Carnegie Libraries 1881 to 1917

Country	Number of libraries built	Total cost per country
United States	1,681	$ 41,233,853.47
United Kingdom and Ireland	660	$ 11,849,457.50
Canada	125	$ 2,556,660
New Zealand	17	$ 194,460
South Africa	12	$ 139,000
West Indies	5	$ 66,500
Australia and Tasmania	4	$ 70,000
Seychelles	1	$ 10,000
Mauritius	1	$ 9,000
Fiji	1	$ 7,500
Total	2,507	$56,136,430.97[1]

[1] Includes $13,067,592.31 paid by the Carnegie Corporation of New York, from 1911 onward.
Source: Robert M. Lester, Forty Years of Carnegie Giving, New York, C. Scribner's Sons, 1941.

Carnegie Hall in New York City opened in 1891.

Carnegie's strategy in the steel business was similar to that he used in earlier ventures. He kept costs low by producing as much as possible, to take full advantage of his machinery and equipment. To sell the large volume he produced, he continually reduced prices, underselling his competitors. He pressured managers to find new ways to save money. He searched for new and better machinery, discarding even recently purchased equipment if a superior product came on the market. Continuing the process of vertical integration, he acquired rights to mine John D. Rockefeller's rich iron ore property in the newly discovered Mesabi iron range in Minnesota. He also signed a 50-year contract to ship the ore to Pittsburgh on Rockefeller steamships and railroads, thus controlling his transportation costs.

Carnegie retired from Carnegie Company in 1901. He and his partners sold the firm to a new corporation, United States Steel, formed by the legendary investment banker J. P. Morgan. Carnegie's share of the sale made him one of the richest men in the world. He spent the rest of his life distributing his fortune to many worthy causes.

In "Wealth," an 1889 article written for the *North American Review*, Carnegie declared that the moral obligation of those reaping the rewards of industrialization is to share those rewards with the larger community. To that end, Carnegie financed the construction of more than 2,000 libraries throughout the United States and the English-speaking world; he also built Carnegie Hall in New York City and the Peace Palace in the Netherlands. Carnegie established hundreds of funds, trusts, and university endowments, giving away approximately $350 million. When he died on August 11, 1919, he had given away most of his fortune. As great as Carnegie's reputation as a philanthropist may be, he deserves equal credit for his accomplishments as a businessman in making low-cost, high-quality steel available to the expanding United States.

This, then, is held to be the duty of the man of Wealth: First, to set an example of modest, unostentatious living, shunning display or extravagance; to provide moderately for the legitimate wants of those dependent upon him; and after doing so to consider all surplus revenues which come to him simply as trust funds, which he is called upon to administer, and strictly bound as a matter of duty to administer in the manner which, in his judgment, is best calculated to produce the most beneficial results for the community—the man of wealth thus becoming the mere agent and trustee for his poorer brethren. . . . in this manner returning their surplus wealth to the mass of their fellows in the forms best calculated to do them lasting good.

Thus is the problem of Rich and Poor to be solved.

—Andrew Carnegie, "Wealth," *North American Review*, 1889.

Further Reading

Livesay, Harold C. *Andrew Carnegie and the Rise of Big Business.* New York: Addison Wesley Longman, 2000.

Meltzer, Milton. *The Many Lives of Andrew Carnegie.* New York: Franklin Watts, 1997.

Wall, Joseph Frazier. *Andrew Carnegie.* New York: Oxford University Press, 1970.

—*Jean Caldwell*

Cartel

A cartel is a group of producers in a particular industry that band together to coordinate their output and prices, sometimes with government support. For cartel members, success requires eliminating competition within the group and preventing new competitors from entering the market. To the extent that they succeed in their anticompetitive practices, cartels typically make prices higher. For this reason, they are generally regarded as undesirable within market economies.

The word *cartel* derives from the Italian word *cartello*, meaning "placard." The French borrowed the word as *cartel* in the sixteenth century and used it to mean "a written challenge or letter of defiance." Its modern meaning in English, suggesting defiance of market competition, has evolved from this French usage.

Cartels originated in Germany in the 1870s, when Germany's economy was growing rapidly. The German government encouraged the formation of cartels prior to and during World War I to foster the production of armaments and other war-related materials. Following the war, in the 1920s and 1930s, German firms formed cartels in many basic industries. The most prominent example was I. G. Farbenindustrie, a group of firms producing chemicals and dyes. At the onset of World War II, the German economy was dominated by cartels, which the government continued to encourage and supervise, again in support of the nation's mobilization for war.

Cartels also may be international, with firms from different countries combining efforts to dominate world markets for their products. Until the late 1930s international cartels existed primarily in the pharmaceuticals and steel industries. However, beginning in the 1960s, some cartels were formed by the governments of oil-rich countries. The most famous of these is the Organization of Petroleum Exporting Countries (OPEC); its 11 members include several Middle Eastern states, including Iraq and Saudi Arabia, as well as countries in Africa, Southeast Asia, and South America.

Increased profits are the goal of cartels. Participating firms enter into agreements to "fix" prices—that is, to raise them above the level that would prevail if the firms competed

See also:
Economies of Scale;
Monopoly; Organization of
Petroleum Exporting
Countries; Sherman
Antitrust Act.

Secretary general of the Organization of Petroleum Exporting Countries Alvaro Silva Calderon of Venezuela at a press conference at the Geneva offices of the United Nations on November 20, 2002.

Cartels, historically common in the pharmaceutical industry, continue to be formed. In 2001 eight firms were fined by the European Union for colluding to inflate the price of vitamins.

with one another in an open market. Such collusive arrangements may be explicit, with firms openly agreeing to form a cartel, or they may be tacit (understood), marked by a pattern of behavior rather than any binding, formal agreement.

To raise prices collectively, cartel members must reduce industry output. This sometimes involves dividing the market into segments and assigning responsibility for supplying each segment to a particular firm. In these cases, the cartel operates as if it were one firm, a monopolist.

Cartels are illegal in the United States because they are deemed anticompetitive. Formal contracts to restrict competition cannot be enforced in court. To succeed, then, cartels must rely on informal arrangements that provide incentives for the member firms to conform to the cartel's policies. In practice, such cooperation can be difficult

to initiate and maintain because each firm has an incentive to cheat—to lower its price slightly by expanding its output at the expense of other firms, thus capturing a larger share of the market.

In the United Kingdom and other countries of Western Europe, some cartels exist legally, but they are monitored by governments to ensure that their monopolistic practices do not become outrageous. In 2001 the European Union fined a pharmaceutical cartel more than 800 million euros (more than $800 million) for keeping vitamin prices artificially high. Although U.S. companies are prohibited by law from forming cartels domestically, they are permitted by U.S. law to "export" a cartel, that is, to coordinate their actions in other markets where they compete.

Cartels have played a major role in the development of several key industries including textiles, pharmaceuticals, and petroleum products. Some argue, moreover, that cartels provide important benefits (contending, for example, that they stabilize markets, reduce costs of production, eliminate high tariffs, and distribute profits equitably). Against these arguments, market-oriented economists and policy makers maintain that, by restricting the competitive process, cartels increase costs for consumers, thus reducing individual well-being and the standard of living for society in general. Accordingly, legal authorities in market-oriented economies will most likely continue to look with disfavor on cartels.

Further Reading

Fleisher, Arthur A. *The National Collegiate Athletic Association: A Study in Cartel Behavior.* Chicago: University of Chicago Press, 1992.

Jones, Geoffrey. *The Evolution of International Business: An Introduction.* London and New York: Routledge, 1996.

LeClair, Mark S. *International Commodity Markets and the Role of Cartels.* Armonk, N.Y.: M. E. Sharpe, 2000.

Levy, Herman. *Industrial Germany: A Study of Its Monopoly Organizations and Their Control by the State.* New York: A. M. Kelley, 1996.

—*Mikhail Kouliavtsev*

Cash Flow

Cash flow is a measurement used by companies to indicate how much ready money is created and consumed by a particular project or by the company as a whole. A company's overall cash flow is considered to be a particularly revealing indicator of its ability to survive—even more than whether the company is profitable. Cash flow is so vital that all publicly owned companies in the United States, as well as in countries that have adopted international accounting standards, must analyze cash flow for their shareholders (in a form similar to the sample at the right) along with revenue and profits).

As the name suggests, cash flow is all about cash. In the world of business, *cash* does not mean actual bills and coins but rather so-called liquid assets, or assets that can be used right away to pay invoices, salaries, or other obligations. A shortage of cash can lead to what is called a liquidity crisis.

People and even countries can also have liquidity crises. Consider this example: a man has no savings and a job at a fast-food restaurant. The job barely pays the rent of $600 a month on his apartment, which he must pay in cash at the end of every month or he will be forced out. His car breaks down; he needs $300 to have the car repaired, but payday is several days away. The man now has a cash-flow problem.

The next day, he buys a winning lottery ticket worth $20 million. He goes down to the lottery office to turn in his ticket. The lottery officials tell him that he will receive several million dollars in cash but not for 18 months, since it will take that long to process the paperwork. How is he going to get the car fixed?

Just as the future lottery payout will not pay the mechanic, a business's buildings, equipment, and long-term investments will not pay landlords, suppliers, and employees—only cash will do that. While the lottery winner probably will not have too

much trouble convincing someone to lend him rent money, the loan will cost him, as it would a company that found itself in a similar situation. A company could also attract additional investors, swapping ownership

See also:
Accounting and Bookkeeping; Budget; Credit; Income Statement.

Sample Consolidated Cash Flow Statement

Consolidated statements of cash flow
(in millions of euros)

	2003	2002	2001
Cash flows from operating activities			
Net income (loss)	(4,963)	1,324	644
Minority interests	5	3	37
Adjustments to reconcile income before minority interests:			
– Depreciation and amortization, net	1,279	1,189	1,050
– Amortization of goodwill and purchased R&D[1]	1,937	597	800
– Changes in reserves for pension obligations, net	41	24	(116)
– Changes in other reserves, net	2,001	(32)	(146)
– Net (gain) loss on disposal of non-current assets	(943)	(915)	(862)
– Share in net income of equity affiliates (net of dividends received)	88	(47)	(133)
Working capital provided (used) by operations	**(555)**	**2,143**	**1,274**
Net change in current assets and liabilities:			
– Decrease (increase) in accounts receivable	1,117	(2,147)	(453)
– Decrease (increase) in inventories	1,186	(3,330)	(333)
– Increase (decrease) in accounts payable and accrued expenses	(1,203)	2,089	588
– Changes in reserves on current assets (including accrued contract costs), net[2]	–	–	–
Net cash provided (used) by operating activities	**545**	**(1,245)**	**1,076**
Cash flows from investing activities:			
– Proceeds from disposal of fixed assets	182	107	191
– Capital expenditures	(1,748)	(1,834)	(1,224)
– Decrease (increase) in loans	299	(962)	(20)
– Cash expenditures for acquisition of consolidated companies, net of cash acquired, and for acquisition of unconsolidated companies	(743)	(834)	(2,173)
– Cash proceeds from sale of previously consolidated companies, net of cash sold, and from sale of unconsolidated companies	3,627	1,579	750
Net cash provided (used) by investing activities	**1,617**	**(1,944)**	**(2,476)**
Net cash flows after investment	**2,162**	**(3,189)**	**(1,400)**
Cash flows from financing activities:			
– Increase (decrease) in short-term debt	(1,401)	(889)	(352)
– Proceeds from issuance of long-term debt	1,744	2,565	1,756
– Proceeds from issuance of shares	8	1,490	110
– Dividends paid	(567)	(508)	(391)
Net cash provided (used) by financing activities	**(216)**	**2,658**	**1,123**
Net effect of exchange rate changes	7	(4)	59
Net increase (decrease) in cash and cash equivalents	1,953	(535)	(218)
Cash and cash equivalents at beginning of year	3,060	3,595	3,813

(1) R&D = research and development
(2) Reclassified under the line "Changes in other reserves, net" in working capital provided by operations.

Cash and Telecommunications

In the late 1990s, the telecommunications market was deregulated, and the industry began to expand rapidly. New companies were entering the market, challenging the local telephone companies that had once operated with no competition.

Investors became enamored of the sector. In 1999 and 2000, U.S. telecommunications companies raised an average of $2 billion every month by making initial public offerings of stock. Many of these new telecommunications businesses took on an enormous amount of debt to build expensive networks.

In 2000, the stock market crashed and investors began to avoid telecommunications stocks, making it very difficult for the upstarts to raise cash by issuing and selling stock. Such companies generally did not have enough customers to get lots of cash from them, and, as they had already borrowed so much money, they could not borrow more. Telecommunications upstarts—even the profitable ones—began to have trouble making the cash payments on the large loans they had taken out in the late 1990s. Many went into bankruptcy, while others were bought out.

Who did the buying? The stodgy, old-fashioned local telephone companies that investors had ignored but that had lots of cash, thanks to the millions of customers who paid their local phone bills every month. Even a relatively small player like Alltel Corp., which mainly offered local service in rural areas, generated $2 billion in cash from business operations in 2001. Such companies were able to buy faltering competitors and pay for other expansions with cash, rather than by borrowing money or selling stock. As the established telephone companies did not have to pay interest on loans, they were more profitable, and, more important, they survived the industry shakeout.

---

of the company for cash. Sometimes, however, a company in a liquidity crisis cannot raise the cash it needs. In that case, the company may go bankrupt.

Liquidity crises are all the more disturbing because revenue and income statements may not indicate that one is approaching. A fast-growing company with strong profits may face a liquidity crisis because it is expanding so quickly that even its growing revenues are not enough to cover the additional costs of more personnel, equipment, and supplies.

In addition, the way that revenues and income are calculated can conceal serious problems. Under standard accounting principles, accounts receivable—payments due for products that have been sold to a customer—are counted as revenues. Customers that owe a company money may not actually pay it, however. Customers may be about to enter bankruptcy, in which case the company may never get paid or get only a small fraction of what it is owed.

Cash flow is designed to help investors and companies spot a potential liquidity crisis before it wipes a company out. Cash flow is very focused on the here-and-now, as opposed to income and revenue, which tend to be more influenced by what has happened in the past and what might happen in the future.

For example, accounts receivable cannot be counted as positive cash flow. Cash flow reflects only money that has actually been received from customers. If a firm is owed a lot of money by its customers but is not actually collecting much money, that tells investors and executives that something is wrong—either the company's main customers are all in serious trouble or the company is not doing a very good job of collecting its debts.

Cash flow and income figures account for major purchases in different ways. In an income statement, the money spent on a factory or expensive piece of equipment must be depreciated, or averaged out, over the expected lifetime of the purchased item. Cash flow simply records how much cash was spent to make the purchase at the time it was made.

Cash flow has limitations. It can be highly volatile; the purchase of, for example, an expensive factory can result in sharply negative cash flow, even if the purchase was a wise long-term business decision. Nevertheless, cash flow provides companies with a valuable planning tool, allowing them to anticipate potential liquidity problems and secure financing in advance. Cash flow also gives investors a method to determine whether the company in which they are investing is likely to be around in the future.

Further Reading

Kallberg, Jarl G., and Kenneth L. Parkinson. *Corporate Liquidity: Management and Measurement.* Homewood, Ill.: Richard D. Irwin, 1993.

Mansonson, Leslie N. *Cash, Cash, Cash: The Three Principles of Business Survival and Success.* New York: Harper Business, 1990.

Plewa, Franklin J., Jr., and George T. Friedlob. *Understanding Cash Flow.* New York: John Wiley & Sons, 1995.

—*Mary Sissor*

Chambers of Commerce

A chamber of commerce consists of business leaders who join together to promote business interests in a community, state, or nation. Its primary goal is to promote the development and continued success of its members while making the area attractive to visitors, investors, and the workforce. It provides a place for members to discuss and act on important business issues and exerts influence in the legal arena by participating in discussions of and action about legislation, regulation, and court rulings.

Chambers of commerce can be found at all levels: international, national, state, and local. Most chambers focus on business and legal issues at their level but can extend their influence to higher levels of government when it serves their interests. Each chamber of commerce exists independently; for example, the U.S. Chamber of Commerce is not an umbrella organization for state and local chambers. However, a local chamber can join a state chamber of commerce, and both local and state chambers can join the U.S. chamber.

The U.S. Chamber of Commerce, located in Washington, D.C., works for businesses on the national level. Established in 1912, it advocates for U.S. business interests before regulatory agencies, all three branches of the government—Congress, the White House, and the courts—and in the media. In 2002 it represented three million businesses, 3,000 state and local chapters, 830 business associations, and 92 American chambers of commerce abroad. In addition to tracking bills in Congress, the U.S. Chamber of Commerce represents business interests in areas like

See also:
Better Business Bureau;
National Black Chamber of
Commerce; Small Business
Administration.

Members of the local chamber of commerce in Brooklyn, New York, pose with President Calvin Coolidge (fifth from right) in 1929.

Sign outside office of the Chinese Chamber of Commerce in San Francisco.

interests in the local community both legal and economically, local chambers may provide community bulletin board information, visitor and relocation information, maps, and a business directory. Other projects can include improving streets, public works, emergency services, schools, and recreation, and tourist facilities. Their goal is to unite business interests for the good of the community. Many times the Convention and Visitor Bureau is part of the chamber of commerce.

State chambers of commerce work on business and legal issues at the state level of government. They ensure that employer opinions are heard in legislative, regulatory, and judicial battles. Issues of concern might include taxation, business and environmental regulation, education and workforce training, technology, and development. State chambers also provide workshops and seminars (both classroom and online), benefits programs like health insurance and discounts on goods and services, and a variety of other services to help businesses stay competitive. Joining the state chamber of commerce allows members to network with similar businesses across the state.

Chambers of commerce abroad are called American Chambers of Commerce (AmChams). There are about 100 AmChams in various foreign countries, all affiliated with the U.S. Chamber of Commerce. Local companies of the host country can outnumber American companies in terms of membership. In most, if not all, cases, AmChams are privately funded, receiving no money from host countries. AmChams concentrate on foreign trade and investment opportunities for U.S. companies abroad. This could include developing services to promote commerce, representing American interests to the host country's government, businesses, and general public, or keeping abreast of current business practices and trends. They work with both U.S. and host country governments to create a mutually favorable trade environment.

Other kinds of chambers of commerce include the U.S. Junior Chamber of Commerce (Jaycees), which is dedicated to developing future business leaders through community service and leadership training.

economic and tax policy, education and workforce training, legal reform, privatization and procurement, transportation, retirement and Social Security, e-commerce and technology, defense, and immigration.

Membership offers benefits: discounted goods and services, retirement plans and insurance, information on business policy issues, and a variety of resources for business owners, especially small businesses. The U.S. Chamber of Commerce does not distribute lists of its members nor does it endorse organizations or provide references for its members.

Local chambers of commerce focus on building the community economically and improving the quality of life in the community. In addition to representing business

Local chambers of commerce often organize events to attract tourists. The Hollywood Chamber of Commerce runs the Walk of Fame, a five-acre stretch of bronze stars commemorating members of the entertainment industry. Actor Jackie Chan, center, received a star in 2002. From left, honorary mayor of Hollywood Johnny Grant, actor Owen Wilson, Chan, director Brett Ratner, chairman of the board of the Hollywood Chamber of Commerce Russ Joyner, and Leron Gubler, president of the Hollywood Chamber of Commerce.

ounded in 1920 in St. Louis, Missouri, the Jaycees focuses on education, networking, and career advancement in addition to community service. The national organization promotes nationwide service projects while local chapters of the Jaycees are involved in community service projects. Jaycees around the country have built parks, playgrounds, and housing for the elderly, and raised millions of dollars for charity.

The United States Hispanic National Chamber of Commerce is specifically concerned with Hispanic-owned businesses, business interests, and networking. In addition to offering support on business development and legislative issues, this organization works with Latin American countries to foster favorable trade agreements. The National Black Chamber of Commerce represents black-owned businesses and has chapters across the United States and abroad. Its primary purpose is to empower black communities and promote participation in the free enterprise system.

The idea of businesspeople banding together for their common good also extends to the Internet. Several Web chambers of commerce serve the interests of companies that do business on the World Wide Web. Some of the Web chambers require adopting a set of Internet business ethics; others focus on issues related to doing business on the Web.

When businesses band together, they gain the advantage of numbers in the legal and economic arenas. Although the main purpose of chambers of commerce is to promote members' business interests, most recognize the importance of giving back to the community, both directly through community projects and information and through improved economic strength. A healthy local or state economy can attract even more businesses to an area, bringing increased opportunity, employment, and tax revenues.

Further Reading

De Soto, William. *The Politics of Business Organizations: Understanding the Role of State Chambers of Commerce.* Lanham, Md.: University Press of America, 1995.

—Stephanie Buckwalter

Chambers of Commerce on the World Wide Web

Canadian Chamber of Commerce. www.chamber.ca

International Chamber of Commerce. www.iccwbo.org

National Black Chamber of Commerce. www.nationalbcc.org

United States Chamber of Commerce. www.uschamber.org

United States Hispanic Chamber of Commerce. www.ushcc.com

Junior Chambers of Commerce

Canada Junior Chamber. www.canadianjrchamber.ca

Junior Chamber International. www.jci.cc

United States Junior Chamber (Jaycees). www.usjaycees.org

See also:
Agriculture Industry;
Labor Union; National Labor
Relations Act; Strikes;
Working Conditions.

Chavez, Cesar

1927–1993
Labor organizer and social activist

Cesar Chavez achieved distinction as a labor organizer committed to reducing racism and poverty. His leadership of the United Farm Workers, a union of agricultural laborers, helped its members earn twice the average farmworker income by the 1980s. Chavez strove to draw attention to the effects that racial and class prejudice had on the status of workers.

Chavez was born near Yuma, Arizona, on March 31, 1927, second of six children of Librado and Juana Chavez. As a young man Librado Chavez had worked on his parents' homestead, but after marrying in 1924, he

and Juana Chavez purchased a combined grocery store, garage, and pool hall. The Great Depression destroyed the Chavez family finances and the parents were forced to sell their business. Returning to the Chavez homestead, they tried to farm, but drought prevented irrigation. In 1937 the state of Arizona took the homestead as compensation for unpaid taxes.

The family moved to California in 1938 to work as migrant agricultural laborers. With his parents and siblings, Cesar Chavez harvested fruit and vegetables across the state. Constant travel meant that the children, like those of most migrant laborers, received only sporadic education. In 1942 Chavez quit school altogether to help support the family.

Chavez sought more opportunities by enlisting in the navy in 1944. However, he

Cesar Chavez with members of the National Farm Workers Association in 1967.

as troubled by the racial discrimination he experienced in the military. During this period, he was arrested for deliberately violating a racial segregation policy at a cinema in Delano, California. No charges were filed, but the incident and the racism he experienced in the navy convinced Chavez that injustice must be challenged directly.

In 1948 Cesar Chavez married Helen Fabela and settled in Delano, California. The couple lived in a one-room shack while Chavez worked on farms. On one occasion, with his father and others, Cesar walked off the job to protest unjust working conditions. Librado Chavez believed in collective labor protests and helped shape his son's growing commitment to activism.

Word spread of the younger Chavez's willingness to take public stands, and in 1952 a recruiter for the Community Service Organization (CSO) asked Chavez to join. The CSO, which promoted civic activism among poor people, soon hired Chavez, and he became its national director in 1958. He learned grassroots methods of organizing people to address inequities and was especially active in helping Chicanos (Mexican Americans) register to vote.

In 1962 Chavez resigned the CSO in protest after the CSO board rejected his plan for organizing farmworkers. He formed the National Farm Workers Association (NFWA); by 1965, several thousand people were members. In that year, NFWA joined with the primarily Filipino American members of the Agricultural Workers Organizing Committee (AWOC) in a strike against farm owners, especially those growing grapes. Drawing inspiration from African Americans' use of nonviolence to challenge racism, Chavez led strikers on a 300-mile march to Sacramento, California, in 1966. The march persuaded smaller farm owners to support unionization of agricultural laborers and led to creation of the United Farm Workers Organizing Committee (UFWOC) when NFWA and AWOC merged with the AFL-CIO.

UFWOC efforts to win recognition from major grape growers were initially thwarted. To persuade growers, Chavez in 1968 promoted a consumer boycott of California grapes. This effort was similar to consumer boycotts that African Americans had organized against businesses practicing racial segregation. The public supported the boycott; polls found that millions of people were not buying grapes. Chavez heightened public awareness of the *huelga* (meaning "strike" in Spanish) with a personal three-week hunger strike inspired by the political fasts of Mohandas Gandhi in India.

By 1970 more grape growers had recognized the UFWOC and agreed to improve workers' pay, health benefits, and working conditions. New challenges emerged for the UFW (the union dropped Organizing Committee from its name in 1973), including a rival organizing effort by the Teamsters and a 1972 grower-led ballot initiative to ban farm-related boycotts in California. Chavez responded by mobilizing voters to defeat the initiative and convincing workers to reject the grower-friendly Teamsters.

By the mid-1970s, Chavez was nationally recognized as a union leader and nonviolent crusader against social injustice. He

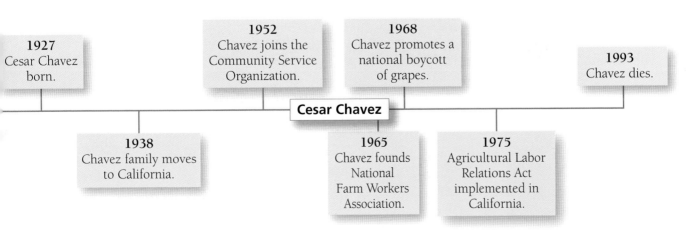

1927
Cesar Chavez born.

1938
Chavez family moves to California.

Cesar Chavez

1952
Chavez joins the Community Service Organization.

1965
Chavez founds National Farm Workers Association.

1968
Chavez promotes a national boycott of grapes.

1975
Agricultural Labor Relations Act implemented in California.

1993
Chavez dies.

In 1973, in New York City, Chavez (third from right) and Coretta Scott King (fourth from right) lead farm workers urging a boycott of lettuce.

helped persuade California's assembly to pass the Agricultural Labor Relations Act (ALRA), which was implemented in 1975. This law allowed collective bargaining and supervised union elections on California farms. Such labor rights existed for most workers nationally under the 1935 National Labor Relations Act (NLRA), but that law specifically excluded farm laborers.

Following passage of the ALRA, Chavez met with further opposition. In 1976 California voters defeated a UFW-promoted initiative to fund monitoring of agricultural workplaces. Growers promoted political resistance to the UFW and supported officials who shared their views. Meanwhile, some UFW members criticized Chavez for combining social justice efforts with straightforward union activities.

Such strains affected UFW support: in the 1980s membership dropped below 12,000 (from an earlier high of 105,000). Chavez especially blamed the California Farm Labor Board, created by the ALRA. The board routinely ruled against farmworkers in labor disputes. To revive public support, Chavez and the UFW initiated a new grape boycott in 1984, although costs of the campaign reduced

funds for union expansion. Chavez engage in a month-long hunger strike in 1988 to su port the boycott. By 1990 grape sales ha dropped in major cities; the UFW, howeve lost two grower-initiated lawsuits for damag incurred during strikes and boycotts.

Despite setbacks, Chavez began anoth hunger strike in 1993 as the UFW appeal one of the lawsuit judgments. Weakenc from previous fasts, Chavez died in h sleep. Thousands marched in his funer procession from downtown Delano to th original UFW headquarters. Union organi ers joined Chicano activists in honorir Chavez for his sustained efforts to reduc racism, social injustice, and oppressiv working conditions on U.S. farms.

Further Reading

Davis, Lucile. *Cesar Chavez: A Photo-Illustrated Biography*. Mankato, Minn.: Bridgestone Books, 1998.

Griswold del Castillo, Richard. "Cesar Estrada Chavez: The Final Struggle." *Southern California Quarterly* 78 (1996): 199–214.

Griswold del Castillo, Richard, and Richard Garcia *Cesar Chavez: A Triumph of Spirit*. Norman: University of Oklahoma Press, 1995.

—*Beth Kra*

Chicago Board of Trade

The Chicago Board of Trade (CBOT) is the oldest futures exchange in the world; it was established in 1848 to enable trade between farmers and merchants. The original purpose of the CBOT was to standardize the quality and quantity of grains that were traded; in 1865 the first futures contract was developed. These contracts became popular because they allowed farmers to lock in a selling price for their grain prior to harvest, and the contracts gave merchants who wished to purchase grain the chance to lock in a price and a supply of grain. The CBOT serves as a meeting place for exchange members to buy and sell contracts on agricultural commodities and financial instruments for their customers and themselves. To become an exchange member, an individual must purchase a seat on the exchange. As of March 2002, the seat price for the CBOT was more than $320,000.

Both futures contracts and options on futures contracts enable individuals to enter into an agreement today that specifies a price, quantity, and date for an exchange of goods that will occur in the future. While futures contracts are legally binding agreements to buy (take delivery of) or sell (make delivery of) a commodity, option contracts do not impose an obligation on the buyer of the contract. Rather, the owner of an option contract has the right to buy or sell the underlying futures contract at a certain price for a limited time.

Futures and option contracts have become popular because they allow traders to hedge their risk by taking a position in the derivatives market that offsets their natural position. For example, wheat farmers are naturally "long" (have a supply of) on wheat. To hedge the risk of falling wheat prices, farmers can go "short" (agree to sell) wheat at the prevailing price in the futures market. This transaction allows the farmer to lock in a selling price for his wheat. Derivatives markets are also used for speculation, which is the practice of buying and selling futures and

See also:
Dow Jones Averages; Futures Markets; Nasdaq; New York Stock Exchange.

Chicago Board of Trade

1848
Chicago Board of Trade (CBOT) established.

1865
First futures contract developed.

1994
CBOT adopts electronic trading with the Project A system.

2000
CBOT replaces Project A with a/c/e system.

2001
Trading volume on the CBOT reaches 260 million contracts.

2002
Value of a CBOT seat reaches $320,000.

The Chicago Board of Trade in session circa 1900.

Brokers on the trading floor are reflected in the ever-changing digital trade board.

options contracts for profit. Speculators have no natural positions in the underlying asset; they simply buy and sell in anticipation of future price movements. While hedging helps to reduce risk, speculating in the derivatives market can be very risky, especially for novice traders.

Many kinds of contracts are traded on the CBOT, including agricultural futures and options (wheat, corn, oats); metal futures and options (gold and silver); financial futures and options (government bonds and municipal bonds); and stock index futures and options (Dow Jones Averages). Each contract trades in a designated area, called a trading pit, on the floor of the exchange. Trading is conducted using an open outcry system during regular trading hours. In an open outcry system, traders verbally communicate their offers to buy and sell to others in the trading pit. In addition to verbal offers, traders also use a system of highly developed hand signals to communicate with each other. Trading volume has grown from four million contracts per year in 1921, when the only contracts were futures contracts on corn, wheat, oats, and rye, to 260 million contracts in 2001.

In contrast to the U.S. stock exchanges and other futures markets around the world, which rely heavily on technology and computers to facilitate trading, very little technology is used to facilitate trading at the CBOT. However, to remain competitive the CBOT has added some electronic trading to its well-established open outcry system. Electronic trading was introduced in 1994 with the Project A system. In August 2000, Project A was replaced with a/c/e (Alliance/CBOT/Eurex). The electronic trading system has been used to expand trading time after the close of the traditional open outcry trading hours.

Throughout its history, the CBOT has chosen to remain relatively low-tech. This choice differentiates the CBOT from many of its global competitors in futures trading, including the London International Futures and Options Exchange and the Eurex, the European Derivatives Market. The coming years will see an interesting experiment as the CBOT with its open outcry system competes head-to-head with global futures exchanges that allow trading around the clock. The question remains: Is technology crucial for the success of futures markets, or can two different trading systems flourish side by side in the twenty-first century?

Further Reading

Hull, John C. *Fundamentals of Futures and Options.* 4th ed. Upper Saddle River, N.J.: Prentice Hall, 2002.

Kolb, Robert W. *Understanding Futures Markets.* 4th ed. Oxford: Blackwell Publishers, 1996.

—*Angeline Lavin*

Child Labor

Child labor has existed throughout recorded history. For most of that time, however, the idea of childhood did not exist as we know it: rather, children were viewed as little adults. In the late eighteenth century, writers like Jean-Jacques Rousseau began to suggest that there is a special period of growth unique to children and that young people, with their special developmental and educational needs, should not be viewed as miniature versions of adults. Although this view of children eventually became the norm, especially among the upper classes, it took more than a century for child labor to be regarded as a social injustice.

Part of the reason that child labor came to be seen as a social ill was the changing nature of work performed by children. Before the Industrial Revolution, all children

See also:
Fair Labor Standards Act;
Globalization; Industrial
Revolution; Lowell Mills;
Working Conditions.

Three young girls outside the Maggioni Canning Company in Port Royal, South Carolina, where they worked as oyster shuckers. This photo was taken by Lewis W. Hine in February 1911.

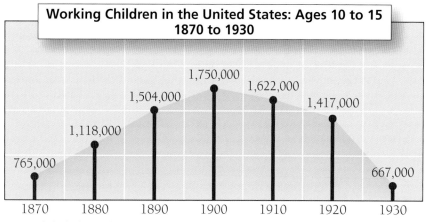

Working Children in the United States: Ages 10 to 15 1870 to 1930

765,000 — 1870
1,118,000 — 1880
1,504,000 — 1890
1,750,000 — 1900
1,622,000 — 1910
1,417,000 — 1920
667,000 — 1930

Note: Includes both agricultural and nonagricultural work. Comparable data not available for later years.
Source: Historical Statistics of the United States, Government Printing Office, Washington, D.C., 1975.

This chart shows the total number of working children aged 10 to 15 in the United States from after the Civil War to the start of the Depression. The Fair Labor Standards Act of 1938 placed strict limits on when children under 16 might be allowed to work.

of the household participated in the family economy. They might work with animals, help with weaving, and perform other tasks critical to the household, supporting the work performed by parents.

At a certain age, children might be apprenticed to a craftsman to learn a trade like shoemaking, pottery, or any number of other artisanal crafts. A master artisan provided apprentices with a place to live, food, and training. The children, who might share a living space with other apprentices, earned no wages but worked at chores usually associated with the trade they were learning. By the time they reached their early twenties, most apprentices, now masters, could start their own businesses. Far from being seen as exploitive, working as an apprentice was usually considered to be a fair arrangement for all involved.

The Industrial Revolution

With the coming of the Industrial Revolution, the nature of child labor changed. Instead of working at home as part of the productive life of the family, or being apprenticed to learn a valuable trade, children were now employed outside the home in factories, mines, and mills. The poet William Blake described these places of toil as "dark, satanic mills." Children as young as five or six would labor 12 to 16 hours a day in hot, poorly ventilated, overcrowded, dimly lit workplaces, sometimes with no breaks.

Children formed an important component in the expanding industrialization of the United States. A large percentage of workers were children, and employers often preferred to hire children rather than adults. Children could be paid less than adults and were more easily managed and more difficult for the emerging labor unions to organize.

Working children had little or no opportunity to attend school. Children who worked long hours in difficult conditions were often pale, undernourished, physically deformed, and sickly. Illness was endemic. Physical and mental fatigue combined with working on dangerous machinery resulted in accidents, maiming, loss of limbs, and death.

Although childhood was beginning to be recognized as a separate stage of life, not until the early part of the twentieth century were meaningful laws protecting children from abusive working conditions enacted in the United States. Even then, many working class families had little choice but to continue to view their children as integral to the family's economic well-being.

Twentieth Century

In 1904 the National Child Labor Committee (NCLC) was formed to address, on a federal level, the abuses of child labor in the United States. In 1908 the group hired photographer Lewis W. Hine to document the faces of children at labor in America. As a former schoolteacher, he was both aware of and critical of the lack of protection for children. Hine worked with the NCLC for eight years and traveled thousands of miles photographing children at work.

As a result of the work of people like Hine, progressive reformer Jane Addams, and others, Congress eventually passed the 1916 Keating-Owen Act, which prohibited the shipping of goods made by firms employing children under age 14. Business leaders challenged the law, and two years later the Supreme Court declared it unconstitutional. More than 20 years would pass before the federal government substantively readdressed the issue of child labor.

ith the Fair Labor Standards Act, passed
1938. Among the act's many provisions,
placed limitations on the hiring of chil-
en under the age of 16 and prohibited
ring children under that age in manufac-
ring and mining.

Although the general population was
owing increasingly opposed to child labor,
any other factors contributed to the
clining number of children in the work-
rce. The economic turmoil of the Great
epression resulted in many unemployed
ults; few were interested in seeing scarce
bs go to children. In addition, as new kinds
machinery were developed, the machines
ok over the simple tasks once done by chil-
ren. This new machinery required semi-
illed adults with some education rather
an unschooled children with small hands.
creasingly it became clear that the United
ates would need literate adults: By the early
ventieth century, all states had laws requir-
g some compulsory education. As a result,
ore children remained in school rather
an entered the labor market.

After World War II, child labor was
ssentially eliminated from the United States.
ome violations remain, however, particu-
rly among migrant agricultural workers. In
ddition, children of illegal immigrants are
metimes a source of low-wage workers for
dustries that compete with imports pro-
uced by low-wage workers, often children,
om other nations.

Contemporary Face of Child Labor

hild labor remains a harsh reality for mil-
ons of children around the globe. The
ternational Labor Organization (ILO),
ounded in 1919 and the first specialized
gency of the United Nations, estimates that
50 million children between the ages of
ve and 14 work in developing nations in
sia, Africa, and Latin America. The num-
ers may, in fact, be higher: As child labor is
sually illegal, it is often kept secret.
In 2000 the ILO created the Statistical
nformation and Monitoring Program on
Child Labor to begin the process of collect-
ng more reliable data.)

Iqbal Masih: Child Labor Activist

Born to impoverished laborers in rural Pakistan, Masih was bound out to a local carpet maker at the age of four to work off his father's debt of 600 rupiah (about $12). For
the next six years, he worked 12-hour days tying knots on a carpet loom. As a result of
the inadequate food and poor working conditions, Masih was left severely underde-
veloped for his age.

At age 10, Masih escaped from his employer and attended a meeting organized by
the Bonded Labour Liberation Front (BLLF), a human rights organization founded in
1988 to pressure the government of Pakistan to enforce laws prohibiting child and
bonded labor. Armed with a new knowledge of his legal rights, Masih refused to return
to the carpet mill. He became an active participant in the organization's campaign to
free child workers, and over the next two years he helped to liberate some 3,000 children from bonded labor. His precocious activism attracted international attention.
Masih was honored by the International Labor Organization in Sweden and awarded
the 1994 Human Rights Youth in Action Award by the Reebok Foundation.

On April 16, 1995, a few months after his return to Pakistan, Masih was gunned
down in front of his grandmother's house in the village of Muridke. The BLLF asserts
that the murder was engineered by the carpet industry, but the Pakistani government
claims that no evidence supports such charges. Masih's murder triggered an international outcry against the use of child labor in the carpet industry, adding to a growing
movement by consumers in Europe and North America to hold industries accountable
for their use of child labor.

—Rebecca Sherman

In November 1989 the Convention on
the Rights of the Child was adopted by the
General Assembly of the United Nations.
This marks the first time in history a community of nations formally addressed the
rights of children in a document of international law. Although the Convention was
signed by 140 nations, some of the signa-
tories are nations where abusive child
labor practices have been reported by the
Children's Rights Division at Human Rights
Watch and the ILO.

Agencies and organizations committed
to ending child labor, or its most abusive
practices, document a wide range of conditions. For example, some employers tie children as young as four to rug looms to keep
them working and restrain them from running away. At the other end of the spectrum,
children who work in family or community
endeavors may learn the value of mutual
responsibility.

Under some circumstances, working
may be beneficial to the child and the family. Indeed, in some instances the money
earned by a child may be the family's only
means of survival. The age of the child, the

Because the international community frowns on the use of child labor, the practice tends to be kept secret, and statistics are hard to come by. These estimates from the International Labour Union show the rate of labor participation among children from the ages of 5 to 14.

Participation Rate of Children in Developing Countries: 5 to 14 Years of Age 1995 (in percent)			
	Both sexes	Boys	Girls
World	24.7	27.0	22.3
Africa	41.4	46.0	36.7
Asia	21.5	22.5	20.4
Latin America	16.5	21.8	11.1
Oceania	29.3	32.7	25.8

Source: International Labour Union Bureau of Statistics, Geneva, 1996.

nature of the work, the effect of the work on the child's health, the conditions under which the child labors, and whether working keeps the child from attending school are all important factors in determining if the child is in a positive situation.

Children who work long hours in dangerous and unhealthy environments are at risk for lasting physical and psychological harm. As a result of working at looms, for example, some children become permanently disabled with eye damage, lung disease, and stunted growth; in addition, they become susceptible to arthritis as they age.

Malnutrition, confinement, beating, and sexual abuse make up only a part of the centuries-old legacy of child labor. In some cases, adults force children into bonded labor. Under such an arrangement, a family receives a small payment from an employer, and the child is expected to work off the payment before being returned to the family. The child usually cannot earn enough to pay the debt, nor does the family have the money to buy the child back from the employer.

International law forbade bonded labor with the 1956 United Nations Supplementary

Abdul Rasheed working as a carpet weaver in Muridke, Pakistan, in 1998. After strong international criticism, Pakistan's carpet weaving industry agreed in 1998 to phase out child labor and send workers like Rasheed to school instead.

Convention on the Abolition of Slavery, the Slave Trade, and Institutions and Practices. Nevertheless, millions of children around the world remain in bondage; the number in India alone is estimated at 15 million children. However, child labor and the exploitation often accompanying it are not restricted to developing nations.

Although the 1938 Fair Labor Standards Act prohibited "oppressive child labor," conditions for the children of agricultural workers in the United States remain little better than those in developing nations. Long hours, limited schooling, and exposure to toxic chemicals characterize the working environment for some of these children. Some states have no minimum age requirements for children employed in agriculture.

Child labor is a complex issue and a harsh reality for many working children, from the United States to Pakistan, who endure it. For those committed to a better future for the world's children, a global economy poses a paradox. Globalization has the potential to either exacerbate or diminish the abuses of child labor.

Further Reading

Freedman, Russell. *Kids at Work: Lewis Hine and the Crusade against Child Labor*. New York: Clarion Books, 1994.

Greene, L. *Child Labor: Then and Now*. New York: Franklin Watts, 1992.

Kielburger, Craig. *Free the Children: A Young Man Fights against Child Labor and Proves That Children Can Change the World*. New York: Perennial, HarperCollins, 1999.

McIntosh, R. G. *Boys in the Pits: Child Labour in Coal Mines*. Ithaca, N.Y.: McGill-Queen's University Press, 2000.

Nardinelli, C. *Child Labor and the Industrial Revolution*. Bloomington: Indiana University Press, 1990.

Taylor, Ronald B. *Sweatshops in the Sun: Child Labor on the Farm*. Boston: Beacon Press, 1973.

—*Connie Tuttle*

In the United States, children under the age of 16 sometimes work in the agricultural sector. This 11-year-old boy was picking chili peppers in Plainview, Texas, in 1997.

Chiquita

Before 1870 bananas were not available in the United States. In that year, Cape Cod merchant sailor Captain Lorenzo Dow Baker purchased 160 bunches of bananas in Jamaica for one shilling a bunch and sold them in Jersey City, New Jersey, for $2 each—a huge profit. Together with Boston businessman Andrew Preston, Baker started the Boston Fruit Company. Today, the company Baker founded is called Chiquita, and every American eats, on average, more than 28 pounds of bananas a year.

In 1871 Minor Keith, an ambitious 23-year-old from Brooklyn, New York, went to Costa Rica with his two brothers to help their uncle Henry Meiggs build a railroad from San José to the port of Limón on the Caribbean coast. When Meiggs and Keith's two brothers died in 1874, Keith was left in charge of the project. To feed his workers, Keith planted bananas on the land easements on either side of the tracks.

When the railway was finally finished, Keith found that few Costa Ricans could afford to travel on it. Keith then used his railroad to transport bananas to the port of Limón instead. Carrying bananas earned Keith more than carrying passengers, and he soon expanded into other Central American countries. By 1899 Keith dominated the banana business in Central America but was facing financial difficulties from old railroad construction debts that were coming due. Keith went to Boston and arranged a merger with his main rival in the banana business, the Boston Fruit Company. The new company, United Fruit, was incorporated on March 30, 1899. United Fruit had plantations in Colombia, Costa Rica, Cuba, Jamaica, Nicaragua, Panama, and Santo Domingo. It owned 112 miles of railroad linking the plantations with ports, along with 11 steamships, known as the Great White Fleet.

Owning Guatemala

In 1901 Guatemalan dictator Manuel Estrada Cabrera granted United Fruit the exclusive rights to transport bananas between Guatemala and the United States. United Fruit was eventually given control of 42 percent of all land in Guatemala, along with almost all means of transport and communication.

Guatemala became the center of United Fruit's empire. The Guatemalan town of Bananera (now Morales) was company headquarters. Over the next 40 years, United Fruit used and expanded on existing local systems of special privileges, bribery, and repression to defeat its business rivals.

United Fruit brought a great deal of economic development and organization to a region that had very little of either. The company built housing, schools, hospitals, and

Chiquita

1871
Minor Keith and family build railroad in Costa Rica; railroad ultimately transports bananas instead of passengers.

1899
United Fruit founded by Keith and his main rival, the Boston Fruit Company.

1901
United Fruit secures exclusive rights to Guatemala's banana trade.

1944
Guatemalan dictator Jorge Ubico overthrown; Juan José Arevalo elected president.

1954
Coup in Guatemala overthrows democratic government.

1970
United Fruit and AMK-John Morrell merge to form United Brands.

1989
United Brands changes name to Chiquita.

1994
Banana trade war between European Union and United States begins.

search laboratories. It sponsored research projects to conquer tropical diseases, like malaria and dengue fever, and to defeat diseases specific to the banana plant. Although the field-workers for United Fruit were paid more than other farmworkers, United Fruit staunchly opposed any attempts to form unions. Whole regions were abandoned at the first sign of union organizing, and company housing and schools torn down.

The Banana Revolution

In 1944 the people of Guatemala overthrew dictator Jorge Ubico and held the first free elections in the country's history. Reformer Juan José Arevalo was elected to the presidency and a new constitution, based on the U.S. Constitution, was written. At this time, over 70 percent of Guatemala's land was owned by just 2.2 percent of the population; most of this land was unused. When Jacobo Arbenz was elected to succeed Arevalo, he proposed redistribution of the unused land to make it available for farming. The largest holder of unused land in Guatemala was United Fruit. The company launched a campaign to convince Americans that the new Guatemalan government was communist.

In the early 1950s, United Fruit used its close connections with the Eisenhower administration and with the media to influence public and government opinion against Guatemala's elected government. The company's campaign succeeded, and in 1954 the Central Intelligence Agency (CIA) orchestrated a coup. The invading force numbered only 150 men, but the CIA convinced the Guatemalan public and President Arbenz that a major invasion was under way. When the government stepped down, the CIA replaced it with a right-wing dictatorship friendly to the United States—and to United Fruit. For the next 40 years, until 1996, Guatemala was run by one brutal regime after another, a civil war raged, and hundreds of thousands were killed or "disappeared." Among the first Guatemalans to be assassinated were 45 men who had attempted to organize unions on United Fruit plantations.

In other countries, workers were fighting back. In 1954 a banana workers strike in Honduras forced United Fruit to negotiate with the workers for increased wages and improved working conditions. For the first time in Honduran history, a private corporation had negotiated a collective agreement. Four years later, the U.S. government found United Fruit guilty of violating antitrust legislation and the company was forced to sell its Guatemalan estates.

A United Fruit Company building in Puerto Barrios, Guatemala, on the day of an anticommunist coup, June 19, 1954. The banner of Guatemala's biggest labor union, the General Confederation of Workers, adorns the building.

A worker washes bananas at a Chiquita plant in Cahuita, Costa Rica.

In 1961, in hopes of protecting its vast holdings in Cuba from Fidel Castro's land reform, United Fruit donated two of its ships to the U.S. invasion of Cuba at the Bay of Pigs. The attempted invasion was a fiasco, and all of United Fruit's Cuban land was appropriated by Castro.

United Fruit Becomes United Brands

On September 24, 1969, Eli Black, a Wall Street banker, made what was then the third largest transaction in Wall Street history by buying 733,000 shares of United Fruit in a single day, thus becoming the company's largest shareholder. The following year Black negotiated the merger of United Fruit and AMK-John Morrell. The new company took the name United Brands and began losing money almost immediately.

The Latin American banana-exporting countries also began to fight United Brands' stranglehold on their economies. In 1974 the governments of Colombia, Costa Rica, Guatemala, Honduras, and Panama formed the Unión de Paises Exportadores de Banano (UPEB)—Organization of Banana Exporting Countries. United Brands now faced export tariffs in those countries.

On February 3, 1975, Black committed suicide by jumping out the window of his office. Investigations of his death revealed a series of bribes. The Securities and Exchange Commission (SEC) accused United Brands of bribing the president of Honduras, Osvaldo López Arellano, in exchange for a reduction in export taxes. The investigation also revealed that United Brands had bribed European and Costa Rican officials. Trade of United Brands stock was halted for almost a week, and the Honduran army removed López Arellano from office. Finally, a federal grand jury brought criminal charges against United Brands and a federal judge granted the SEC permanent access to United Brands' records.

Over the next 10 years, United Brands narrowed its focus to tropical fruit, changing the company name to Chiquita in 1989. (United Fruit had been putting Chiquita stickers on its bananas since 1959 to distinguish them from competitors' fruit.) During the 1990s, Chiquita and the U.S. government became involved in a trade war with Europe over banana imports. In 1994 the European Union established a quota system giving preference to bananas imported from former European colonies in Africa. The United States eventually won its claim of unfair trade restrictions, but skirmishes in the banana trade wars are frequent.

A great deal of argument has arisen about whether Chiquita was a benefit or a scourge to Central America. The company brought modernization and opportunities to a corrupt and poorly run region. Many argue, however, that it also brought increased corruption and violence that delayed land reform, labor reform, and modern industry and led to widespread poverty. Today, Chiquita says that the controversies of the United Fruit days are behind it, although many groups around the world continue to boycott Chiquita.

Further Reading

Dosal, Paul J. *Doing Business with the Dictators: A Political History of United Fruit in Guatemala, 1899–1944.* Wilmington, Del.: Scholarly Resources, 1997.

Langley, Lester D., and Thomas D. Schoonover. *The Banana Men: American Mercenaries and Entrepreneurs in Central America, 1880–1930.* Lexington: University Press of Kentucky, 1996.

Schlesinger, Stephen C., et al. *Bitter Fruit: The Story of the American Coup in Guatemala.* Cambridge, Mass.: Harvard University Press, 1999.

—Lisa Magloff

Cisco Systems

The Internet enables information to travel between tens of millions of computers. Without a way to move that information and to direct specific information to specific computers, the Internet would not exist. Computer networks are controlled by devices called routers. More than 80 percent of the information that moves along the Internet's electronic superhighway travels through computer routers built by Cisco Systems. Within 15 years of its founding in 1984, Cisco had become not only the most valuable company in Silicon Valley, but also one of the most valuable in America, with a worth (based on stock market capitalization) of more than $40 billion.

The Beginnings of Cisco

Len Bosack and Sandy Lerner were a husband and wife who both worked for Stanford University. They wanted a way to communicate with each other over their separate computer networks. With help from some friends, they first ran network cables between the buildings, and then connected them with routers that they had designed themselves.

The routers, which were essentially small computer switches, would transmit only the traffic that was meant to get out and accept only the traffic that was meant to get in. This allowed separate computer systems to be linked together into a network. When Stanford refused to fund further development, Lerner and Bosack founded Cisco Systems, named after nearby San Francisco.

They used their credit cards to pay all the start-up costs, and their house became company headquarters. Despite the lack of a real sales staff, they were soon earning hundreds of thousands of dollars every month. With little business experience, in 1987 Lerner and Bosack turned to venture capitalist Don Valentine to provide financing, management, and a process that would move Cisco out of the living room.

From the start, tension was evident between the independent-minded Lerner and Bosack and the management team Valentine hired to run Cisco. In 1990 seven of the vice presidents went as a group to Valentine and gave an ultimatum: either Lerner left or they would leave. Lerner was asked to leave the company, and Bosack left with her. They both immediately sold their shares of company stock, at that time worth about $170 million.

With the money she made, Sandy Lerner left California and bought Ayershire Farms, the 40-room house where Jane Austen wrote her novels. Bosack started his own company, XKL, in Redmond, Washington, and also funded charities and nonprofits, including SETI (the Search for Extra-Terrestrial Intelligence).

Expanding the Company

Cisco captured a huge share of the networking market right from the start and has kept that market share not only with a broad range of products and good customer service but also by being the biggest. Because Cisco products dominate the market, they are a "safe" choice. Cisco

See also:
Computer Industry;
E-Business; Information
Technology; Internet.

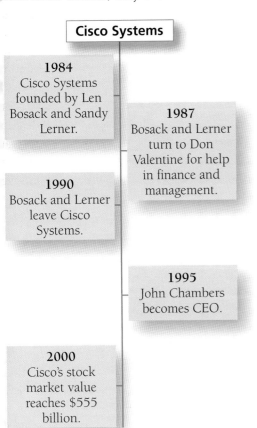

Cisco Systems

1984
Cisco Systems founded by Len Bosack and Sandy Lerner.

1987
Bosack and Lerner turn to Don Valentine for help in finance and management.

1990
Bosack and Lerner leave Cisco Systems.

1995
John Chambers becomes CEO.

2000
Cisco's stock market value reaches $555 billion.

Connection Center: Video

Connection Center: Voice

Data/V...

Tract, Semi-Custom Homes and Multiple Dwelling Units

...none and ...stem

Connection Center: Burglar/Fire Alarm

In 2000 Cisco employee Jerrod Headly displays the Residential Gateway router, which can connect data, voice, and video streams in the home.

has also bought other businesses and successfully integrated them into its huge conglomerate. What Cisco cannot (or does not have time to) build itself, it buys. The company has adopted an "anything that builds a network" strategy, and any small company that develops an innovative network product is soon presented with a generous offer by Cisco. Since 1993 Cisco has acquired more than 50 companies—17 in 1999 alone—that specialize in networking, data, or wireless services.

John Chambers took over as chief executive officer in January 1995, and his vision of an Internet-centered world helped drive the huge boom in Internet businesses. Chambers helped push the idea that the new Internet technology would help everyone work faster and more efficiently. So confident was Wall Street in Chambers's vision that Cisco's stock market value in March 2000 reached $555 billion, briefly making it the most valuable company on the planet.

Because its products are used by almost every Internet company, Cisco also acts as a barometer for the industry. In a downturn, companies first cut back on new networking technology. Cisco received a lot of criticism for not foreseeing the bursting of the Internet bubble at the end of 2000; Cisco had more than $2.5 billion in unsold inventory by December of that year. Cisco's stock value plummeted. Analysts now watch Cisco closely in hopes of predicting when swings in the Internet economy will occur.

To avoid being caught in future Internet slumps, Cisco is working to move beyond Internet routers and build a single, giant, global communications system, based on the Internet, that would make the current telephone system obsolete. Cisco is conducting research to develop the hardware and software infrastructure of this new network, which will combine computer networks with telephones, television, radio, and satellite communications. More than just the backbone of the Internet, in the future Cisco aims to become the backbone of the entire communications industry.

Any company that thinks it's utterly unbeatable is already beaten. So when I begin to think we're getting a little bit too confident, you'll see me emphasizing the paranoia side. And then when I feel that there's a little bit too much fear and apprehension, I'll just jump back to the other side. My job is to keep those scales perfectly balanced.

We can't change how people behave. And we ought to listen to constructive criticism, because there are areas that we need to improve in. That said, we focus on customers who really believe that this is the future and who are willing to invest the time with us. Others will say, "You know, I'm going to put this on the back burner." All you can do at that time is educate them and get them to realize that they are making a very conscious decision not to pay attention to the Internet.

—John Chambers, interview with *Fast Company* magazine, July 2001

Further Reading

Bunnell, David, and Adam Brate. *Making the Cisco Connection: The Story behind the Real Internet Superpower.* New York: John Wiley & Sons, 2000.

Paulson, Ed. *Inside Cisco.* New York: John Wiley & Sons, 2001.

Stauffer, David. *Nothing But Net: Business the Cisco Way.* Milford, Conn.: Capstone, 2000.

Young, Jeffrey S. *Cisco Unauthorized.* Roseville, Calif.: Forum, 2001.

—Lisa Magloff

John Chambers addresses Cisco employees.

See also:
Americans with Disabilities Act; Equal Employment Opportunity Commission; Pay Equity; Women in the Workforce.

Civil Rights Legislation

The U.S. Constitution guarantees civil rights for all citizens of the United States. Included among these rights are several freedoms: the right to speak one's mind, the right to assemble in groups, the right to equal treatment in public places, and freedom from involuntary servitude. As these guarantees are stated, they explicitly prohibit discriminatory actions by the federal government; the First Amendment, for example, prohibits the government from restricting expressions of speech. Prior to the Civil War, however, whether these guarantees also protected citizens from discriminatory actions made by state governments or private organizations and businesses was not always clear. Constitutional amendments granted Congress new powers to enact far-reaching civil rights legislation. Civil rights legislation has had a profound effect on both employers and employees, especially females and racial minorities.

Rosa Parks being fingerprinted by Deputy Sheriff D. H. Lackey after her arrest for refusing to move to the back of a bus in Montgomery, Alabama, in 1955.

The Foundations of Civil Rights

Historically, the most important foundations civil rights legislation in the United States a the 13th and 14th Amendments to the U. Constitution. In 1865 the 13th Amendme abolished legal slavery throughout th United States. The practice of slavery ha been primarily concentrated in the 11 state of the Old Confederacy and was limited African Americans. In efforts intended nullify the 13th Amendment in practice, va ious states then enacted "Black Code designed to limit, by new means, the civ rights of the freed slaves.

In response, the 14th Amendment wa ratified in 1868. It sought to ensure that n citizen's rights could be abridged withou due process of law and that all citizen would have equal protection of the law The amendment also authorized Congres to enforce its provisions by enactment appropriate legislation. Subsequently, du ing Reconstruction in the late 1860s an early 1870s, Congress enacted several civ rights statutes that remain in force today.

No constitutional amendment could en discrimination entirely. On December 5, 195 the modern civil rights movement aros in Montgomery, Alabama, at the first mas meeting of the Montgomery Improvemen Association (MIA). Only days before, a blac seamstress, Rosa Parks, had been arrested fo refusing a white bus driver's order to surrende her seat to a white male and to move to th back of the city bus. Parks's act of courag touched a nerve in the local black communit and in black and white communities through out the United States. The MIA called for a boy cott of the public transit system; its leader, Di Martin Luther King, Jr., was propelled int national and international prominence. Durin the next four decades, boycotts, sit-ins, an other nonviolent protests led to passage of civ rights laws at every level of government.

Of these legislative initiatives, the mos prominent is the Civil Rights Act of 1964 President John F. Kennedy went on televi sion to address the nation on civil rights o June 11, 1963; he then sent a comprehen sive package of civil rights legislation t

To enforce the constitutional right to vote, to confer jurisdiction upon the district courts of the United States to provide injunctive relief against discrimination in public accommodations, to authorize the Attorney General to institute suits to protect constitutional rights in public facilities and public education, to extend the Commission on Civil Rights, to prevent discrimination in federally assisted programs, to establish a Commission on Equal Employment Opportunity, and for other purposes.

Be it enacted by the Senate and House of Representatives of the United States of America in Congress assembled, That this Act may be cited as the "Civil Rights Act of 1964."

UNLAWFUL EMPLOYMENT PRACTICES
SEC. 2000e-2. [Section 703]
(a) It shall be an unlawful employment practice for an employer—
   (1) to fail or refuse to hire or to discharge any individual, or otherwise to discriminate against any individual with respect to his compensation, terms, conditions, or privileges of employment, because of such individual's race, color, religion, sex, or national origin; or
   (2) to limit, segregate, or classify his employees or applicants for employment in any way which would deprive or tend to deprive any individual of employment opportunities or otherwise adversely affect his status as an employee, because of such individual's race, color, religion, sex, or national origin.

(b) It shall be an unlawful employment practice for an employment agency to fail or refuse to refer for employment, or otherwise to discriminate against, any individual because of his race, color, religion, sex, or national origin, or to classify or refer for employment any individual on the basis of his race, color, religion, sex, or national origin.

(c) It shall be an unlawful employment practice for a labor organization—
   (1) to exclude or to expel from its membership, or otherwise to discriminate against, any individual because of his race, color, religion, sex, or national origin;
   (2) to limit, segregate, or classify its membership or applicants for membership, or to classify or fail or refuse to refer for employment any individual, in any way which would deprive or tend to deprive any individual of employment opportunities, or would limit such employment opportunities or otherwise adversely affect his status as an employee or as an applicant for employment, because of such individual's race, color, religion, sex, or national origin; or
   (3) to cause or attempt to cause an employer to discriminate against an individual in violation of this section.

(d) It shall be an unlawful employment practice for any employer, labor organization, or joint labor–management committee controlling apprenticeship or other training or retraining, including on-the-job training programs to discriminate against any individual because of his race, color, religion, sex, or national origin in admission to, or employment in, any program established to provide apprenticeship or other training.

(e) Notwithstanding any other provision of this subchapter,
   (1) it shall not be an unlawful employment practice for an employer to hire and employ employees, for an employment agency to classify, or refer for employment any individual, for a labor organization to classify its membership or to classify or refer for employment any individual, or for an employer, labor organization, or joint labor–management committee controlling apprenticeship or other training or retraining programs to admit or employ any individual in any such program, on the basis of his religion, sex, or national origin in those certain instances where religion, sex, or national origin is a bona fide occupational qualification reasonably necessary to the normal operation of that particular business or enterprise, and
   (2) it shall not be an unlawful employment practice for a school, college, university, or other educational institution or institution of learning to hire and employ employees of a particular religion if such school, college, university, or other educational institution or institution of learning is, in whole or in substantial part, owned, supported, controlled, or managed by a particular religion or by a particular religious corporation, association, or society, or if the curriculum of such school, college, university, or other educational institution or institution of learning is directed toward the propagation of a particular religion.

Congress. Following Kennedy's assassination in November 1963, President Lyndon B. Johnson took aggressive steps to push a more comprehensive civil rights bill through Congress in 1964. The 1969 act strengthened voting rights for blacks and barred racial

President Lyndon Johnson (seated) shakes the hand of Martin Luther King, Jr., after signing the Civil Rights Act on July 2, 1964.

discrimination in employment and places of public accommodation. It also authorized the U.S. attorney general to bring suit to force the desegregation of public schools, and it created an Equal Employment Opportunity Commission to monitor and enforce the implementation of its various provisions.

Civil Rights and Employment

Congress passed the Civil Rights Act of 1991 to amend the Civil Rights Act of 1964. The 1991 act strengthened and improved federal civil rights law by providing for damages in cases of intentional discrimination and by clarifying provisions regarding "disparate impact" cases (cases involving allegations of discrimination based upon evidence about

discriminatory effects, as opposed to di criminatory intentions).

The 1991 act was specifically designe to address several decisions by the U.S Supreme Court, including *Wards Cove Packir Co. v. Antonio* (1989). The *Wards Cove* cas had reinterpreted the disparate impact star dard, holding that an employer could avoi liability in a claim of disparate impact (fc example, fewer promotions for black employ ees) by establishing a business reason for th practice. This decision was viewed by many a making the winning of discrimination case against employers more difficult.

By adding a new subsection to Title V (which addresses gender discrimination), th act codified the disparate impact theory iscrimination, essentially restoring the law o what it had been prior to the *Wards Cove* uling. The act also provided protection from iscrimination in employment to employees f Congress and to some high-level political ppointees, and it extended Title VII pro- ections to employees of U.S. and U.S.– ontrolled companies operating in foreign ountries. Upon proof of violations under he act, employees may obtain punitive and ompensatory damages (capped at $300,000 er person for large firms).

Critics of the 1991 act charge that it cre- tes powerful financial incentives to sue, urning corporations and other "deep ocket" organizations into targets. An alter- ative interpretation is that litigation is riven by ongoing problems of discrimina- ion. Either way, the consequences for busi- ess and industry are very real.

mpact on Industry

acial discrimination charges filed with the qual Employment Opportunity Commission EEOC) increased from approximately 10,000 n the 1980s (before passage of the 1991 act) o nearly 50,000 during the 1990s, a fivefold ncrease. These charges made up 3 percent of all race-based complaints in the 1980s—the remainder were complaints about sex dis- crimination, workplace harassment, age dis- crimination, and so on—as compared with 23 percent of all race-based complaints in 2000. The business arena appears to be rapidly becoming the new civil rights battleground.

The monetary amounts of both judicial and out-of-court settlements in race-discrim- ination cases before and after passage of the 1991 act suggest that this observation has merit. For example, AT&T paid a $15 mil- lion settlement in a racial discrimination complaint in 1973; in 1991 the same com- pany paid $66 million.

The surge in discrimination cases since 1991 suggests that more workers are taking advantage of the easier burden of proof and the greater financial incentives to sue their employ- ers for real or perceived discrimination. As the vast majority of these cases have been settled out of court, it remains arguable that more cor- porate discrimination has been brought to light or that more litigation has been initiated against corporations under what many businesses deem the litigation-friendly Civil Rights Act of 1991. The overall costs of the settlements have increased substantially.

Key Modern Civil Rights Legislation

Date	Name of Law	Purpose
1963	Equal Pay Act (EPA)	Protects both men and women from sex-based salary discrimination
1964	Civil Rights Act	Prohibits discrimination based on race, color, religion, sex, or national origin in employment and in public places; creates the Equal Employment Opportunity Commission; authorizes the U.S. attorney general to enforce desegregation in public schools
1965	Voting Rights Act	Prohibits the refusal or abridgment of the right to vote to any citizen on the basis of color or race; suspends literacy tests as basis for voting rights
1967	Age Discrimination in Employment Act (ADEA)	Prohibits employment discrimination against workers over the age of 40
1973	Rehabilitation Act	Prohibits discrimination against federal workers with disabilities
1978	Civil Service Reform Act (CSRA)	Prohibits any discriminatory personnel practices on the basis of race, color, age, sex, religion, marital status, and political affiliation; enforced by the Office of Special Counsel (OSC) and Merit Systems Protection Board (MSPB)
1990	Americans with Disabilities Act (ADA)	Prohibits employment discrimination against qualified individuals with disabilities; requires employers to provide reasonable accommodation for persons with disabilities
1991	Civil Rights Act	Amends Civil Rights Act of 1964 by providing for damages in cases of intentional discrimination, ensuring protection against discrimination for congressional employees and other political appointees; also extends the protection to include American companies outside the United States

Corporate Payments in Racial Discrimination Cases

Before the Civil Rights Act of 1991		
1973	AT&T	$15 million
1974	AT&T	$30 million
1980	Ford Motor Company	$30 million
1983	General Motors	$42 million
After the Civil Rights Act of 1991		
1991	AT&T	$66 million
1993	Shoney's	$132.5 million
1996	Winn-Dixie	$28.1 million
1997	Texaco	$176 million
1998	Mitsubishi of America	$34 million
1999	Boeing	$15 million
1999	CSX Transportation	$25 million
2001	Coca-Cola	$192.5 million

Note: Includes both judicial and out-of-court settlements.

The Civil Rights Act of 1991 significantly affected the financial penalties paid by businesses convicted of racial bias.

Derrick Washington (right), a former Microsoft employee, at a press conference about a $5 billion racial discrimination suit he filed against the company in January 2001. His attorneys look on.

The trend seems likely to continue. In early 2002, plaintiffs had filed major race-discrimination charges against Cargill, Lockheed Martin, Johnson & Johnson, Microsoft, and several other major U.S. corporations. Typical charges include discrimination in promotion and compensation, termination discrimination, and reverse discrimination.

In the twenty-first century, civil rights cases argued in the courts or receiving negotiated settlements are still concentrated in the traditional race- and gender-discrimination arenas. However, the number of suits involving discrimination based on disability, religion, language, sexual orientation, and age are also increasing. The Civil Rights Act of 1991, coupled with the rapidly changing demographics of the corporate workplace, has resulted in U.S. corporations facing an increasing number of lawsuits alleging discrimination even as business attempts to produce more goods and services and create more jobs.

Further Reading

Egerton, John. *Speak Now against the Day.* New York: Alfred Knopf, 1994.

Franklin, John H., and Gena R. McNeil. *African Americans and the Living Constitution.* Washington, D.C.: Smithsonian Institution Press, 1995.

Grofman, Bernard, ed. *Legacies of the 1964 Civil Rights Act.* Charlottesville: University Press of Virginia, 2000.

Klinker, Phillip A., and Rogers M. Smith. *The Unsteady March: The Rise and Decline of Racial Equality in America.* Chicago: University of Chicago Press, 1999.

Lewis, John, and Michael D'Orso. *Walking with the Wind.* New York: Simon & Schuster, 1998.

Thernstrom, Stephan, and Abigail Thernstrom. *America in Black and White: One Nation Indivisible.* New York: Free Press, 1997.

—*Walter C. Farrell, Jr., and Renee Sartin Kirby*

Clark, Jim

1944–

high-technology entrepreneur

Jim Clark has successfully guided three separate technology companies from inception to public stock offering. An intellectual nomad who jumps from idea to idea, Clark is seen as a visionary, salesman, and savvy manipulator of the media.

Clark was born in 1944 in Plainview, Texas. His father was an abusive alcoholic; after his parents divorced in 1958, his mother struggled to provide for Clark and his sister. At school Clark preferred playing the clown to studying. Clark decided to escape Plainview by joining the navy, where he was quickly labeled a problem recruit.

While in the navy, Clark was tested for math skills. He scored the highest grade in the class; until then he had no idea he had any mathematical inclination. Clark was encouraged to pursue college after the navy. Within eight years, he had earned a bachelor's degree and a master's in physics from the University of New Orleans; in 1974 he earned a doctorate in computer science from the University of Utah.

By 1979 Clark had been divorced twice and was teaching at Stanford University. Clark set a group of students to developing a computer chip he called the Geometry Engine. The chip made possible the creation of models on the computer screen, using three-dimensional graphics. In 1982 Clark and his students formed a company, Silicon Graphics, around the chip.

Silicon Graphics took five years to achieve significant sales. Hollywood was one of the company's first customers, using the software to create special effects for films. Clark was eventually forced out of his company and was denied a large portion of the profits because of his naïve arrangements with the venture capitalists who had provided the additional cash needed for development. He received only 3 percent of Silicon Graphics's profits because of the machinations of the "velociraptors," as Clark called the investors. Clark vowed to find (in a phrase made famous by Michael Lewis's book about Clark) the "new, new thing."

Clark looked to the Internet, which was then used by approximately 25 million people. Clark partnered with Marc Andreessen, a student at the University of Illinois at Urbana-Champaign. Andreessen had created Mosaic, a user-friendly browser for the World Wide Web that he released to the Internet in 1993. Clark approached Andreessen about starting a business together; with Clark's funding, Andreessen and the team that had worked with him on the Mosaic project reunited to create what would come to be known as Netscape Navigator. They released the first version in October 1994. By the following spring, six million people around the world were Netscape users. Netscape's

See also:
Health Care Services Industry; Information Technology; Internet; Venture Capital.

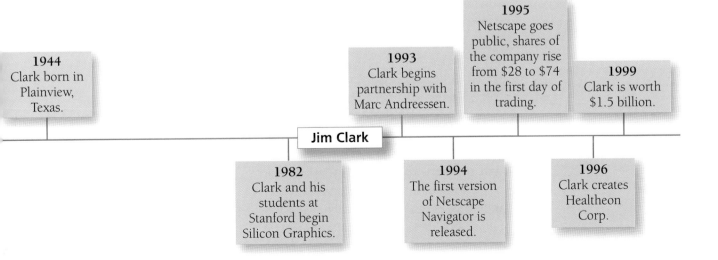

1944 Clark born in Plainview, Texas.

1982 Clark and his students at Stanford begin Silicon Graphics.

1993 Clark begins partnership with Marc Andreessen.

1994 The first version of Netscape Navigator is released.

1995 Netscape goes public, shares of the company rise from $28 to $74 in the first day of trading.

1996 Clark creates Healtheon Corp.

1999 Clark is worth $1.5 billion.

Jim Clark

Jim Clark, left, with Netscape cofounder Marc Andreessen.

1995 debut on the stock market made history, with shares soaring from $28 to $74 and bringing Netscape's value to $2.3 billion at the end of the first day.

Other companies were soon chasing Netscape, developing competing browsers; among them: Oracle, Sun Microsystems, AT&T, and, most significant, Microsoft, which announced the availability of its Internet Explorer browser in August 1995. Clark was still chairman of the board of Netscape but had little to do with running the company. He was too preoccupied with making another billion to replace the billion he feared he would lose to Microsoft.

Clark began eyeing the $1.5 trillion health care industry. He was well acquainted with the frustrating and complicated system; in the 1990s he had crushed his leg in a motorcycle wreck and was diagnosed with a blood disease that required regular trips to the doctor. In 1996 Clark created Healtheon Corp., aiming to eliminate paperwork and waste by connecting doctors, insurers, pharmacies, and patients to one another via the Internet. Venture capitalists clamored to fund the start-up, based on Clark's track record with Silicon Graphics and Netscape. At the time of Healtheon's initial public offering in 1999, the company was worth nearly $100 million. Including his stake in America

Online, which had purchased Netscap[e] Clark himself was worth $1.5 billion.

Three successful ventures only fuele[d] Clark's desire for the next big opportunit[y.] His preoccupation with tracking wealth le[d] to his next company, myCFO, an onlin[e] portfolio management service for the ver[y] rich. He has also had a hand in other suc[-]cessful ventures including Shutterfly, th[e] leading provider of online photo services fo[r] digital and film cameras; DNA Sciences, [a] leader in pharmaco-genetics (helping t[o] determine the safety and efficiency of drugs[)] and Neoteris, which offers secure Interne[t] access services.

Clark is the product of ambition and res[t]less creativity. Easily bored once his ideas tak[e] shape, he tends to leave day-to-day manage[-]ment to others. Clark is an impatient vision[-]ary who has the ability to persuade those wit[h] money to back his next "new, new thing."

Further Reading

Clark, Jim, with Owen Edwards. *Netscape Time: The Making of the Billion-Dollar Start-Up That Change[d] the World.* New York: St. Martin's Press, 1999.

Cusumano, Michael A. *Competing on Internet Time: Lessons from Netscape and Its Battle with Microsoft.* New York: Free Press, 1998.

Lewis, Michael. *The New New Thing: A Silicon Valley Story.* New York: W. W. Norton, 1999.

—*Sheri Rehwol[d]*

Coca-Cola Company

Coca-Cola is often touted as the second most universally understood term in English—exceeded only by the expression "OK." Coke is sold in more countries (195) than the number belonging to the United Nations (184), and it is a globally recognized symbol of what some admire most and some admire least about American culture.

Coca-Cola was invented in 1886, when John Styth Pemberton, a pharmacist and patent medicine inventor in Atlanta, Georgia, blended extracts from coca leaves, kola nuts, caffeine, and sugar in an iron tub in his backyard. Pemberton did not create Coca-Cola as a beverage; instead, he sold the syrup to local pharmacies as a headache tonic. This was not Pemberton's first attempt at creating a patent medicine. His earlier products included Globe of Flower Cough Syrup and French Wine Coca. In 1886, after Pemberton had spent $76.96 on advertising (some hinting discreetly that Coca-Cola was a potent aphrodisiac), sales of Coca-Cola averaged only nine drinks per day, and Pemberton grossed only $50 in sales revenue.

Pemberton became ill in 1887 and sold his business to Willis Venable for $283.29. Venable had the idea of mixing the Coca-Cola syrup with soda water and serving it as a refreshing beverage. As a beverage, Coca-Cola sold better than had the headache tonic, and on the strength of some early success Venable was able to sell his Coca-Cola formula to an Atlanta businessman named Asa Candler. Candler began to sell Coca-Cola in franchise operations he owned, plowing most of his profits back into his business. He sold nine thousand gallons of Coca-Cola syrup in 1891. Within nine years his sales reached 281,000 gallons, and Candler began selling Coca-Cola bottling franchises. His decision to franchise the bottling operation enabled the company to concentrate on developing a national distribution system for the syrup, while leaving the mixing of the syrup and soda water, along with bottling, sales, and distribution of the finished product, to the franchise owners. By 1909, nearly 400 Coca-Cola bottling plants were in operation, most of them family-owned businesses. Some operated only during summer months when demand was highest.

From the outset, advertising was crucial to the success of Coca-Cola. Candler spent more than 25 percent of Coca-Cola's annual budget on advertising, and as early as 1904 Coca-Cola had become the most recognized brand name in the United States. Pemberton's first slogan had been simply "Drink Coca-Cola." In 1906, capitalizing on the growth of the temperance

See also:
Advertising, Business Practice; Brand Names; Franchise; Globalization; Trademark.

Coca-Cola Company

1886
John Styth Pemberton invents Coca-Cola syrup.

1887
Willis Venable buys business from Pemberton, mixes syrup with soda water.

1904
Coca-Cola is the most recognized brand name in America.

1941–1945
Coca-Cola distributes product to U.S. soldiers overseas.

1985
New Coke is introduced, only to be pulled three months later.

1997
Coca-Cola develops "think local, act local" management policy.

1886	Drink Coca-Cola
1904	Delicious and Refreshing
1905	Coca-Cola Revives and Sustains
1906	The Great National Temperance Drink
1917	Three Million a Day
1922	Thirst Knows No Season
1925	Six Million a Day
1927	Around the Corner from Everywhere
1929	The Pause That Refreshes
1932	Ice-Cold Sunshine
1938	The Best Friend Thirst Ever Had
1939	Coca-Cola Goes Along
1942	Wherever You Are, Whatever You Do, Wherever You May Be, When You Think of Refreshment, Think of Ice-Cold Coca-Cola
1942	The Only Thing Like Coca-Cola Is Coca-Cola Itself. It's the Real Thing.
1948	Where There's Coke, There's Hospitality
1949	Coca-Cola . . . Along the Highway to Anywhere
1952	What You Want Is a Coke
1956	Coca-Cola . . . Making Good Things Taste Better
1957	Sign of Good Taste
1958	The Cold, Crisp Taste of Coke
1959	Be Really Refreshed
1963	Things Go Better with Coke
1970	It's the Real Thing
1971	I'd Like To Buy the World a Coke
1975	Look Up America
1976	Coke Adds Life
1979	Have a Coke and a Smile
1982	Coke Is It!
1985	We've Got a Taste for You (Coca-Cola and Coca-Cola Classic) America's Real Choice
1986	Catch the Wave (Coca-Cola) Red White & You (Coca-Cola Classic)
1989	Can't Beat the Feeling
1990	Can't Beat the Real Thing
1993	Always Coca-Cola

movement (a movement aimed at discouraging or banning the drinking of alcoholic beverages), the slogan became "The Great National Temperance Drink." In 1919, when Candler sold the business to a consortium of Atlanta businessmen for $25 million, Coca-Cola advertising emphasized Coca-Cola's high volume sales with the slogan, "Three million bottles a day."

The company's success soon caused host of competing brands to spring up, wit names like Co Kola, Coke-Ola, and Okl Cola. By 1926 Coca-Cola had resorted t the courts no fewer than 7,000 times t protect its trademark name, logo, and dis tinctive bottle design. Coca-Cola also wo the right to trademark protection for it alternative name, Coke, in 1930.

When the United States entered World War II, wartime sugar rationing severely limited business for all soda beverage companies. Coca-Cola president Paul Woodruff responded with an idea for turning the war into an opportunity—to raise morale and increase future business. "We'll see that every man in uniform gets a bottle of Coca-Cola for five cents, wherever he is and whatever it costs our company," Woodruff proposed. Coke then successfully lobbied the United States government for the right to buy sugar so that it could distribute Coke to U.S. soldiers overseas. The company shipped Coke concentrate to be bottled in plants on army bases; the men who ran these plants were given the pseudo-military title of technical officer, and each received a military rank commensurate with his company salary.

The availability of Coke did boost morale among soldiers, just as the military authorities had hoped. Coca-Cola also profited hugely. Not only did Coke cement its position as the all-American drink, but also Coke was able, after the war, to convert most of its 64 overseas bottling plants to civilian, commercial use. People around the world had learned to associate Coca-Cola with the United States. The association was so strong, in fact, that by 1950 the word *Coca-colonization* had been coined, referring to the growing prevalence of American culture throughout the world. *Time* magazine printed a picture of a globe drinking a Coke on a 1950 cover, titling it "World and Friend."

New Coke vs. Old Coke

Coke continued to prosper, but in the 1980s the company learned something about consumer sovereignty and the cost of tampering with an established, very popular product. Cuban-born chemist Roberto Goizueta became the president of Coca-Cola in 1980, and he immediately outlined his business philosophy, suggesting an intention to make big changes: "A company starts to worry about holding on to success when it has decided that it has

more to lose than it has to gain. At that point, it gets overly timid and concerned with appearances."

Goizueta had experimented with a new formula for Coke earlier in his career, and he believed that a new formula would usher in a new, more modern image for Coke. The formula change was announced in 1985 in a tidal wave of publicity, spawning articles like *Newsweek* magazine's "Coke Tampers with Success," referring to the old drink as "the American character in a can." Crowds booed advertisements for New Coke on video screens at football games, and Goizueta soon found himself under siege. Three months later Goizueta gave up, and the old formula returned as Classic Coke. When news of the return of the original formula leaked, television programming was interrupted to make the announcement. One Arkansas senator described the turnaround in a speech as "a meaningful moment in American history." Coke would later make changes in management policy, but it left its formula alone.

Coca-Cola's changes included new, centralized management, standardized practices, and a consolidation of its network of local bottling partners. The changes paid off in increased profits and enabled Coca-Cola to take greater advantage of new markets opening in Africa and Eastern Europe. Its global presence was such that, in May of 1993, *Fortune* magazine's cover story called Coke "the world's best brand." The movement away from its traditional, local bases of strength also caused new problems, however, and during the 1990s Coke began to see a backlash

Some people would say our business is selling soft drinks. Others would go a bit deeper and say our business is delivering refreshment. But if you want to get to the bottom of what our business really is, I would say our business is actually building relationships.

Making sure we are operating as a model citizen is essential to making sure the reputation of our company is a positive part of the strength of our brands. You cannot communicate about your brand in one way . . . and then behave as a company in another.

—Doug Daft, CEO, Speech to the British & U.S. Chambers of Commerce, October 5, 2000

A Coca-Cola bottling plant in Ho Chi Minh City, Vietnam, in April 2000.

against the product in foreign countries. Abroad, some people began to associate the brand less with "The Real Thing" and more with cultural imperialism.

Explained Doug Daft, who replaced Goizueta as chairman and chief executive officer on Goizueta's death in 1997, "A very real backlash developed . . . which in hindsight was predictable, natural and relatively healthy. . . . The very forces that were making the world more connected and more homogeneous were simultaneously triggering a desire to preserve what was uniquely local." In response, the company adopted a "think local, act local" philosophy, which attempts to place decision making in the hands of local managers. Coke hopes this shift will distance the brand from charge of coca-cultural imperialism.

Further Reading

Allen, Frederick. *Secret Formula: How Brilliant Marketing and Relentless Salesmanship Made Coca-Cola the Best-Known Product in the World.* New York: Harper Business, 1998.

Enrico, Roger, and Jesse Kornbluth. *The Other Guy Blinked: How Pepsi Won the Coke Wars.* New York: Bantham, 1996.

Greising, David. *I'd Like the World to Buy a Coke: Th Life and Leadership of Roberto Goizueta.* New York: John Wiley & Sons, 1999.

Pendergrast, Mark. *For God, Country and Coca-Cola The Definitive History of the Great American Sof Drink and the Company That Makes It.* New York: Basic Books, 2000.

—Lisa Maglo

Collective Bargaining

Collective bargaining is the process through which union leaders representing specific groups of workers negotiate written terms of employment with representatives of management. Terms of employment negotiated often include wages and benefits, hours of work, job classifications, effort required, work practices, seniority, discipline procedures, promotion and layoff procedures, methods of enforcement, and grievance resolution.

Collective bargaining has existed in various forms in the United States for more than 200 years. In 1792 shoemakers in Philadelphia formed a local trade union to bargain for higher wages. Modern practices, however, evolved in the 1930s and 1940s and were codified by federal laws and court decisions in those decades.

Labor relations in the United States and elsewhere have often been characterized by confrontation. More than 90 percent of collective bargaining, however, is peaceful, resulting in contracts acceptable to both sides. The media often report on those cases involving picketing, strike activities, or other work disruptions. The public rarely sees reports on employers like the Baghdad Copper Mine in Arizona, which has offered lifetime employment since 1929 and has not encountered significant labor unrest.

Some people assume, because they are not union members, that labor–management activities do not affect them. However, baseball fans saw the 1994 World Series canceled because of an impasse in negotiations between team owners and the players' union. Businesses and individuals had delivery of packages disrupted by the 1997 strike involving United Parcel Service workers, and airline passengers have had their travel plans disrupted by airline employee strikes many times.

Labor conflicts and contracts also have numerous indirect effects. More workers are affected by collective bargaining agreements than are actually unionized. For example, nonunion employers who wish to keep unions out of their companies may set wages or other benefits at a particular level as a direct, albeit informal, reaction to union activity; experts refer to this as a union-substitution strategy. Union contracts can also be extended to wider groups of workers through what are known as prevailing wage provisions.

Overview of the Collective Bargaining Process

The collective bargaining process is long and complex. Prior to bargaining, the union must attain the status of exclusive or sole bargaining agent. The usual route is an organized campaign ending in an election supervised by the National Labor Relations Board (NLRB). The first step in the union organizing procedure involves identifying and meeting with key workers in the unit to be organized. If the workers contact the union, the identification is simple. If the union targets the employees, union leaders must pinpoint the key people. The first contact is usually made without the knowledge of the employer.

Once the organizing is actually underway, union organizers usually distribute

See also:
Labor Union; National Labor Relations Act; Strikes.

Leaders of the National Women's Trade Union, meeting in Waukegan, Illinois, in 1929.

In 1949 John Bugas (left), director of industrial relations for Ford Motor Company, and Walter P. Reuther (right), president of the United Auto Workers, join hands to signal they have reached an agreement.

authorization cards to employees. Such cards show support for the union. When a union has signed authorization cards from at least 30 percent of the employees, it can petition the NLRB to conduct a certification, or representation, election. Upon filing the petition, the election process and campaign begin.

The NLRB will convene a meeting with the employer and union and obtain a list of all employees. At this meeting, the details of the election are set. The campaign then commences under rules defined in the law. Both union and management can be expected to use a variety of methods, not always pleasant or legal, to sway workers to one side or the other. The election is conducted through secret ballot by the NLRB. If the union wins the election, it is certified as the exclusive bargaining agent for the workers. Certification is binding for 12 months. The employer must then bargain with the union.

Prior to actual bargaining, both parties undertake extensive preparations for the bargaining process. Successful negotiations depend upon the knowledge and skill of the

negotiators. Each side must, through careful preparation, become knowledgeable about their own and the other side's positions on the bargaining issues. Both sides will define a series of positions on numerous issues that are each assigned a priority. The collection of large amounts of information to support arguments is crucial. After preparation, the parties are ready for the first stage, the bargaining stage.

In the initial phase of negotiations, the party that is pressing for a new contract (usually the union) presents its demands. This stage sometimes involves a certain amount of posturing; for example, the union may make excessive demands to set the stage for later trade-offs and compromise. Posturing is important as it allows a certain amount of face-saving for the party with the lesser bargaining power.

Demands presented by both sides are classified as mandatory, permissive, or illegal bargaining subjects by the NLRB and the courts. Subjects deemed mandatory by labor law include rates of pay, wages, hours of employment, and other conditions of employment. As a category, wages may include pensions and insurance benefits, profit-sharing plans, Christmas and other bonuses, stock purchase plans, merit wage incentives, and sometimes company housing and meals, and discounts. Hours of employment involve start and stop times, lunch and rest periods, and other scheduling rules. Conditions of employment include issues such as employment security (hiring and firing), job performance (for example, absenteeism and dress codes), drug testing, union security, and union–management relationships.

If a subject is permissive, a party must withdraw it from bargaining if the other party objects to its inclusion in bargaining. Permissive subjects may include prices in the company cafeteria, pension benefits of retired employees, employee child care, use of the union label, and plant closings.

Subjects deemed illegal under the labor laws may not be proposed for discussion. Even if agreed to by both sides, an illegal subject provision in a collective bargaining greement would not be enforceable in court. Illegal bargaining subjects include closed shops (union membership required before a person is hired), racial separation of employees, and discrimination against nonunion members.

The first stage shifts to the second, or middle, stage when serious discussions commence. Agreements are often made immediately on less important items (usually nonfinancial). At this point, each side narrows the list of demands and establishes a set of priorities. Both sides are required to negotiate in "good faith," which sounds vague but actually is a fairly specific term, the meaning of which has been established and refined through a variety of court decisions going back to the 1940s. Management and unions must both make their best effort to consider the proposals of the other side, they must disclose relevant information to the other side, and they must not act in such a way as to undermine the authority of the appointed representatives or the bargaining process itself. When each side bargains in good faith, the outlines of a potential settlement usually begin to emerge.

The final stage of bargaining involves more compromises and trade-offs. Flexibility is important in this stage, with exchanges between negotiators taking place at the table and away from it. Both union and management may have to bend on issues more than they wish to in trying to reach a tentative agreement. If agreement cannot be reached,

the negotiators have arrived at a point of crisis. Techniques for resolving such a crisis include mediation (a neutral third party suggests solutions to both sides) and arbitration (submission of a dispute to a neutral third party whose decision is binding).

If collective bargaining, arbitration, and mediation fail, a strike may result. Strikes play an important role in collective bargaining, but usually as an implicit or explicit threat, rather than as an actual occurrence. Indeed, experts have found that when the threat of a strike is credible, unions tend to get good results for their members. Strikes are seldom used to solve disputes, but they are nearly always a part of the bargaining process, if only implicitly.

If a tentative agreement is reached, the union leadership holds informational meetings with employees to present details of the tentative labor contract and answer questions. Next, union members vote by secret ballot on whether to accept or reject the agreement. If the proposed agreement is ratified, then a contract is written. Contract language should be precise to minimize labor grievance actions that can arise from different interpretations of ambiguous wording.

Bargaining Techniques

Bargaining techniques or approaches are classified into three categories: distributive bargaining, integrative bargaining, and attitudinal structuring. The bargaining behavior or approach of a party usually changes

Collective Bargaining Achievements 1970 to 1995						
	1970	1975	1980	1985	1990	1995
Total number of workers receiving a wage rate increase (in millions)	10.2	9.7	8.9	5.5	4.9	4.2
Average wage rate increase (in percent)	9.4	9.0	10.1	4.2	4.2	3.1
Wage rate increase by industry (in percent)						
Manufacturing	7.1	8.5	10.2	2.8	4.4	2.3
Construction	NA	8.1	9.9	3.0	3.4	2.8
Transportation and public utilities	NA	9.7	10.8	3.6	2.2	2.2
Wholesale and retail trade	NA	9.2	7.6	3.3	3.6	2.3
Services	NA	6.4	8.1	5.1	4.3	2.2

Note: NA = Not available.
Source: U.S. Department of Labor, Bureau of Labor Statistics, Compensation and Working Conditions, Washington, D.C.

Northwest Airlines pilots picket the terminal at Detroit's Metropolitan Airport in 1998 to call attention to a contract dispute.

during the course of negotiations in response to the attitudes of the other party.

Two parties are involved in distributive bargaining when they view negotiations as a "win–lose" situation (the goals of the two parties are in direct conflict). Resources are viewed by negotiators as limited, and each side wants to get the greatest share of those resources. Limited resources include the monetary assets of the firm and unfilled positions. Hence, those issues often subject to distributive bargaining include almost all economic issues like wages and fringe benefits.

Integrative bargaining occurs when the negotiators' goals are not in conflict; rather the negotiators focus on an issue of common concern. For example, integrative bargaining would be used to establish an alcohol or drug abuse program for employees. Exact details of such a program might

bring the union and management into conflict, but they share a common goal.

Unlike distributive and integrative bargaining, attitudinal structuring is a social process. It involves the activities that occur during negotiations aimed at influencing the relationship between the parties. In fact the two parties will both negotiate and administer the collective bargaining agreement. In attitudinal structuring, economic issues are not directly involved.

Further Reading

Kearney, R. C., and R. Carnevale. *Labor Relations in the Public Sector.* 3rd ed. New York: Marcel Dekker, 2001.

Lo Faro, Antonio. *Regulating Social Europe: Reality and Myth of Collective Bargaining in the EC Legal Order.* Portland, Ore.: Hart Publishing, 2000.

Troy, Leo. *Beyond Unions and Collective Bargaining.* Armonk, N.Y.: M. E. Sharpe, 1999.

—*Carl Pacin*

Commodities

In broad terms, commodities are any products that can be traded and that are used for commerce. More narrowly, commodities are products that are traded on an authorized commodity exchange. Major commodities of this kind include wheat, rice, corn, pork bellies, oilseeds, sugar, coffee, cocoa, tea, oil, natural gas, cotton, wool, jute, sisal, rubber, copper, zinc, lead, and tin.

The practice of buying and selling commodities in an open marketplace began in ancient times. The Agora in Athens and the Forum in Rome were originally commercial marketplaces; medieval fairs were their successors. These regional fairs were gradually replaced by the establishment in cities of specialized trading centers. In Japan, commodity exchanges arose in the eighteenth century. In these markets the purchase of commodities was generally made on the basis of immediate delivery ("spot" trading). Gradually, however, the merchants developed the practice of forward contracting, or futures, which is today one of the most crucial functions of a commodity exchange.

Commodity futures, which are contracts for delivery of specific commodities at a stated price at a specified future date, perform several important functions. The buying and selling of futures tends to even out price fluctuations (caused, for example, by seasonal availability) by allowing the market to mirror expectations about future harvests (or other variables in supply) and changes in demand. Futures are not usually employed for the buying or selling of the actual commodity, but for hedging price fluctuations. Hedging is a method by which individuals or businesses gain protection against future price changes.

For example, say that a coffee dealer knows that six months down the line he will buy 10,000 pounds of coffee to send to a processor, and he has promised to sell that coffee to the processor at a certain price. To protect himself, the coffee dealer buys coffee futures contracts representing 10,000 pounds of coffee. If the price of coffee is higher six months later, the value of the futures contracts rises too. By selling the futures at a higher price than he paid for them, the coffee merchant offsets the extra money he has to pay for the coffee. Hedging thus not only helps to even out gains and losses incurred by fluctuating prices, it also helps contribute to an even flow of business.

The number of commodity markets is not fixed. In mid-2002, the Chicago Board of Trade, the largest futures and options exchange in the United States, counted 85 exchanges worldwide, while noting that others were being developed. In addition to the Chicago Board of Trade, major commodity markets include the Chicago Mercantile Exchange, the New York Cotton Exchange, the New York Commodity Exchange, the New York Mercantile Exchange, the New York Metal Exchange, the New York Sugar Exchange, and the London Metal Exchange.

See also:
Capital; Chicago Board of Trade; Futures Markets; Inventory; Supply and Demand.

Kinds of Commodity Futures

Livestock / meat products	• Propane
Examples:	• Unleaded gas
• Cattle	**Financial and index futures**
• Hogs	Examples:
• Pork bellies	• Dow Jones industrial average futures
Grains, cereal / oilseed	
Examples:	• NASDAQ 100 index futures
• Canola	• NYSE composite index
• Corn	• S&P 500
• Cotton	**Currencies**
• Flaxseed	Examples:
• Oats	• Australian dollar
• Rice	• British pound
• Soybeans	• Canadian dollar
• Wheat	• Japanese yen
Metals	**Miscellaneous commodities**
Examples:	Examples:
• Copper	• Butter
• Palladium	• Cocoa
• Silver	• Coffee
Soft commodities / energy	• Lumber
Examples:	• Milk
• Heating oil	• Orange juice
• Natural gas	• Sugar

The interior of the Chicago Board of Trade.

Important commodity markets are located in Winnipeg, Canada (rye, barley, and oats); Brazil, India, and Egypt (cotton); and Australia, New Zealand, and South Africa (wool).

Most commodities do not pass through commodity exchanges but are sold by direct contact between exporter and importer, who agree on a contract. Commodity exchanges are of great global importance, nevertheless. Commodity markets are the hubs where buyers and sellers trade information and opinions, and their mutually reinforcing expertise tends to determine world prices of a particular commodity. The basic function of a commodity exchange is to ensure the regular and reliable flow of commodities by establishing accepted markets and determining current prices. Properly organized commodity markets strive to establish prices that are in line with demand and that do not fluctuate widely; in addition, as commodities often must be transported great distances from their point of origin to their point of use, commodity markets make certain that products are delivered reliably. Commodities markets are probably best known as the places where futures contracts are traded.

The futures market relies on individuals who are willing to accept risk. Futures attract speculators, persons who usually have no direct contact with the specific commodity but who get into the market in the hopes of making a profit by buying low and selling high. Because of the high risk and great potential profits of their activities, speculators have often been considered as buccaneers who add little value to business. Yet speculators play an important role in the commodities world. They are willing to bear the risk that hedgers seek to avoid and thus act as a kind of insurance underwriter.

Further Reading

Greenaway, David, and C. W. Morgan. *The Economics of Commodity Markets.* Northampton, Mass.: Edward Elgar, 1999.

Markham, Jerry W. *The History of Commodity Futures Trading and Its Regulation.* New York: Praeger, 1987.

Rose, Frank, ed. *Commodity Trading Manual.* New York: Amacom, 1999.

Wasendorf, Russell R., and Thomas A. McCafferty. *All About Commodities.* New York: McGraw-Hill, 1992.

—Joseph Gustaitis

Communism

Communism is a political ideology that maintains that all property, and the wealth derived from its use, should be owned collectively and equally by the whole community. It is a recurrent idea in the history of political thought; in practice, communisim has taken two principal forms: primitive and modern.

Primitive communism has existed in certain highly egalitarian preindustrial societies. Some of these are known to us only through the archaeological record, while others continue to exist in parts of the developing world. Primitive communism can also refer to small-scale experimental communities, for example, those created at New Lanark, Scotland, and New Harmony, Indiana, by the nineteenth-century utopian socialist Robert Owen.

Modern communism has its origins in the writings of the German revolutionaries Karl Marx and Friedrich Engels. They analyzed history as a series of class struggles that would culminate in the revolutionary overthrow of the bourgeoisie (ruling class) by the proletariat (working class). Marx wrote that the new society created by this revolution would come to be organized on the principle of "from each according to his capacity, to each according to his needs."

In *The Communist Manifesto* (1848), Marx and Engels rejected the small utopian experiments of the past and called for a large-scale revolution. They also listed a number of immediate demands, including a progressive income tax, free education, and the abolition of inheritances. "The proletarians have nothing to lose but their chains," they declared. However, the actual experience of modern communist societies in the twentieth century differed markedly from Marx's vision.

The Russian Revolution

The first state to be created on the principles of modern communism was the Soviet Union. The regime of Tsar Nicholas II began to lose its legitimacy after Russia's defeat in the Russo–Japanese War (1904–1905) and failure to meet the political demands of the Revolution of 1905. The regime was weakened further by defeats in World War I, and the tsar abdicated in February 1917. Radical workers, inspired by Marxist revolutionaries, formed workers' councils (or *soviets*) across the country. The revolutionary communist Bolshevik Party, led by Vladimir Lenin, took control in October 1917.

Lenin withdrew Russia from the war, shut down all political opposition, and set about creating a communist state. He transferred ownership of industry, commerce, and

See also:
Capitalism; Competition;
Marx, Karl; Private Property;
Rule of Law; Socialism.

In 1975, a banner of three icons of communism hung in Moscow's Red Square: from left, Vladimir Lenin, Friedrich Engels, and Karl Marx.

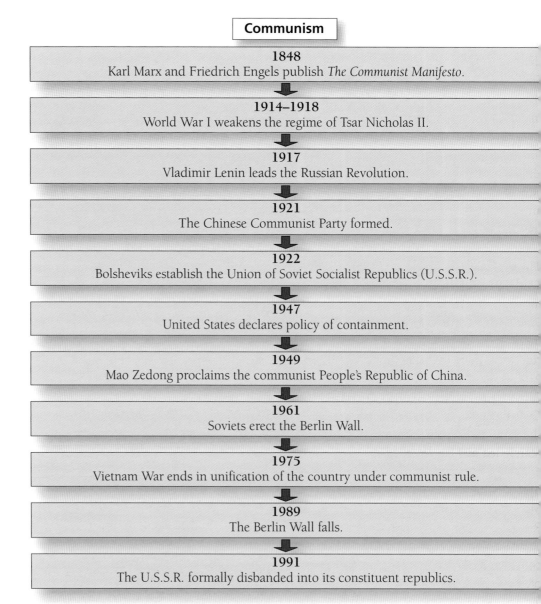

Communism

1848
Karl Marx and Friedrich Engels publish *The Communist Manifesto*.

1914–1918
World War I weakens the regime of Tsar Nicholas II.

1917
Vladimir Lenin leads the Russian Revolution.

1921
The Chinese Communist Party formed.

1922
Bolsheviks establish the Union of Soviet Socialist Republics (U.S.S.R.).

1947
United States declares policy of containment.

1949
Mao Zedong proclaims the communist People's Republic of China.

1961
Soviets erect the Berlin Wall.

1975
Vietnam War ends in unification of the country under communist rule.

1989
The Berlin Wall falls.

1991
The U.S.S.R. formally disbanded into its constituent republics.

banking to the state. When these actions, coupled with a civil war, threatened economic collapse, Lenin was forced to introduce the more market-based New Economic Policy (NEP) to stimulate production.

The Bolsheviks established a new political entity—the Union of Soviet Socialist Republics (U.S.S.R.)—in December 1922. Lenin's death in 1924 triggered a power struggle between Joseph Stalin, who wanted to pursue a policy of "socialism in one country," and Leon Trotsky, whose priority was an international communist revolution. By 1929, Stalin had emerged as leader; Trotsky went into exile and was later assassinated.

Stalin instituted a series of Five Year Plans to accelerate industrialization and to collectivize agriculture. In the process, millions of *kulaks*—independent peasant proprietors—were killed. In the mid-1930s, Stalin completed his control over the Communist Party, and he established the party's totalitarian dominance over society through the creation of an extensive secret police network. He also used the Comintern (or Third International) to establish Soviet control over Communist Parties in other countries.

As World War II was beginning, Stalin, wanting to expand Russia's territory, entered into the Nazi–Soviet Pact (1939), under which the Soviet Union and Germany agreed to partition Poland. By the end of 1940 Stalin had also annexed the Baltic states and parts of Finland. The Nazi–Soviet act did not hold, however, and German forces invaded Russia in June 1941; Stalin then joined the Western Allies. By 1945 Soviet forces had pushed westward against the Germans, occupying and installing communist governments in most of Eastern Europe and the Balkans. Alarmed by a new threat of Soviet domination in Europe, the United States in 1947 declared its policy of containment, under which it would resist any further expansion of Soviet power, and the cold war began.

The Chinese Revolution

The Chinese Communist Party (CCP) was formed in 1921. Initially it cooperated with Sun Yat-Sen's nationalist republican movement, the Kuomintang, against imperial rule and the foreign penetration of China. After Sun died in 1925, his successor, Chiang Kai-Shek, sought to annihilate the CCP. Encircled by Chiang's forces in 1934, the communists began the famous Long March, led by Mao Zedong. Thereafter, Mao concentrated on building a revolutionary organization among the rural peasantry. Mao proclaimed the communist People's Republic of China (PRC) on October 1, 1949.

The communists quickly established control over the whole country and occupied Tibet in 1950. The PRC relied on Soviet aid and adopted the Stalinist model of economic planning. In 1958, frustrated with the slow pace of economic development, Mao launched the "Great Leap Forward." This rush to boost industrial and agricultural productivity through state mandates was an unmitigated disaster, resulting in famine and the deaths of millions.

After a brief period of normalization following this disaster, Mao established personal domination through the "Cultural Revolution" (1966–1976)—a long campaign to purge the party of critics and establish control over all aspects of Chinese life. As many as half a million people are believed to have died as a result of hardships and punishments imposed by Mao's regime during this time. When Mao died in 1976, he left China at the brink of fundamental change.

Third World Communism

As the Asian and African colonial empires of the European powers began to disintegrate at the end of World War II, communism presented itself to leaders of important anticolonial movements as an ideology of national liberation. This view was strengthened whenever the United States, pursuing its policy of containment, intervened in anticolonial struggles to prop up collapsing imperial regimes or postcolonial dictatorships. Both the Soviets and the Americans couched their Third World interventions in ideological language; in reality, both acted on the basis of cold war strategic calculations.

In the Korean War (1950–1953), the United States led a United Nations campaign to repel an invasion of South Korea by the communist North. The United States then sided with the pro-Western government in South Vietnam against Ho Chi Minh's North Vietnam, which was supported by the Soviet Union and China. The result was the

Fidel Castro (center) and fellow revolutionaries enter Havana, Cuba, on January 1, 1959.

President Josip Tito of Yugoslavia in 1962.

In Africa, the United States and the U.S.S.R. competed to install compliant governments in unstable countries, often exacerbating local conflicts in the process. For example, the two superpowers supported opposing sides in the civil wars that broke out in the mid-1970s in the former Portuguese colonies of Mozambique and Angola. In the Middle East, the United States traditionally supported Israel and the religiously conservative oil-rich states of the Persian Gulf, while the Soviets backed the Palestinian cause and various radical Arab states.

Tensions within the Communist World

During the cold war years, the communist world itself was seriously weakened by internal tensions. Sino–Soviet relations were damaged by a border dispute and by rivalry for leadership of the communist world. By 1971, the rift was sufficient for U.S. president Richard Nixon to visit Beijing, driving a permanent wedge between China and the U.S.S.R.

The Soviet Union's recurring problems in Eastern Europe were highlighted in Yugoslavia, where President Josip Tito's communists owed their position not to Soviet imposition but to their leading role in the resistance to the Nazi occupation. Titoism therefore emerged as an independent communist model, characterized by an economy relatively liberal by communist standards—that emphasized worker self-management over centralized planning. Expelled from the communist bloc in 1948, Yugoslavia went on to play a leading role in the creation of the Non-Aligned Movement.

Other Eastern European countries had less success resisting Soviet control. In East Berlin in 1953, demonstrations against increased work quotas were put down by the East German authorities. In 1961, to solidify control over East Berlin, the Soviets built the Berlin Wall, which became the ultimate symbol of the cold war. In 1956, when Hungary tried to assert a greater degree of national independence by withdrawing from the Soviet-dominated Warsaw Pact, the Soviets

Vietnam War (1964–1975), which ended with the unification of Vietnam under communist rule. Elsewhere in Southeast Asia, the Pathet Lao brought communism to power in Laos, and in Cambodia Pol Pot's Khmer Rouge instituted a murderous brand of agrarian communism.

Communism also made inroads into Latin America. In Cuba, Fidel Castro and Che Guevara overthrew the Batista dictatorship in January 1959 and embarked on a thoroughgoing communist revolution that served as a model for Third World revolutions elsewhere. To the Kennedy administration, Cuba exemplified the threat of communist expansionism and, in October 1962, an American naval blockade forced the Soviets to withdraw their missiles from the island.

invaded. The "Prague Spring" of 1968, Czechoslovakia's experiment in liberal communism, was crushed by Soviet tanks. In Poland in 1980, shipyard workers formed Solidarity, an independent trade union movement, which challenged the communist government's economic policy. Solidarity was banned after the imposition of martial law in late 1981.

Within the Third World, conflict among communists was usually the result of communism's encounter with preexisting local antagonisms. A series of border skirmishes between China's ally Cambodia and Soviet-backed Vietnam began in 1975 and ended in 1979 with the Vietnamese invasion of Cambodia and the destruction of the Khmer Rouge government. Also in 1979, the Soviet Union invaded Afghanistan to prevent ethnic and religious opposition groups from overthrowing that country's communist government.

The Decline and Fall of Communism

Communism failed for four main reasons. First was economic inefficiency. Industry and agriculture were state-owned, and economic activity was planned from the center by a bureaucratic hierarchy. Economic decisions were, therefore, made subordinate to political considerations. The Soviet economy was subject to what has been called "diseconomies of scale" and characterized by the production of shoddy goods, continuous economic shortages, and the inefficient distribution of goods and services. Officially, unemployment was abolished in the Soviet Union. However, underemployment was extremely common.

After the fall of communism, statues of Lenin (right) and Dr. Petra Groza (first communist prime minister of Romania) were left abandoned in a field in the suburbs of Bucharest, Romania.

A McDonald's restaurant in downtown Beijing, 2000.

the Soviet Union. Gorbachev aimed to democratize Soviet politics through a policy of *glasnost* (opening) and to liberalize the economy through a policy of *perestroika* (restructuring). The Gorbachev program also fueled demands for reforms in Eastern Europe, where communist governments began to fall in the face of a series of "people's revolutions." On November 9, 1989, the end of communism was marked by the fall of the Berlin Wall. The Soviet Union itself then began to break up into its constituent republics and formally came to an end on December 31, 1991.

Communist Parties exist today in several countries throughout the world, but communism is no longer a major force in world politics. China, Cuba, and North Korea are the only remaining countries dominated by communism. The brutal suppression of the pro-democracy demonstrations in Tiananmen Square in 1989 demonstrated that the Chinese Communist Party remains intolerant of political dissent. However, China has increasingly turned toward a liberalized, market-oriented economy, encouraging free enterprise and joining the World Trade Organization. Cuba also remains under Communist Party rule, but it also has liberalized its economy and has taken steps toward normalizing its relations with the United States. North Korea remains a closed and isolated communist society, though it has improved its relations with capitalist South Korea. In eastern Europe, voters in some countries have supported Communist Parties, but these parties appear to be influenced increasingly by democratic thought and market-oriented economic policy.

Some workers did little more than punch time cards on their way in and out.

Experiments in economic liberalization like those made under Nikita Khrushchev (1953–1964) stimulated innovation and productivity, but they also jeopardized the political dominance of the Communist Party. Consequently, Khrushchev gave way to Leonid Brezhnev (1964–1982), who used state directives to focus the economy on heavy industry, regardless of consumer demand for other goods and services.

Second, the ideals of communist internationalism clashed with the realities of a world divided into nation-states. Marxist–Leninist ideology could not override nationalism and the desire for self-determination. Third, despite state censorship, communications technology made the citizens of communist countries aware of the higher living standards and greater political freedoms of the West. Fourth, after 1980, greater Western defense spending placed unbearable strains on the inefficient communist economies, as did the unwinnable war the Soviets had undertaken in Afghanistan.

All these problems confronted Mikhail Gorbachev (1985–1991), the last leader of

Further Reading

Brzezinski, Zbigniew. *The Soviet Bloc: Unity and Conflict.* Cambridge, Mass.: Harvard University Press, 1960.

Figes, Orlando. *A People's Tragedy: A History of the Russian Revolution.* New York: Viking, 1997.

Marx, Karl, and Frederick Engels. *The Communist Manifesto: With Related Documents.* Edited with an introduction by John E. Toews. Boston: Bedford/St. Martin's, 1999.

—*Peter C. Grosvenor*

Comparative Advantage

Comparative advantage is an economic concept that helps explain why people and countries trade with one other. If one country can grow bananas at a lower cost than another country, and the second country can make computers at a lower cost than the first, the reasonable course would seem to be that they should specialize in what they do best and most economically and then trade with one another.

What, exactly, does lower cost mean? This concept has two important interpretations. If one country can produce a good using fewer resources than another country, then its costs, measured in terms of resources used, are lower. If one country can produce a good by giving up less of other goods than another country, then its costs, measured in terms of goods given up, are lower. These sound very much the same, but they are not. If the first statement is true, the country is said to have an absolute advantage in producing that good. When the second is true, then the country is said to have a comparative advantage.

Distinguishing between Absolute and Comparative Advantage

Consider the simple world of Robinson Crusoe and Friday. Suppose Robinson needs an average of 20 minutes to either gather a basket of berries or catch a fish, while Friday needs, on average, one hour

See also:
Globalization; International Trade; Opportunity Cost; Trade Policy.

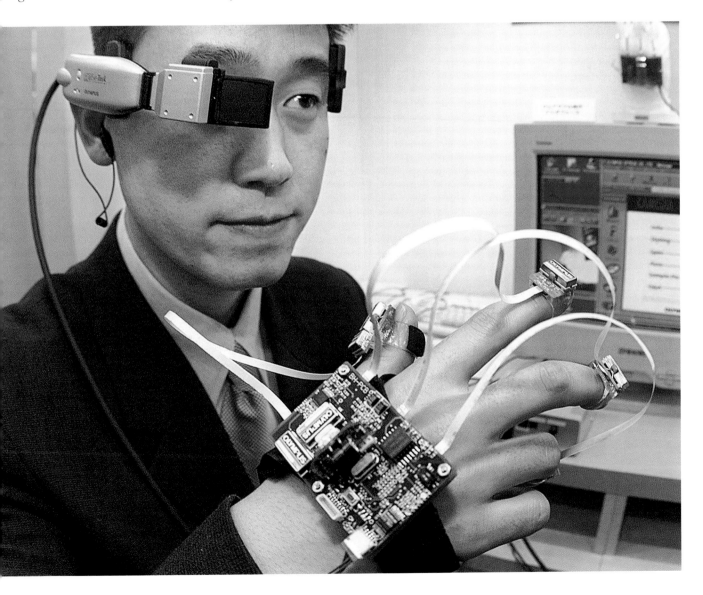

An employee of Olympus Optical in Japan demonstrates the company's prototype for a wearable computer. Japan has a comparative advantage in producing high technology products because of its large number of skilled workers.

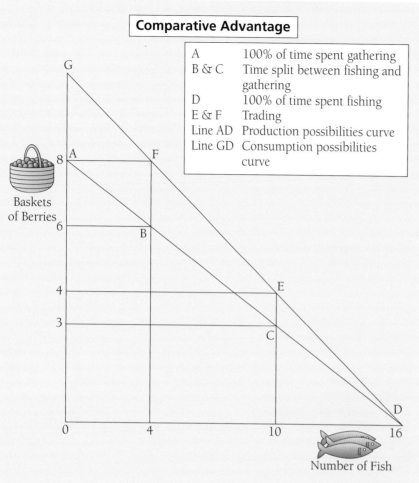

Comparative Advantage

A	100% of time spent gathering
B & C	Time split between fishing and gathering
D	100% of time spent fishing
E & F	Trading
Line AD	Production possibilities curve
Line GD	Consumption possibilities curve

Baskets of Berries

Number of Fish

Suppose Friday wishes to work (gathering berries and catching fish) only eight hours each day. The figure shows all the combinations of berries and fish he could produce on his own. As shown, he could produce 8 baskets of berries if he spent all of his time gathering (Point A) or he could catch 16 fish if he spent all of his time fishing (Point D). He could also choose to split his time between these two activities and end up with some of each of the goods, like 6 baskets and 4 fish (Point B) or 3 baskets and 10 fish (Point C). Line AD is called Friday's production possibilities curve. It shows those combinations of fish and berries possible for Friday to produce in eight hours without trading.

Suppose Friday and Robinson decide to specialize in what they do best and trade at the rate above, one basket of berries for one-and-a-half fish. Friday could put all his efforts into fishing and produce 16 fish (Point D). Given the terms of trade, he could then trade away 6 of his fish for 4 baskets of berries and end up with 4 baskets of berries and 10 fish (Point E) or he could trade away 12 of his fish for 8 baskets of berries and end up with 8 baskets of berries and 4 fish (Point F). In fact, he could now end up with any combination of berries and fish on Line GD (called his consumption possibilities curve). He can now get combinations that offer him more berries and fish than he could get before trading. A similar diagram could be drawn for Robinson. Both are able to enjoy more berries and fish by specializing and trading because now their resources are used to produce what they do best according to their comparative advantage.

has the absolute advantage in producing berries? Since gathering a basket of berries takes 20 minutes of Robinson's time, but an hour of Friday's, Robinson does. He uses 40 minutes less of his labor resource. Who has the absolute advantage in producing fish? Again, Robinson does as he can catch a fish in just 20 minutes while Friday takes 30 minutes. As Robinson can do both things faster than Friday, he would seem to gain no advantage from trading with Friday. Trade, however, is based on comparative advantage, not absolute advantage.

Who has the comparative advantage in producing each good? To determine the answer, one needs to look at what must be given up in terms of other goods. Economists refer to this as the opportunity cost. Each time Robinson decides to gather one basket of berries he loses the opportunity to catch one fish, as 20 minutes spent gathering means 20 minutes unavailable for fishing. Thus, each basket of berries costs Robinson one fish. Each time Friday decides to gather a basket of berries he loses the opportunity to catch two fish, as the one hour required to gather one basket means one hour he cannot be fishing (in which time he could have caught two fish). Thus, each basket of berries costs Friday two fish. In terms of fish that must be given up, Robinson has to give up less than Friday, so Robinson has the comparative advantage as the producer of berries.

However, consider the respective opportunity costs of producing fish. For each fish Robinson produces, he must give up the opportunity to produce one basket of berries. But for each fish Friday produces, he gives up only half a basket of berries. With respect to fishing, Friday has the comparative advantage.

One way of thinking about this is to note that Friday's absolute disadvantage at fishing is not as great as it is for berry gathering. Robinson can gather a basket of berries three times faster than Friday can, but he can fish only one-and-a-half times faster. Hence, Robinson's time is better spent in gathering berries. Both Robinson and

to gather a basket of berries and 30 minutes to catch a fish. Robinson and Friday are both using their labor resources (themselves) to produce berries and fish. Who

riday could be made better off (that is, each ave more fish and more berries to consume) if they specialized and traded with ne another. Each person should specialize i producing that good for which he has a omparative advantage: for Robinson it is erries, for Friday it is fish.

International Trade

he same principles of the example above ay be applied to countries and their productive resources. Productive resources are ot distributed evenly throughout the orld or even within a country. Saudi rabia has few timber resources but does ave large oil reserves. Japan has little oil eserves but does have many highly skilled orkers. Costa Rica has few skilled workers ut does have a tropical climate. Most of the nited States does not have a tropical climate but does have a vast stock of technologically advanced equipment.

The mix and quality of productive esources a country has depends on its initial ndowment of natural resources and on the nvestment a country makes in capital goods nd in the education and training of its people. This mix in turn determines what goods nd services that country possesses a comparative advantage in producing. Countries vill generally export those goods they have comparative advantage in producing and mport those they do not. Japan will export lectronic goods and import oil from Saudi rabia. Costa Rica will export bananas and mport manufactured goods from the United States. In doing so, total world production will rise as more efficient use is nade of the world's resources—in much he same way Robinson and Friday were ble to produce more berries and fish.

Note that although trading on the pasis of comparative advantage does benefit both countries in terms of them both peing able to produce more, it does not nean all groups within both countries are nade better off. Consumers usually benefit rom the lower prices resulting from ncreased competition and production, but workers in those industries where a country

A plantation worker harvests bananas in Costa Rica. Costa Rica has a comparative advantage in growing bananas because of its warm climate.

does not have a comparative advantage would likely start to lose their jobs. Of course, workers in those industries where a country does have a comparative advantage would start seeing more opportunities. On the whole, for a country, the gains from trade tend to outweigh the losses, but to those losing their jobs, such trade may not seem beneficial.

Further Reading

Blinder, Alan S. *Hard Heads, Soft Hearts.* Boston: Addison-Wesley, 1987.
Mankiw, N. Gregory. *Principles of Economics.* New York: The Dryden Press, 1998.
McConnell, Campbell R., and Stanley L. Brue. *Economics: Principles, Problems, and Policies.* 15th ed. New York: McGraw-Hill, 2002.

—Curt L. Anderson

Compensation

When most people think of compensation, they think of wages—the amount of money that a person receives per hour of work or per year worked, generally received in regular paychecks. However, compensation—what a company gives employees in exchange for their labor—includes a wide variety of remuneration. Compensation can be structured in many different ways and has changed considerably as the economy, businesses, and social norms have altered.

Although compensation is usually not the only reason an individual chooses a certain career or joins and remains with a particular employer, how employees are compensated and whether they feel that compensation is fair can have a critical effect on how hard employees work, how loyal they are, and what kind of work they do. Companies have almost always considered compensation to be a means of helping the business achieve certain goals, especially to attract and retain good workers.

Wages and Benefits

Traditionally, an employee's wages were calculated using base pay—the amount of money a person received when first hired. Usually the base pay a person received depended on the kind of job. Often companies had explicit policies governing base pay—an electrician earned a certain amount, while a marketing executive earned a different amount. Usually a company would survey similar companies in the area or the industry to determine what the standard base pay was for a particular job.

A person's base pay also depended on the individual, however. An electrician with 10 years of experience, for example, would receive a higher base pay than one with six months of experience. Until the practice was effectively outlawed, a person's gender, race, or ethnic background would also be taken into consideration. For example, when it was uncommon for married women to work, a man would often receive a higher base pay than a woman because the assumption was that he was supporting a family and she was single.

Once a worker accepted the base pay and began working for a company, he or she would receive raises, often annually. Raises were of two kinds: cost-of-living increases and merit raises. Cost-of-living increases were initially designed to compensate for the effect of inflation on salaries. As a result, all workers usually got the same percentage raise.

As the name suggests, merit raises gave management more discretion to reward better workers with bigger raises. Both kinds of raises tended to award seniority—the longer employees stayed with a company, the more raises they would get and the higher their salary would be.

If workers wanted to earn dramatically more money, they usually needed to seek promotion. Many companies had a set salary range for each kind of job—a line worker could make only up to a certain amount, but a supervisor could make

Components of Compensation		
Wages and salaries		72.8%
Paid leave	6.6%	
Supplemental pay	2.7%	
Insurance	6.5%	
Retirement and savings	2.8%	
Legally required benefits	8.3%	
Other benefits	.3%	

Source: U.S. Department of Labor, Bureau of Labor Statistics, Washington, D.C.

Of the different kinds of compensation received by U.S. workers, almost three-quarters is received in the form of wages, with paid vacation, insurance, and other kinds of compensation rounding out the mix.

Benefit Programs by Industry 1997
(in percent)

	All industries	Professional, technical, and related	Clerical and sales	Blue collar and service		All industries	Professional, technical, and related	Clerical and sales	Blue collar and service
Paid time off					*Tax-deferred savings*				
Holidays	89	89	91	88	With employer contribution	46	56	51	38
Vacations	95	96	97	94					
Personal leave	20	23	33	13	With no employer contribution	9	11	8	8
Funeral leave	81	84	85	76					
Jury duty leave	87	92	89	83	*Income continuation plans*				
Military leave	47	60	50	38	Severance pay	36	48	43	26
Sick leave	56	73	73	38	Supplemental unemployment benefits	5	2	2	7
Family leave	2	3	3	1					
Unpaid family leave	93	95	96	91	*Family benefits*				
Disability benefits					Child care	10	14	10	7
Short-term disability	55	54	52	58	Adoption assistance	10	16	12	6
Long-term disability	43	62	52	28	Long-term care assistance	7	10	11	4
Insurance					Flexible workplace	2	5	3	(Z)
Medical care	76	79	78	74	*Health promotion programs*				
Dental care	59	64	59	56	Wellness programs	36	44	36	32
Vision care	26	28	25	24	Employee assistance programs	61	75	63	52
Life insurance	87	94	91	81					
Retirement	79	89	81	72	Fitness center	21	31	19	16
Defined benefit	50	52	49	50	*Miscellaneous benefits*				
Defined contribution	57	70	63	46	Job-related travel accident insurance	42	56	46	32
Savings and thrift	39	49	45	30					
Deferred profit sharing	13	15	15	12	Nonproduction bonuses	42	43	43	40
Employee stock ownership	4	6	6	3	Subsidized commuting	6	10	7	3
					Educational assistance				
Money purchase pension	8	12	6	6	Job-related	67	81	68	58
					Not job-related	20	25	18	18

Z) = Less than 0.5 percent.
Note: Covers full-time employees in privately held establishments with more than 100 workers. Covers only benefits for which the employer pays part or all of the premium or expenses involved, except unpaid family leave.
Source: U.S. Department of Labor, Bureau of Labor Statistics, *News,* USDL 99-02, January 7, 1999.

more. Like regular raises, promotions tended to reward seniority. An industrious line worker who knew the production line well because she had worked on it for many years was an obvious candidate to supervise that line. Employees who did well could "rise through the ranks," going ever higher in the management hierarchy and receiving ever-higher levels of pay.

In addition to wages, employees could expect to receive benefits—noncash items of value to employees. Following World War II, companies began to offer benefits like health insurance, life insurance, paid vacations, and retirement pensions. (Such benefits are distinct from perquisites or "perks"—free use of a company car, for example—that are reserved for high-ranking executives or given as rewards to exceptional performers.) Benefits are not only of value in themselves, but also, unlike wages, they are not ordinarily subject to income tax.

The many kinds of benefits received and what kind of jobs receive them are shown above.

As the cost of health care increased, benefits became more important to employees. In 2002 they accounted for roughly a quarter of the average compensation package. In addition, new forms of benefits have become popular. As more women have entered the workforce, demand for employee-sponsored child care has become very strong—indeed, many companies have found that employees would rather have free or low-cost child care than higher wages.

The seniority system was the norm in most professions; however, in some professions, alternate compensation systems were always common. For example, many salespeople had a very low or nonexistent base pay; instead, they were paid through commissions, essentially a share of the sales they generated. Very high-ranking executives were often given an ownership stake in the company. For both, the potential risks and the potential rewards were higher—if sales went well, a salesperson could earn lots of money; if they went poorly, he could earn little. The intent of such systems was to motivate salespeople and high-ranking executives to work very hard to make the company successful.

Performance versus Seniority

Beginning in the 1980s, increasing numbers of companies began to shift away from compensation systems that rewarded seniority to systems more like those traditionally used to compensate salespeople and high-ranking executives. Instead of basing compensation on seniority, these systems were intended to base compensation on performance.

Performance-based compensation appealed to companies for many reasons. For one, the technological advances and economic pressures of the late twentieth century caused companies to restructure to eliminate many layers of management. With fewer ranks to rise through, promotion was less likely. If a worker was unlikely to be promoted, he or she had little motivation to work hard under a traditional compensation system.

Basing compensation on performance could also mean increased financial flexibility for the employer. Under the seniority system, the only way to trim payrolls in lean years was to lay off workers. When the market recovered, companies had to

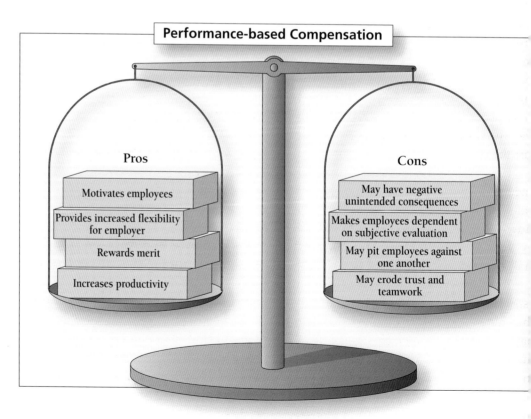

Performance-based Compensation

Pros	Cons
Motivates employees	May have negative unintended consequences
Provides increased flexibility for employer	Makes employees dependent on subjective evaluation
Rewards merit	May pit employees against one another
Increases productivity	May erode trust and teamwork

ramble to find new workers. However, if company's financial performance is a criterion in determining employee compensation, payrolls automatically shrink when the company is not doing well, reducing the need for layoffs.

In addition, basing pay on performance held the promise of rewarding genuine merit. Under a seniority system, any worker who manages not to get fired for a long time gets more pay and is more likely to get promoted—even if the worker is not particularly industrious or talented. Critics of the seniority system charged that employees were motivated to do the bare minimum required not to get fired, but not much more. Compensating performance, however, seemed to give employees a motivation to work harder and be more productive because they would be recognized and rewarded in a manner consistent with their accomplishments.

Performance-pay systems seem like they would work well; however, designing and implementing an effective system is actually quite challenging. Companies must choose what kind of performance they wish to encourage. One common strategy is to base payments on a company's profits. Profit sharing is intended to make employees feel like they have a stake in the overall well-being of their company, making them more willing to work in teams, be more productive, and generally behave in a way that benefits the entire company, not just the employee or his department.

However, profit sharing can actually be bad for employee morale because a company may have no profits for reasons outside employees' control—mistakes made by top management, for example, or a generally poor economic climate.

Another strategy, which has become especially popular in fields like health care that require specialized knowledge, is to pay people for obtaining new skills. A nurse who undertakes additional training in a particular field of medicine, for example, would get paid more than one who did not. Companies usually rely on outside

Employer Costs per Hour for Employee Compensation September 2002	
	Cost per hour
Total compensation	$23.44
Wages and salaries	16.93
Total benefits	6.51
Paid leave	1.60
Supplemental pay	.56
Insurance	1.67
Retirement and savings	.80
Legally required benefits	1.85
Social security	1.36
Federal unemployment insurance	.03
State unemployment insurance	.09
Workers' compensation	.38
Other benefits	.03

Source: U.S. Department of Labor, Bureau of Labor Statistics, Washington, D.C.

certification to verify that the new skill has, in fact, been acquired.

Other kinds of performance pay are based on accomplishing certain goals, for example, devising a cost-saving strategy or finishing a project under budget and before deadline. Companies usually give bonuses—one-time payments made in addition to regular wages—when a goal is met, but noncash awards are sometimes also given, which can range from valuable goods like paid vacations to plaques and mentions in a company newsletter.

As performance pay has become more widespread, the potential drawbacks of such systems have become apparent. Poorly designed performance-pay systems can have unintended consequences. For example, consider a data-processing company that decides to give a lavish bonus to the employee who types the most data from handwritten input sheets into the computer over the next six months. The expectation is that this will motivate all the workers to be more productive. The employees do type faster, but because they are going to be rewarded for speed, not accuracy, the result is more mistakes that the company must pay people to track down and fix later. In addition,

The average cost to U.S. businesses for employee compensation.

The amount of compensation received by workers differs widely depending on location. The map shows the average hourly costs to businesses for employee compensation in selected countries; wages are listed in U.S. dollars for easy comparison. Note that although compensation costs have risen throughout the world, they have risen far more slowly in developing nations like Mexico and Korea.

employees neglect other important tasks, including meeting with clients, to spend more time typing.

As the end of the six-month period approaches, the more competitive employees take to sabotaging the computers and hiding the input sheets of people who type faster than they do. By the end of six months, the company experiences greater costs, alienated clients, and has a department full of employees who do not trust each other and cannot work together.

Another issue with performance pay is assessing an employee's performance.

Such judgments may use measurable c[r]i teria, but performance is often subje[c] tively judged by other employees, openi[ng] up the process to bias and politics. F[or] example, a white male manager may gi[ve] favorable performance reviews only [to] other white men—and give especially ro[sy] reviews to white men who belonged to h[is] college fraternity.

Managers who have worked with a re[l] atively small group of employees for a lo[ng] time often feel guilty about giving out unf[a] vorable performance reviews to peop[le] they know well, so they hand out favorab[le]

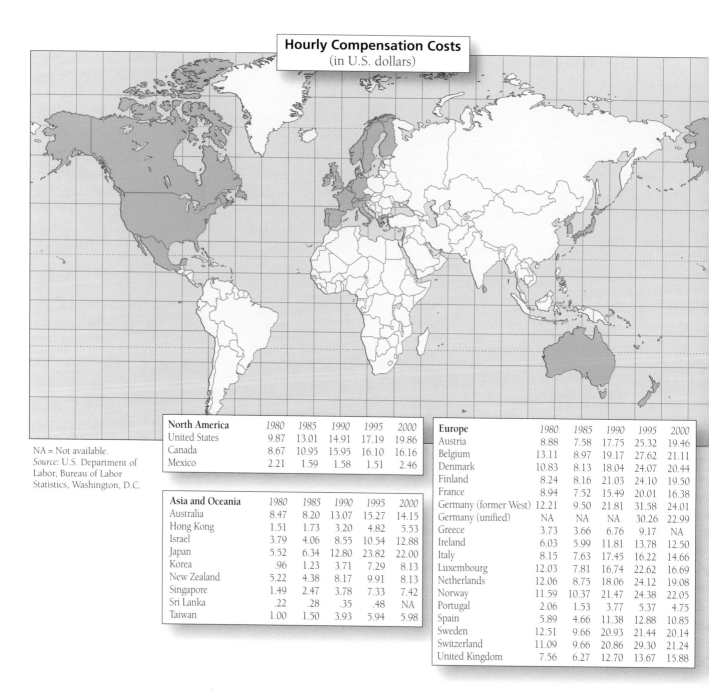

Hourly Compensation Costs
(in U.S. dollars)

NA = Not available.
Source: U.S. Department of Labor, Bureau of Labor Statistics, Washington, D.C.

North America	1980	1985	1990	1995	2000
United States	9.87	13.01	14.91	17.19	19.86
Canada	8.67	10.95	15.95	16.10	16.16
Mexico	2.21	1.59	1.58	1.51	2.46

Asia and Oceania	1980	1985	1990	1995	2000
Australia	8.47	8.20	13.07	15.27	14.15
Hong Kong	1.51	1.73	3.20	4.82	5.53
Israel	3.79	4.06	8.55	10.54	12.88
Japan	5.52	6.34	12.80	23.82	22.00
Korea	.96	1.23	3.71	7.29	8.13
New Zealand	5.22	4.38	8.17	9.91	8.13
Singapore	1.49	2.47	3.78	7.33	7.42
Sri Lanka	.22	.28	.35	.48	NA
Taiwan	1.00	1.50	3.93	5.94	5.98

Europe	1980	1985	1990	1995	2000
Austria	8.88	7.58	17.75	25.32	19.46
Belgium	13.11	8.97	19.17	27.62	21.11
Denmark	10.83	8.13	18.04	24.07	20.44
Finland	8.24	8.16	21.03	24.10	19.50
France	8.94	7.52	15.49	20.01	16.38
Germany (former West)	12.21	9.50	21.81	31.58	24.01
Germany (unified)	NA	NA	NA	30.26	22.99
Greece	3.73	3.66	6.76	9.17	NA
Ireland	6.03	5.99	11.81	13.78	12.50
Italy	8.15	7.63	17.45	16.22	14.66
Luxembourg	12.03	7.81	16.74	22.62	16.69
Netherlands	12.06	8.75	18.06	24.12	19.08
Norway	11.59	10.37	21.47	24.38	22.05
Portugal	2.06	1.53	3.77	5.37	4.75
Spain	5.89	4.66	11.38	12.88	10.85
Sweden	12.51	9.66	20.93	21.44	20.14
Switzerland	11.09	9.66	20.86	29.30	21.24
United Kingdom	7.56	6.27	12.70	13.67	15.88

views to everyone. If executives review each other, they may have an unspoken agreement that everyone gives everyone else positive performance reviews to ensure that everyone gets good raises and nobody gets fired.

Although performance pay is far from a perfect method for calculating compensation, most observers expect it to be adopted and refined further. The financial flexibility it gives companies and the positive effect a well-designed system can have make performance-based compensation extremely attractive to companies.

Stock Options

Another compensation scheme, which was particularly popular among the high-tech industries of the late twentieth century, was offering company shares to large numbers of employees for free or at low cost. The thinking was that if an employee has a stake in the company, he will work to further the best interests of the company over the long term.

Another way to share ownership of a publicly held company is to grant stock options, which are the right to buy shares of the company's stock at a certain price at some point in the future. Stock options are designed to reward a rising stock price. Say a company's stock is worth $20 a share, and the company grants an employee the right to buy the stock at $30 a share in five years. If the company's stock reaches $40 a share at that point, the employee can buy those $40 shares for the bargain price of $30. However, if the company's stock is under $30 five years later, the option is "under water," or worthless.

Such programs are intended to make employees focus on the company's long-term prospects, but they have not always done so. Indeed, critics argue that employees, especially senior executives, who wish to sell their stock in the company are motivated to "pump and dump"—exaggerate earnings or talk up the company to get the price of the stock up, then sell all their shares while the market is high.

CEO Pay

Chief executive officers (CEOs) of large corporations get paid large amounts of money—and a lot more than they used to. During the 1990s, CEO compensation increased by more than 550 percent—far more than the rise in pay for the average worker.

CEOs have traditionally been the recipients of performance pay, receiving bonuses, stock, and stock options if the company meets certain goals. In theory, CEO pay is supposed to go up when the company does well, and go down when the company does poorly. In practice, this happens to a degree, but critics argue that the system of CEO compensation hands ever-higher rewards to CEOs, especially in companies where the CEO is a particularly powerful figure. Defenders of performance pay argue that companies can ill afford to alienate CEOs in tough economic times, when leadership is more important than ever.

One practice that has received tremendous criticism is that of moving performance targets to make them easier to meet. For example, a company's board of directors has set a target of 20 percent revenue growth or the CEO loses his bonus. However, the year looks slow, so the board resets the target for 10 percent growth, and the CEO keeps his bonus. (The validity of using a growth target could itself be questioned because a CEO might try to reach that goal by sacrificing profits or overexpanding.) The practice infuriates shareholders' rights activists, who charge that it rewards the incompetent as well as the capable.

Another issue is CEO stock options, which are the right to buy a stock at a certain price in the future. Stock options are not counted as an expense, so boards of directors have been very generous in approving them. By the early twenty-first century, about 80 percent of executive compensation was in stock options, and a large portion of the rapid increase in CEO pay was attributable to ever-larger packages of options. Stock options can further weaken the link between pay and performance. For example, in 2001 the price of the stock of the technology company Oracle Corp. fell by more than half, and CEO Lawrence Ellison received no salary or bonus. That same year, Ellison exercised stock options awarded years before that were worth $706 million, making him the best compensated CEO ever.

Further Reading

Farr, J. Michael, and LaVerne L. Ludden. *Best Jobs for the 21st Century*. Indianapolis: JIST, 2000.

Flannery, Thomas P., et al. *People, Performance and Pay: Dynamic Compensation for Changing Organizations*. New York: The Free Press, 1996.

Hall, Brian J. *The Pay to Performance Incentives of Executive Stock Options*. Cambridge, Mass.: National Bureau of Economic Research, 1998.

Kohn, Alfie. *Punished by Rewards: The Trouble with Gold Stars, Incentive Plans, A's, Praise, and Other Bribes*. New York: Houghton Mifflin, 1993.

Monks, Robert A., and Nell Minow. *Corporate Governance*. 2nd ed. Malden, Mass.: Blackwell Publishers, 2001.

Rynes, Sara L., and Barry Gerhart, eds. *Compensation in Organizations: Current Research and Practice*. San Francisco: Jossey-Bass, 2000.

—Mary Sisson

Competition

Whenever two or more people want the same thing and only one can have it, the usual result is competition, as they try to outdo one another in attaining the desired affect or goal. In its simplest sense, competition in the business world occurs in a similar situation: two or more companies want to sell the same thing to a person, who is going to buy it from one. Like competition among people, competition among business divides observers. Some argue that competition is too stressful and destructive, but others claim competition is healthy and the surest way to get good results.

Kinds of Competition
People can compete in many different arenas—in sports, academically, professionally. Likewise businesses have many modes of competition. For example, imagine two Chinese restaurants, the Lucky Dragon and the Golden Temple, located across the street from each other. The two are the only restaurants on the block, and their food, ambience, and service are almost indistinguishable. The proprietor of the Lucky Dragon decides he wants to take business away from the Golden Temple, so he slashes the prices of his lunches and dinners. He is engaging in price competition, probably the most familiar form of business competition.

The proprietor of the Golden Temple is not going to let her customers go next door without a fight, so she matches the Lucky Dragon's prices. In response, the Lucky Dragon cuts prices again. The proprietor of the Golden Temple wants to avoid an all-out price war, so she decides to take a different tack.

Instead of cutting prices, she fires her chef, hires a better one, and upgrades the quality of her food. She also renovates the restaurant's interior, making it larger and more luxurious, and hires more staff so that service is always speedy. The proprietor then advertises the improvements, and more customers start coming in, seeking a nicer, albeit slightly more expensive, dining experien than provided by the Lucky Dragon. Th proprietor of the Golden Temple has com peted through investing—spending mon to improve her product—rather tha through price-cutting.

The Lucky Dragon is not going to ta this lying down. The proprietor does n like his restaurant becoming known as th place to get cheap, lousy Chinese food, b if he upgrades his service, interior, and foo to match the improvements at the Gold Temple, he will be right back where h started. Instead, the proprietor replaces h chef and begins offering fusion cuisine— a mix of traditional Chinese food an European and American regional cuisine Fusion cuisine is new to the town, and soo adventurous diners are flocking to th Lucky Dragon. The Lucky Dragon is no competing by innovating—offering som thing new that people will buy instead the old product.

By this point, the block that houses th Lucky Dragon—the town's first fusio restaurant—and the Golden Temple—hom of the finest Chinese cuisine—has a certai cachet among diners who like Asian foo Whereas before only people who live nearby ate at the Lucky Dragon or th Golden Temple, now people come from a over town and even from other towns to ea at these two restaurants, lining up outside t wait for a table.

Other would-be restaurateurs tak notice. The two fired chefs open an inexpen sive Chinese restaurant halfway down th block called Original Temple and Drago Soon, other Chinese and fusion restauran are opening on the block, along with a sus bar, a Thai restaurant, and a Korean barbe cue, until every storefront houses some kin of Asian restaurant. While the concentratio of restaurants attracts more diners, the pro fusion of restaurants means less business fc the Lucky Dragon and the Golden Templ Even worse, now the two proprietors do nc have to worry just about each other, the have to compete against a dozen othe restaurants, all on the same block.

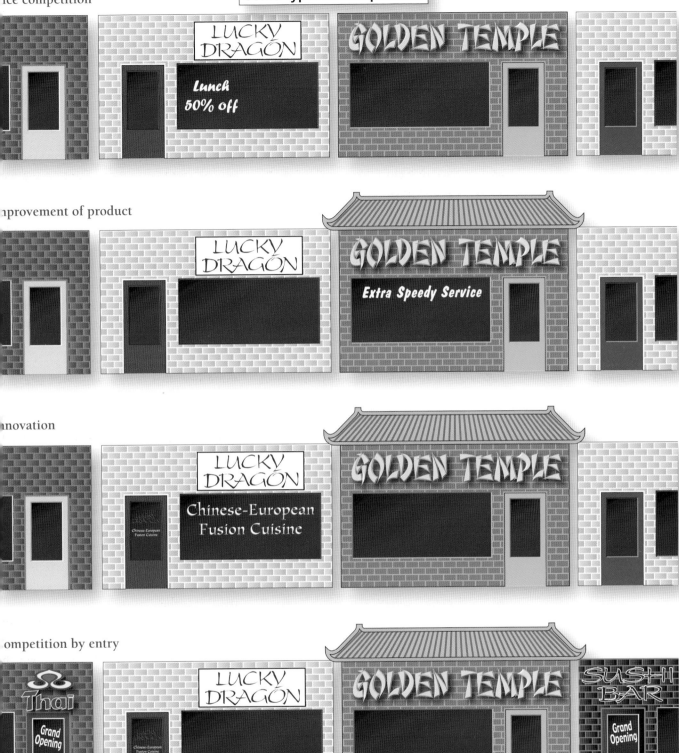

The two restaurants are facing another mode of competition—the entry of new businesses into the market. Competition-by-entry is especially disconcerting for businesses because it tends to happen when a business is successful and can come in unexpected forms. Imagine that the Lucky Dragon and the Golden Temple occupy the only two storefronts on the block, and no one else can open a restaurant near them. They still might suffer if someone opens a take-out and delivery Chinese-and-fusion food place five blocks away, or if an Asian market opens and people start cooking Chinese and fusion cuisine at home instead of going to restaurants, or if the diners who once flocked to their restaurants discover a restaurant in another town and go there instead.

As the proprietors of both the Lucky Dragon and the Golden Temple have discovered, life is a lot easier for businesses when there is no competition. Profits are usually higher too—some economists even define competition as actions that drive down profits in an industry, although others disagree. Economic theorists often refer to "perfect competition," a situation where many companies are offering the same products to consumers who know everything about the products and their prices. In a situation of perfect competition, profits are almost nonexistent.

Eliminating Competition

Fortunately for businesses, perfect competition does not exist in the real world. Indeed, plenty of businesses, like Intel Corp., manage to operate in areas with little or no competition. Intel, which manufactures computer microprocessors, has accomplished this largely through being in an industry that, unlike the restaurant business, has high barriers to entry. Developing and building microprocessors are expensive and require specialized expertise, thus, few companies are likely to try to compete with Intel.

Nevertheless, even Intel has some competitors. Intel has had to remake itself repeatedly to stay on the cutting edge of technology where competitors are few. Indeed, the mere prospect of serious competition can be as great a motivator as actual competition.

Another way to eliminate competition is to create a monopoly or a cartel. A monopoly is a single company that controls an entire

Examples of Anticompetitive Practices

- Restricting trade or commerce.
- Preventing competition in manufacture, transportation, or sale.
- Creating a monopoly.
- Fixing or restricting prices.
- Giving kickbacks to suppliers.
- Restricting customers or markets.
- Agreeing with other suppliers not to compete against each other.
- Instituting exclusive supply or purchasing agreements.

market; as customers cannot go elsewher the company has the power to raise prices will. A cartel is created when a group of com petitors gets together and agrees on wh prices to charge.

Monopolies and cartels are usual more appealing to businesses than compet tion. Say that instead of cutting prices nab business from the Golden Temple, th proprietor of the Lucky Dragon instea decides that he and the proprietor of th Golden Temple need to start a Chines restaurant cartel. They get together an agree to charge $50 a plate for sweet-an sour pork, expecting to make more mone without the trouble of cutting prices, reno vating, or making over their menus.

The cartel will work, however, only the Golden Temple and the Lucky Drago remain the only two Chinese restaurants i the area. Accordingly, the two proprieto start taking steps to keep out other com petitors. They lobby the town council t deny business licenses to new Chines restaurants. They buy out the only area sup plier of Asian food or offer the supplie bribes to refuse to sell to other Chines restaurants. They may refuse to buy fro the supplier if he does supply other Chines restaurants. If a new Chinese restaurar opens in the area, the proprietors try to bu it so they can shut it down. If their offer i refused, the staff of the Golden Temple an Lucky Dragon go to the new restaurant a night and burn it to the ground.

Obviously the proprietors of the two Chinese restaurants are breaking the law. Indeed, they are engaging in a range of what are known as anticompetitive practices, including price fixing and giving kickbacks to suppliers, that can run afoul of antitrust laws (not to mention anti-arson laws). However, the proprietors' other actions—lobbying the town council, for example—are perfectly legal, albeit anticompetitive. Actions like buying out competitors and suppliers can be legal depending on the size of the market the two restaurants control and whether they form part of a pattern of anticompetitive behavior.

Governments tend to have a highly ambivalent attitude toward competition. The United States, for example, is known for its embrace of competition, but the country also allows certain monopolies and cartels, subsidizes industries, and erects trade barriers, all to protect certain industries against competition, especially foreign competition. Such protections against competition are widespread in other countries as well.

Why might a government entity like a town council agree to protect two Chinese restaurants from competition? The restaurants pay taxes, they employ people, and they are a legal and desirable kind of business. The council might do what it can to make sure they thrive, because the restaurants benefit the town.

Protection of industry from competition, especially from foreign competition, is often motivated by job preservation and survival of industry. In a wealthy country like the United States, wages are higher than in many poorer countries. As a result, the products produced in those countries are cheaper, and U.S.-made products cannot compete on price, so industry falters and workers are laid off. Those who wish to ensure that a domestic industry survives tend to support the levying of tariffs on imported goods and other barriers to foreign competition.

Industry protection was also once seen as important for products, electricity, for one, that were considered too vital for people to do without, although this view is beginning to change. Monopolies in areas like electricity and telecommunications were long encouraged to prevent utilities from experiencing financial problems that could lead to interruptions of these important services. Countries often protect nascent industries, especially ones that have high initial costs, like airlines, by granting monopolies or barring the entry of new competitors in an industry. Protecting industries from competition avoids the risk that companies in the industry will be unable to respond to competitive threats and will fail.

The Benefits of Competition

Supporters of greater competition argue that the protectionist approach is short-sighted and defends the present at the expense of the future. Consider the Lucky Dragon and the Golden Temple. If the two are protected from competition by the town council, then the town gets two mediocre, pricey Chinese restaurants. If they are forced to compete, then the town gets an entire restaurant district, one that attracts diners from miles around. From the town's point of view, the latter outcome is obviously preferable—the two restaurants are

---

Major Provisions of Key Antitrust Legislation

"Antitrust laws . . . are the Magna Carta of free enterprise. They are as important to the preservation of economic freedom and our free-enterprise system as the Bill of Rights is to the protection of our fundamental personal freedoms."

Supreme Court, *United States v. Topco Associates, Inc.* (1972)

Sherman Antitrust Act (1890)
- Outlaws "every contract, combination . . . or conspiracy, in restraint of trade."
- Makes illegal a company's effort to "monopolize or attempt to monopolize" trade or commerce.

Federal Trade Commission Act (1914)
- Outlaws "unfair methods of competition."

Clayton Act (1914)
- Prohibits mergers and acquisitions where the effect "may be substantially to lessen competition, or to tend to create a monopoly."
- Requires the prior notification of large mergers to both the Federal Trade Commission and the Justice Department.

What Makes an Industry Competitive?

Regulators have long faced the problem of deciding when an industry is so dominated by a single company or a handful of companies that it can no longer be considered competitive. For a long time the answer seemed simple: Look at the number of companies in an industry; the fewer the companies, the less competitive the industry.

This view has come under fire, in part because competition tends to take place between industries, not simply within them. For example, the Federal Communications Commission (FCC) has long restricted the number of broadcast television or radio stations a single company can own in a single market, with the idea of ensuring that competing views can get aired. The rise of cable television and the Internet, however, has led the FCC to relax these restrictions because alternatives to broadcast television and radio are available.

Likewise, relatively few U.S. companies manufacture steel, but they compete with foreign steel suppliers as well as suppliers of aluminum and other materials that can be used instead of steel. Indeed, one reason for the lack of U.S. steel manufacturers is that the market is so competitive that it tends to discourage new entrants. Presumably the U.S. steel industry could dwindle to one manufacturer—the survivor would almost certainly not be considered an anticompetitive monopoly. Indeed, despite the small number of companies in the steel industry, in 2002 the United States took steps to reduce competition in the industry by placing tariffs on imported steel.

still open (in fact, they serve better food than they did before), and the town has more businesses paying taxes and employing people. Even the two fired chefs have become restaurant owners. Obviously such positive outcomes are not guaranteed, but defenders of competition argue that the benefits of a competitive market almost always outweigh the risks.

Competition forces companies to be disciplined about costs. A monopoly electricity utility, for example, traditionally passed along cost increases to customers. As a result, such utilities had no reason to discover the cheapest way to produce and distribute electricity; in a competitive electricity market, a utility can be undercut on price by a more efficient competitor. Such price competition forces the utility to seek out cost-efficient ways of doing business.

Of course, price competition has another benefit—lower prices for consumers. Long-distance telephone service, for example, was once a monopoly granted to AT&T. The service was thrown open to competition in the early 1980s, and, as a result, prices consumers pay for long distance calls dropped considerably.

Competition is also an especially potent means to force companies to innovate. New products—especially technically advanced ones that are hard for other companies to duplicate—essentially give businesses temporary monopoly pricing power; as a result such advances are extremely lucrative. A company that is constantly innovative can charge a premium for each new product it creates because, by the time competitors enter the market, the company has moved on to the next new thing. Such movement is critical in fields like technology: If a company creates one innovative device and then just keeps producing it without substantial improvements, the company will see other competitors enter the market and its profit will eventually suffer—a common fate of many short-lived high-tech firms. Technical innovation not only helps the originating company, it also makes new technology available to society at large.

Advocates of competition appear to have gotten the upper hand over advocates of protectionism in the United States. Since the 1970s, many industries, including airlines, telecommunications, and electric utilities, have been deregulated to encourage competition. A series of free trade pacts have been signed to open U.S. and foreign markets to competition. Nonetheless, the desire to protect industries and jobs from the ravages of the competition remains a potent political force, one that will likely continue to shape policy to at least some degree in the decades ahead.

Further Reading

Armentano, Dominick T. *Antitrust and Monopoly: Anatomy of a Policy Failure.* 2nd ed. Oakland, Calif.: The Independent Institute, 1990.

Auerbach, Paul. *Competition: The Economics of Industrial Change.* Oxford: Basil Blackwell, 1988.

Hunt, Shelby D. *A General Theory of Competition: Resources, Competences, Productivity, Economic Growth.* Thousand Oaks, Calif.: Sage Publications, 2000.

Moore, James F. *The Death of Competition: Leadership & Strategy in the Age of Business Ecosystems.* New York: HarperBusiness, 1996.

—Mary Sisson

Compound Interest

Becoming a millionaire is fairly easy for those who start saving early in life. If Michael, a 10-year-old, begins to deposit $22 every week in an account that earns 10 percent interest and continues to invest $22 every week until he is 65, he will accumulate $1 million. Compound interest is the key.

What is interest? Interest is the cost of borrowing money. If a customer borrows money to buy a car, the bank will charge the customer interest on the amount borrowed. Bank customers also may earn interest. If a customer puts money into a savings account, the bank will pay interest on the amount deposited. Interest thus encourages both lending and saving. It compensates lenders for the risk they take when they make loans, and it compensates savers for giving up consumption today in exchange for the ability to have more money and be able to purchase more goods in the future. Although bank savings accounts rarely offer 10 percent interest, a 10 percent return on other investments may be attainable. According to the *Stocks,*

Bonds, Bills, and Inflation 1999 Yearbook™ published by Ibbotson Associates, Inc., the average annual return on investment in large-company stocks between 1926 and 1998 was 13.2 percent.

Simple interest and compound interest differ. Simple interest is interest earned on the original principal (that is, the amount saved) only. Compound interest is interest earned on the original principal and on interest reinvested from prior periods.

For example, 50 years ago Phoebe invested $100 in a savings account at 5 percent simple interest rate. Today, that $100 is worth $350 because Phoebe earned 5 percent, or $5 per year, on the account for 50 years. The ending value of her investment is the original $100 principal plus $250 simple interest. If Phoebe had deposited her $100 in an account paying compound interest at a rate of 5 percent, however, her account would be worth $1,146.74 after 50 years. That is $796.74 more than she earned from the simple interest account; the difference is explained by compounding, or interest earned on interest.

To gain the most from compound interest, one should invest early and often. The more frequently individuals make investments, the sooner the money will be available

See also:
Finance, Personal; Interest; Savings and Investment Options.

Compound Interest vs. Simple Interest

Year	Beginning Value of Investment Account	Annual Compound Interest	Ending Value of Investment Account	Annual Interest Earned on Interest (Compound interest minus simple interest of $5 per year)
1	$100	.05 x 100 = $5	100 + 5 = $105	5 – 5 = $0
2	$105	.05 x 105 = $5.25	105 + 5.25 = $105.25	5.25 – 5 = $0.25
3	$110.25	.05 x 110.25 = $5.51	110.25 + 5.51 = $115.76	5.51 – 5 = $0.51
25	$322.51	.05 x 322.51 = $16.13	322.51 + 16.13 = $338.64	16.13 – 5 = $11.13
50	$1092.13	.05 x 1092.13 = $54.61	1092.13 + 54.61 = $1146.74	54.61 – 5 = $49.61

In the first year simple and compound interest are the same because the amount of interest earned on interest is $0. However, in the twenty-fifth year, interest earned on interest is $11.13; and, in the fiftieth year, interest earned on interest totals $49.61.

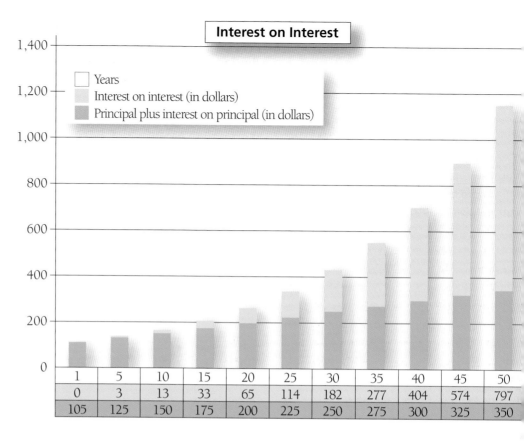

Interest on Interest

	1	5	10	15	20	25	30	35	40	45	50
	0	3	13	33	65	114	182	277	404	574	797
	105	125	150	175	200	225	250	275	300	325	350

☐ Years
☐ Interest on interest (in dollars)
■ Principal plus interest on principal (in dollars)

Earning interest on interest greatly increases wealth over time.

for the accumulating effects of compound interest. In other words, investing regularly throughout a given time period, say a year, is preferable to waiting to invest a lump sum at the end of a year, because the incremental investments start earning compounding interest immediately.

Returning to the millionaire example: if Michael does not start investing $22 per week until age 30, he will accumulate only $366,130 by age 65. He pays a $633,870 penalty for waiting 10 years to begin investing. If he waits until age 30 to begin investing, and he still wants to accumulate $1 million by age 65, he will need to invest $60 per week at 10 percent. If he waits until he is 40 to start saving, he will need to invest $172 per week to become a millionaire by age 65.

If Michael waits until age 30 to begin investing and wants to invest only $22 per week, he will need to earn 13.72 percent on his money to accumulate $1 million by age 65. Although a 13.72 percent return on investment may be feasible, it will require investment in riskier assets than investing for a 10 percent average return.

The key to earning compound interest is to reinvest interest payments rather than spend them. The primary benefit of forgoing consumption today in return for future consumption is the overall increase in earnings gained. Compound interest provides savers with an opportunity to assert control over their financial future.

Further Reading

Brain, Marshall. "Understanding and Controlling Your Finances." BYG Publishing. http://www.bygpub.com/finance/finance0.htm (January 1, 2003).

Ibbotson Staff. *Stocks, Bonds, Bills, and Inflation 1999 Yearbook: Market Results for 1926–1998.* Chicago: Ibbotson Associates, 1999.

Kapoor, Jack, Les Dlabay, and Robert J. Hughes. *Personal Finance.* New York: McGraw-Hill, 2001.

Kiyosaki, Robert T., and Sharon Lechter. *Rich Dad, Poor Dad.* New York: Warner Books, 1997.

Lynch, Peter. *Beating the Street.* New York: Simon & Schuster, 1993.

Stanley, Thomas J. *The Millionaire Mind.* Kansas City Mo.: Andrews McMeel Publishing, 2000.

Stanley, Thomas J., and William D. Danko. *The Millionaire Next Door: The Surprising Secrets of America's Wealthy.* Atlanta, Ga.: Longstreet Press, 1996.

—*Angeline Lavin*

Computer Industry

Stand-alone computers are used by businesses, governments, and individuals to perform innumerable tasks. The so-called Information Revolution has produced environments in which computers are as common as telephones, plus others in which computers are essentially invisible—tucked away inside automobile transmissions, for example. The huge international market for computers, software, printers, and related products supports thousands of companies.

Modern computers are used to assist in everything from managing household finances to animating cartoons; however, computers were originally designed to do only mathematical calculations. Long before the development of electronic computers, humans used mechanical tools including abacuses (believed to have been invented some 6,000 years ago) and slide rules to perform fairly complex calculations.

Creating an Industry

The building of true computers was stymied by an early reliance on mechanical technology. For example, in the 1820s, English inventor Charles Babbage envisioned a mechanical device that could be programmed to perform a wide variety of calculations. Babbage spent years and a vast sum of money trying to build his "engine," which had thousands of moving parts, but he could never create a working device. His ideas, however, inspired scientists more than a century later, and by the 1930s mass-produced mechanical calculators that could add, subtract, multiply, and divide were found in many business offices, supporting companies like International Business Machines Corp. (IBM). By then a new technology had emerged, however—electronics. Radios and telephones were using vacuum tubes and relays to harness electrical power without relying on clunky mechanical gears.

Scientists became interested in using electronics technology to create machines that could perform calculations too complicated or tedious for humans. The first such

See also:
Hewlett-Packard Company;
IBM; Information Revolution;
Intel Corporation; Internet;
Microsoft; Technology.

The gross income of U.S. hardware and software makers, plus the percentage growth in income from year to year is shown in the graph below. Note that the software industry has consistently had a higher rate of income growth.

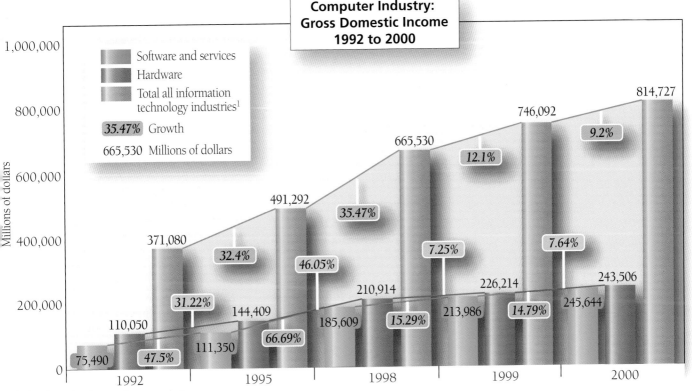

**Computer Industry:
Gross Domestic Income
1992 to 2000**

Legend:
- Software and services
- Hardware
- Total all information technology industries[1]
- 35.47% Growth
- 665,530 Millions of dollars

Y-axis: Millions of dollars

Total all information technology industries:
- 371,080
- 491,292 (32.4%)
- 665,530 (35.47%)
- 746,092 (12.1%)
- 814,727 (9.2%)

Software and services:
- 110,050
- 144,409 (31.22%)
- 185,609 (66.69%)... 210,914 (15.29%)
- 226,214 (7.25%)
- 245,644 (7.64%)

Hardware:
- 75,490 (47.5%)
- 111,350
- 213,986 (14.79%)
- 243,506

Years: 1992, 1995, 1998, 1999, 2000

[1] Includes other industries, not shown separately.

Source: U.S. Department of Commerce, Economics and Statistics Administration, *The Digital Economy*, Washington, D.C., June 2000.

The ENIAC, 1946, an all-electronic calculator.

devices, like the Mark I, unveiled at Harvard University in 1944, were hybrids that combined electronic and mechanical technology. Such hybrids were noisy and prone to breakdowns and were soon supplanted by faster, all-electronic devices like the ENIAC (Electronic Numerical Integrator and Calculator). Early computers were commonly referred to as calculators because, in the 1940s, the term *computer* referred to a person (usually a woman) who performed calculations, generally with the help of a mechanical calculator.

The early computers differed in details of design but shared some common features. They filled entire rooms, and they were custom-built, making them enormously expensive. Building computers was such an immense undertaking that Howard Aiken, who designed the Mark I, predicted that only a small number of computers would ever be built—and, indeed, until 1950, only 60 had been.

Nonetheless, computers quickly showed their worth both in science and in national defense, a field of special interest during the 1940s. Computers could rapidly handle the complex calculations needed, for example to design artillery systems and atomic bombs. Construction on many early computers began during World War II, and the cold war between the United States and the Soviet Union after World War II ensured that the U.S. government would remain a major buyer and developer of computers. Many computing breakthroughs, including the development of the first networked computers and the Internet, resulted from defense projects.

In large corporations, meanwhile another, much larger market for computers had begun to develop. In 1951, the first computer produced on an assembly line the UNIVAC-1, was installed. While no smaller than a custom-built machine, the UNIVAC-1, produced by Remington Rand Corp., was cheaper. Other mass-produced computers soon followed. IBM eventually dominated the market for what became known as mainframe computers. Initially very large, taking up the better part of a room, mainframe computers became smaller and cheaper throughout the 1950s and 1960s, thanks largely to the invention of transistors, which were considerably smaller than vacuum tubes.

Banks and other companies that needed to process large quantities of numerical information increasingly turned to computers. Even with transistors, however, computers were neither cheap nor small. The cheapest mainframe cost more than $100,000, and prices for particular models could go up to several million dollars. Nonetheless, corporate demand for computers was strong enough to prompt companies like IBM to abandon their old mechanical calculators and refocus their efforts on manufacturing computers.

The market attracted upstarts as well. In 1965, Digital Equipment Corp. introduced the first so-called minicomputer—named after the miniskirts popular in the 1960s. The minicomputer was less powerful than a mainframe, but it sold well because it was smaller and considerably less expensive (a mere $18,000) than the larger devices.

The minicomputer was made possible by the development of the integrated circuit, a technological advance that basically placed many transistors on a single silicon chip. Ironically, the integrated circuit eventually caused problems for computer manufacturers. Advances in integrated-circuit technology made possible the manufacture of more powerful but less costly mainframe computers and minicomputers. This was good news for businesses that bought computers—and even relatively small businesses soon began to buy them—but bad news for the companies that made them. Computer makers saw their sales revenues fall even as the number of computers sold increased.

In the mid-1970s, however, another new market began to emerge, a market for computers that people could use in their homes. Upstarts like Commodore International and Apple Computer, Inc., began to manufacture computers that cost less than $5,000 and were small enough to fit on a desk. Initially called microcomputers, these personal computers were made possible by ongoing technical advances in the manufacture of computer chips. By 1971, a computer's

entire central processing unit could be placed on a single chip, and chips became more powerful as the decade progressed. The new personal computers attracted businesspeople, too, drawing small-business customers away from IBM. In 1980, IBM responded by deciding to enter the personal computer market; it introduced its first personal computer a year later.

Consumer Commodity

IBM's entry into the personal computer market had an unexpected side effect. To facilitate production, IBM built its personal computer using an open architecture, that is, the specifications were available to the public and any other manufacturer could copy them. IBM dominated the world of mainframe computers, causing other manufacturers to fear that IBM's architecture would become the standard and their noncompatible computers would be left out. Other manufacturers of personal computers cloned IBM's architecture. Such cloning ensured that, for example, Compaq computers could use the same software and peripherals used in IBM computers. IBM's architecture became the standard among personal computers; Apple's personal computers remain the principal exception.

In 2000, at the University of Sarawak in Bario, Malaysia (on Borneo Island), a tribal Kelabit man learns how to use Microsoft Excel.

Until the late 1970s, a customer buying a computer usually received some software—its cost included in the purchase price. That policy had already begun to change when Microsoft, a Seattle company, was contracted to create software for the first IBM personal computer. When the IBM architecture became standard, Microsoft's software followed suit. The popularity of personal computers combined with a standard architecture opened the field to a number of new companies to sell computer peripherals like printers and memory drives.

During the 1980s the personal computer became widespread. In 1981 fewer than two million personal computers were in use in the United States; by 1991 that number had increased to more than 60 million. By 1992 the dollar value of personal computers equaled that of all larger computer systems in operation. Easy-to-use software and peripherals drove sales of personal computers, as consumers with no special knowledge of computing discovered, for example, that word processing programs were easier to use than typewriters.

The rise of the Internet in the mid-to-late 1990s proved to be a boon to computer manufacturers. The new service spurred individuals and companies to upgrade their computers—the new demand was often driven by an upsurge of interest in e-mail—and some manufacturers branched out into production of Internet hardware such as servers. Sales increased in response to fears that older computers would not be able to correctly process information referenced to the years following 1999—an issue called the Year 2000 or Y2K, problem—which prompted customers to replace older computers.

The flurry of computer upgrades preceding the year 2000 resulted in a slowdown in computer sales after 2000. The slump was worsened by the onset of a recession in 2001 and a by a dearth of popular new applications requiring a computer upgrade. The downside of standardization also became apparent, as manufacturers of personal computers found their products increasingly becoming a commodity, indistinguishable by consumers except in regard to price. Hoping to capitalize on the situation, Dell Computer Corp.—known for its low-cost manufacturing and relative financial strength—began a price war, aggressively lowering prices on its personal computers in an effort to drive its competition out of the business. By 2001 consumers could buy a fairly powerful personal computer for less than $1,000.

Computers are ubiquitous in the United States. Families and businesses depend on them to conduct everyday affairs. Will new technology continue to revitalize the industry and generate demand for new products or will intense price competition and ever-shrinking profit margins discourage investment and industry growth?

Careers in the Computer Industry

The phrase computer industry usually brings to mind a computer programmer. There are two main types of programmer: applications programmers write computer code for software that performs a specific task, such as tracking inventory; systems programmers write computer code that runs a computer (its operating system) or an entire network. The microchip revolution led to an explosion in career opportunities for computer programmers, but that trend appears to have peaked at the end of the twentieth century. While skilled programmers will always be needed, the U.S. Department of Labor predicts a slowdown in job growth in the field, due partly to innovations in computer programming that have streamlined the process of writing code.

However, the need for software engineers, those who analyze user needs and design systems to meet those needs (as opposed to writing the code itself), is expected to expand. So too will the need for computer hardware engineers, who design the computers themselves—hardware engineers comprise a smaller but nonetheless vital component of the industry. Businesses will also demand systems analysts, who solve computer problems and help firms realize the benefits of networking technology. Skills in specific areas of computer technology, such as Web design or database management, will continue to make well-trained employees especially desirable.

Further Reading

Ceruzzi, Paul E. *A History of Modern Computing.* Cambridge, Mass.: MIT Press, 1998.

Cohen, I. Bernard. *Howard Aiken: Portrait of a Computer Pioneer.* Cambridge, Mass.: MIT Press, 1999.

Pugh, Emerson. *Building IBM: Shaping an Industry and Its Technology.* Cambridge, Mass.: MIT Press, 1995.

Strathern, Paul. *The Big Idea: Turing and the Computer.* New York: Anchor Books, 1997.

—*Mary Sisson*

Constitution, U.S.

Constitutions provide the fundamental laws of society, structure the government, and delineate the rights of citizens. Constitutions may be written, as in the United States, or unwritten, as in the United Kingdom. As the defining document of a society, a constitution is critical for business and industry.

Unlike many countries' constitutions, the U.S. Constitution is relatively short. Rather than describing the details of government in exact language, the founding fathers established general principles, leaving many of the details to be described in statutes. Also unlike the constitutions of many countries, the U.S. Constitution is long-lived. The general nature of much of the Constitution's text has allowed it to function even as American society has changed dramatically.

The U.S. Constitution has four features that are especially important for business: limits on central government authority; separation of powers; federalism; and protection of individual rights. These features help create a climate in which businesses can rely on stable conditions and limited government interference with their operations.

Limiting Authority

The U.S. Constitution created a central government of limited powers. Any action of the national government must, therefore, rest upon a specific grant of authority within the Constitution. Article 1, section 8, for example, lists the powers of Congress; Congress may not enact legislation that is not authorized by one of the Constitution's provisions.

Some government powers are defined in specific terms. For example, the power to "establish . . . uniform Laws on the subject of Bankruptcies throughout the United States" would be difficult to misinterpret. Other grants of powers are written broadly. Congress's power "to regulate Commerce with foreign Nations, and among the several States, and with the Indian Tribes" has been the subject of long-standing controversy. Over time this commerce clause has been interpreted to be the source of Congress's authority for most national regulation and has been the subject of more litigation than any other provision of the Constitution. For example, in 2000 the Supreme Court reopened the debate over the extent of Congress's power under the commerce clause by deciding that the 1994 Violence against Women Act was unconstitutional. Congress had asserted that fear of violence inhibited women's participation in the economy, thus justifying federal criminal penalties for crimes against women. In *United*

See also:
Environmental Regulation;
Hamilton, Alexander;
Regulation of Business and
Industry; Rule of Law.

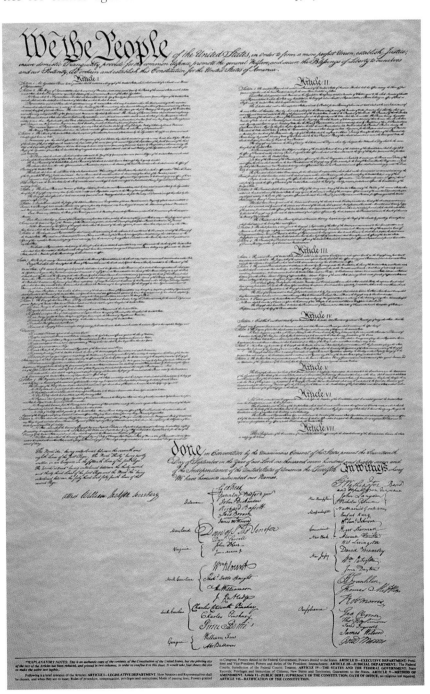

A photograph of an original copy of the U.S. Constitution.

States v. Morrison, the Supreme Court rejected this position as too tenuous a connection to commerce to give Congress authority to enact the legislation.

The structure of the Constitution, which limits the federal government to powers explicitly granted, restricts the federal government in the United States in ways that many countries' governments are not restricted. As a result, business and industry face fewer regulatory restrictions in the United States than elsewhere.

Separation of Powers

An important innovation in the U.S. Constitution was the explicit separation of powers among multiple branches of government. The Constitution divides national government authority among legislative (Article 1), executive (Article 2), and judicial branches (Article 3). Each branch also has important powers that allow it to check actions by the others. For example, the president can veto congressional action, Congress must approve the budget for the executive branch, and the courts can strike down actions by either the president or Congress.

The drafters of the Constitution used the separation of powers to address two problems: majority and minority factions. The founders feared the tyranny of the majority—that a large group would use the government to oppress a minority. Debtors, for example, might seek relief from their obligations to creditors. The founders also feared minority factions that might obtain special favors from government by gaining temporary control of part of the government.

Separation of powers protects against both by making government less efficient. By slowing down the process and placing roadblocks in the way of action, the Constitution denies either majorities or minorities easy use of the government for advancing particular interests. For example, the founders allowed the president to appoint the members of the Supreme Court but required that he do so only with the approval of the Senate, where all states are represented equally.

Few businesses would divide authority among executives as does the Constitution. Running a government "like a business," as politicians often promise, is difficult because the U.S. government is not structured like businesses. The separation of powers can also create obstacles for firms that do business with the government.

For example, obtaining the approvals necessary to work with the government can be difficult. Defense contractors often face problems because selection of weapons systems requires approval from both the president and the Congress. Contractors, therefore, sometimes choose a site for their plants or work with particular subcontractors to cultivate favor with key senators and

---

U.S. Constitution: Overview

Article 1: Legislature
- Section 1 Establishment of the Legislature
- Section 2 The House of Representatives
- Section 3 The Senate
- Section 4 Congressional Elections and Meetings
- Section 5 Legislative Proceedings
- Section 6 Compensation, Privileges, and Restrictions
- Section 7 Procedures for Passing Laws
- Section 8 Powers Granted Congress
- Section 9 Powers Denied to the Federal Government
- Section 10 Powers Denied to the States

Article 2: Executive Branch
- Section 1 Establishment of the Office of President and Vice President
- Section 2 Presidential Powers and Duties
- Section 3 Other Duties of the President
- Section 4 Impeachment

Article 3: Judicial Branch
- Section 1 Establishment of the Judiciary
- Section 2 Federal Court Jurisdiction
- Section 3 Treason

Article 4: The States and the Federal Government
- Section 1 State Records
- Section 2 Rights of Citizens within States
- Section 3 New States and Territories
- Section 4 Federal Duties to States

Article 5: Amending the Constitution

Article 6: Supremacy of National Law

Article 7: Ratification of the Constitution

Although the U.S. Constitution provides for the separation of powers, the president does have some power over Congress in the form of the veto. Here, President Bill Clinton vetoes the Nuclear Waste Policy Amendments Act of 2000. Joining Clinton were (left to right) Sen. Harry Reid, Rep. Shelley Berkley, and Sen. Richard Bryan.

epresentatives. A new plane might be assembled from components manufactured in a number of congressional districts rather han from the least expensive sources.

Doing business with the government also can be challenging because the separation of powers forces engagment with different branches of government to obtain work. Different branches may have varied concerns. This is particularly true when one political party controls all or part of Congress and another controls the presidency. Congressional committees can investigate executive branch actions by holding hearings, demanding documents, and restricting the use of funds in appropriations bills. The president can retaliate, for example, by omitting projects favored by particular congresspeople from his budget or by dragging his feet on projects in their congressional districts. Differences over regulatory agendas can prove especially troubling for businesses, as the political parties may compete by attempting to show that each is tougher on a particular issue—the environment, for example, or corporate fraud—than the other.

Federalism

Another important form of division of power is the federal nature of the U.S. Constitution. The Constitution represents an agreement of the people of the states to form a national government that would coexist with, not replace, their existing state governments. Such a structure is quite different from that of countries with a strong central government, like France. By creating a new layer of government, the Constitution gave the United States tools to deal with national problems (for instance, commerce between the states) while leaving the individual states to address local issues. To be sure, the dividing line between local and national is not always clear and has certainly shifted over time, but the idea of federalism remains an important part of U.S. constitutional life.

Dividing authority among different levels of government solved important political problems for the founders and has two important implications for businesses. First, businesses that operate in more than one state face the potential problem of inconsistent state regulations. Consider, for example, product labels. Consumer protection and other regulations often require specific information to be placed on product labels in a particular format. The U.S. Department of Agriculture requires nutrition information on many food products, listing the ingredients, fat content, and other data. If each state required its own label, rather than having a single national label, food processors hoping to sell nationally could potentially have to create 50 separate labels. As many regulations affect products in even more substantial ways, inconsistency among state requirements has been a powerful motive for multistate businesses to seek national solutions to problems. The automobile industry, for example, backed early air pollution legislation out of fear of inconsistent state regulation of auto emissions.

Second, competition among jurisdictions operates as a constraint on state government activity. States with high business taxes, for example, are at a disadvantage in recruiting new businesses. At times, businesses have used the threat of relocation against states with lower taxes or higher regulatory burdens to convince state governments to change laws or offer incentives to offset tax and regulatory costs.

Protecting Individual Rights

One of the most important parts of the Constitution is the Bill of Rights, as the first 10 amendments are known collectively. Some of the parts of the Bill of Rights sound archaic today—the Third Amendment's ban on quartering soldiers on citizens seems irrelevant in a day when communities vigorously compete

for military bases. Others remain the subject of extensive controversy. The religion clause of the First Amendment, for example, are still the subject of regular lawsuits.

From a business perspective, the most important parts of the Bill of Rights are the takings clause of the Fifth Amendment, the speech protections of the First Amendment, and the protections against searches and seizures of the Fourth Amendment.

The takings clause requires the government to pay "just compensation" whenever it "takes" private property. Courts have begun to extend this assurance beyond requiring compensation when the government actually acquires property, for example, for highways. The regulatory takings doctrine now requires the government to compensate property owners when government regulations result in loss of property rights under some circumstances. For example, in *Lucas v. South Carolina Coastal Commission* (1992), the owner of beachfront property successfully forced South Carolina to purchase his property when environmental regulations prevented him from building on it.

The speech protections are important to businesses because they provide some

The Bill of Rights and Business and Industry

Amendment 1 Guarantees freedom of religion, assembly, speech, press, and right to petition government

Amendment 2 Guarantees right to bear arms and organize state militias

Amendment 3 Prohibits quartering of soldiers in homes in peacetime

Amendment 4 Forbids unreasonable searches and seizures

Amendment 5 Guarantees due process of law. Requires grand jury indictment for arrest in serious crimes, protects against self-incrimination, bars double jeopardy

Amendment 6 Guarantees right to counsel in criminal cases and right to speedy public trial

Amendment 7 Guarantees jury trial in civil cases

Amendment 8 Prohibits excessive bail or fines; forbids cruel or unusual punishment

Amendment 9 Stipulates that the rights of the people are not confined to those enumerated in the Constitution

Amendment 10 Stipulates that powers not expressly delegated to the federal government or prohibited to the states are reserved to the states and people

Amendment 1: "Congress shall make no law . . . abridging the freedom of speech, or of the press . . ."

Amendment 4: "The right of the people to be secure in their persons, houses, papers, and effects, against unreasonable searches and seizures, shall not be violated . . ."

Amendment 5: ". . . nor shall private property be taken for public use, without just compensation . . ."

protection for commercial speech, which includes advertising. However, less protection is granted commercial speech than is provided to other kinds of speech. The search and seizure protections are important because they limit the government's ability to seize business records and other documents as part of criminal investigations.

Interpreting the Constitution

Because the Constitution is written in general terms, understanding how to interpret its provisions often requires doing more than simply reading the text. For example, how should the First Amendment's statement that "Congress shall make no law . . . abridging freedom of speech" be read? Does it mean no laws concerning speech can be written by Congress? (Answer: no.) Does it mean that only Congress is so restricted? (Answer: no.) Does it refer to laws relating only to verbal speech or printed materials or conduct? (Answer: printed materials and conduct are included.) Does it mean that advertisements cannot be regulated? (Answer: no.)

Two main schools of constitutional interpretation exist. Some judges, commentators, and academics argue for an "originalist" interpretation of the Constitution, contending that where the text is unclear, history should be the guide to what the founders intended when they wrote the Constitution. By examining sources like the *Federalist Papers* and the ratification debates, originalists believe the intent of the Constitution can be made clear. An example of originalist jurisprudence is Justice Clarence Thomas's analysis of the Eighth Amendment's prohibition of cruel and unusual punishment. Thomas examined founding-era criminal punishment practices in his dissent in *Hudson v. McMillian* (1992).

Others argue that the Constitution must be seen as a living document, capable of adapting to modern conditions and circumstances. The founders' intent is thus evidence, but only some evidence, of underlying principles that may find different expression in today's world. An example of a living constitution approach is the series of decisions beginning with

Constitutional Features Important to Business

- Limits on central government authority
- Separation of powers
- Federalism
- Protection of individual rights

Griswold v. Connecticut (1965) and proceeding through *Roe v. Wade* (1973) and various other abortion rights cases. In those cases, the Supreme Court's decisions rested on a right to privacy derived indirectly from various provisions of the Constitution rather than any explicit statement in the text.

The divide over interpretation has important consequences for businesses. As the national economy has grown in size and importance, so has the role of the national government. An originalist view of the Constitution would sharply restrict national government activities with respect to many regulatory practices. While lessening regulation by the national government might ease regulatory burdens for some businesses, others would face increased, and potentially inconsistent, state-level regulatory burdens. The ongoing controversies over the proper method of interpreting the Constitution suggest that the debate is far from settled and the implications for business are large.

Further Reading

Ackerman, Bruce. *We the People: Foundations.* Cambridge, Mass.: Belknap Press, 1993.
Borden, Morton. *The Antifederalist Papers.* East Lansing: Michigan State University, 1965.
Currie, David P. *The Constitution of the United States: A Primer for the People.* Chicago: University of Chicago Press, 2000.
Epstein, Richard. *Takings.* Cambridge, Mass.: Harvard University Press, 1985.
Fisher, Bruce D., and Michael J. Phillips. *The Legal, Ethical, and Regulatory Environment of Business.* Cincinnati, Ohio: West Legal Studies in Business, 2001.
Kurland, Philip B., and Ralph Lerner, eds. *The Founders' Constitution.* Chicago: University of Chicago Press, 1986. Also available: http://press-pubs.uchicago.edu/founders/ (December 29, 2002).

—*Andrew Morriss*

See also:
Accounting and Bookkeeping;
Management; Strategic
Planning; Technology.

Consulting

In its narrowest definition, the consulting industry is a pure service industry that offers one thing to clients: advice. Getting paid to give advice is by no means a new profession, yet in many respects consulting is a new industry, one that emerged only in the last 20 years of the twentieth century. Since the early 1980s, consulting has grown rapidly; as of 2000, it was a $100 billion industry in the United States, attracting a large minority of graduates from business schools. The definition of consulting has expanded as well. Consulting firms now provide clients with temporary labor and valuable equipment as well as advice.

No simple generalization is sufficient to describe what consultants do. Some specialize in questions of strategy, helping a business expand and develop. Others focus on how a company can improve particular business operations—handling the payroll, for example. Still others focus on implementing specific projects, for instance, creating an inventory-tracking system, that are too specialized for a client company to do on its own.

Some consultants work only for start-up businesses or only for hospitals, some only help companies apply for government contracts, and others work only for companies that are about to go bankrupt. In some cases, the consulting is so specialized that a consultant must possess a special expertise or a professional license—consulting engineers must be licensed engineers, for example—but in general consulting is not licensed o subject to special regulations.

Most consultants work for themselves o in partnership with one or two other consultants. Often, independent consultant join with other independent contractors, t create a consulting network that can handl a variety of tasks. Some consultants do wor for large consulting firms, however, an some are employed "in house" by companie that maintain consulting divisions to suppo their main productive activity. Still others— often academics or other experts—consul only part time.

The field has not always been as mult faceted as it is today. Consulting firms lik Booz-Allen & Hamilton, Inc., and McKinse & Co. date to the 1910s and 1920s, but con sulting then was a different profession. In th first half of the twentieth century, consultant were often called efficiency experts or man agement engineers. As those titles suggest consultants during this period often focuse on business management, interacting mostl with high-level executives, sometimes on th basis of close, exclusive relationships wit top management. In this context consultant might be called upon to advise a compan about how it might respond to exceptiona business situations—an impending bank ruptcy, a period of slumping profits, merger, or a strategic decision about refocus ing a company or expanding operations to foreign market, for example.

Starting in the 1980s, however, oppor tunities for consulting began to expand rapidly. Management consulting alon expanded from a $3 billion industry i 1980 to a $22 billion industry in 1990, an businesses began to use consultants in ne ways. By the end of the 1990s, many larg companies employed full-time consultants just as many employed attorneys, regard less of whether any unusual busines events were pending. In addition, clien companies turned increasingly to employ ing consultants from several different firm some working with senior management some with middle management, and som

Examples of Consulting Services

- Accounting, tax preparation, bookkeeping, and payroll services
- Advertising and public relations services
- Architectural, engineering, and testing services
- Legal services
- Human resources
- Information technology services
- Interior design services
- Management, scientific, and technical services
- Scientific research and development services

with line workers. Consulting also became less limited. In some fields, including management consulting, providing advice is still a mainstay, but consultants now also work directly on project implementation, providing temporary supplemental staff (both managerial and operational) and special expertise essential to completion of a given project.

The explosion in demand for consultants was the result of several different trends affecting businesses in the 1980s and 1990s. Certain kinds of consulting, for example, computer and technology consulting or international consulting, expanded rapidly as applications for computers and the Internet became widespread and more companies went global. Also, as the government took a stronger stance on social issues like environmental quality and racial equality, consultants emerged to help businesses comply with new regulations. More fundamentally, many businesses altered their operations in ways that made them more reliant on consultants. The changes included downsizing, undertaken by many businesses in efforts to cut costs by employing a slimmed-down, flexible workforce, and an increasing trend toward tightly focusing business operations on core objectives. Both these trends led to corporations frequently finding themselves in need of help from extra workers who could fill staffing gaps in a small, full-time workforce or provide focused assistance with special projects. Consultants seemed to provide the solution in these cases, especially consultants offering expertise in a narrow specialty that meshed well with specific corporate needs.

The expansion of consulting has generated a backlash in some parts of the business world. The lack of licensing bothers some critics (and some consultants), who argue that the quality and experience of unlicensed consultants are highly uneven. Some critics also contend that consultants deliberately foster a client company's dependence on their services so that they will continue to get work from that client.

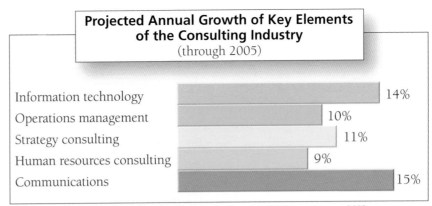

Projected Annual Growth of Key Elements of the Consulting Industry
(through 2005)

Information technology	14%
Operations management	10%
Strategy consulting	11%
Human resources consulting	9%
Communications	15%

Source: Perry Capell, "Have You Considered a Career in Consulting?" IMDiversity.com, 2002, http://www.imdiversity.com/Article_Detail.asp?Article_ID=7856 (January 6, 2003).

Others, including disgruntled shareholders, charge that companies sometimes hire consultants to rubber-stamp a decision that has already been made by management. In response to these complaints, some new organizations of professional consultants have been formed, many of them offering certification and ethical guidelines.

The reliance of businesses on consultants has one major drawback for consultants themselves: The highly cyclical consulting industry will, in good times, grow phenomenally; 20 percent annual growth was the norm through much of the 1980s and 1990s. In bad times, however, the consulting industry tends to do worse than the overall economy because consultants are often sacrificed by their client companies to cut costs.

Nonetheless, consulting has proved to be lucrative for many practitioners, and their success continues to draw new specialists into the field. An obvious example is provided by computer software and hardware companies that now offer consulting services to help businesses decide how best to deploy and utilize the high-tech goods they buy.

Not all forays into this burgeoning field have been without controversy, however. In the 1990s, the five biggest U.S. accounting firms—PricewaterhouseCoopers, Ernst & Young International, KPMG International, Andersen Worldwide, and Deloitte Touche Tohmatsu—all had large consulting businesses. Their consulting businesses arose out of efforts to sell accounting services to small

Many businesses rely on computer consultants for software and hardware installation, troubleshooting, and computer training.

and Exchange Commission (SEC). The SEC oversees the accounting industry, monitoring its performance in the vital task of reviewing the finances of publicly owned companies. This process, called auditing, is crucial to the workings of the stock market because it provides some assurance that companies are not lying about their finances to attract investors. In the 1990s SEC chairman Arthur Levitt, Jr., charged that the melding of consulting and accounting was compromising the integrity of the Big Five auditing services. Levitt worried that accounting firms would perform favorable audits to win consulting contracts—especially, lucrative contracts to install large computer systems. The Big Five responded that they were structured to avoid such conflicts of interest, but the accusation nonetheless resulted in damaging publicity.

At one point Levitt appeared ready to force accounting firms to shed their consulting businesses. In November 2000, however, the two sides reached a compromise that allowed accounting firms to retain their consulting businesses. Under the agreement, the audit committee of a client company—which oversees the auditing process—must review and approve any consulting contract with a firm that also performs the client company's audits. Despite the agreement, the pressure from the SEC led KPMG, Ernst & Young, and Andersen to sell or spin off all or part of their consulting businesses voluntarily by the end of 2000. The anticipated protections came too late for Arthur Andersen, however, which collapsed in 2002 mostly as a consequence of its relationship with the scandal-ridden Enron Corporation.

businesses, which often wanted advice as well. As the consulting industry expanded its presence in accounting, it threatened to overshadow accounting as it had previously been provided. By 2000, consulting revenues accounted for just over half of total revenues for the so-called Big Five accounting firms, and revenues from consulting were growing at three times the rate of revenues from traditional accounting services.

This melding of accounting and consulting raised concern in the U.S. Securities

Choosing a Consultant

Both public and private organizations use consultants for a variety of reasons. Some lack the internal resources needed to handle a project, while others need a consultant's expertise to determine what resources will be required and what problems may be encountered if they pursue a particular opportunity.

To retain a consultant, a company first solicits proposals from a number of consulting firms specializing in the area in which it needs assistance—for example, biotechnology, health care, information technology, human resources, engineering, or telecommunications. These proposals include the estimated cost and scope of the project, staffing requirements, references from a number of previous clients, and a completion deadline. The company then selects the proposal that best suits its needs. An increasingly popular trend is the use of consulting teams rather than individual consultants. The team structure permits examination of a variety of different issues and problems within an organization.

—*John Riddle*

Further Reading

Freedman, Arthur M., and Richard E. Zackrison. *Finding Your Way in the Consulting Jungle.* San Francisco: Jossey-Bass/Pfeiffer, 2001.

McGonagle, John J., and Carolyn M. Vella. *How to Use a Consultant in Your Company: A Managers and Executives' Guide.* New York: John Wiley & Sons, 2001.

Tuller, Lawrence W. *Cutting Edge Consultants: Succeeding in Today's Explosive Markets.* Englewood Cliffs, N.J.: Prentice Hall, 1992.

—*Mary Sisson*

Consumer Confidence Index

Because economists cannot see into the future, they look to so-called leading indicators to predict upward and downward movements of the economy. Leading indicators reflect the economic indicators that fall before a recession and rise prior to a recovery. Consumer confidence is such an indicator. As consumer spending makes up about two-thirds of total spending in the United States, accurate predictions about consumer spending play an important role in predicting broader economic trends. Measures of consumer confidence are also used to gauge reactions to economic and political events, like wars and declines in the stock market.

Several regional, national, and international measures of consumer confidence are available. The Conference Board's Consumer Confidence Index (CCI) and the University of Michigan's Index of Consumer Sentiment (ICS) are the primary national measures. Both of these measures gather and assess consumers' opinions about current and future economic conditions—both of the general economy and their own financial situations.

The CCI is calculated by the Conference Board's Consumer Research Center. The Conference Board is a not-for-profit organization started in 1916 to conduct research and examine issues important to business and society. The Conference Board began tracking consumer opinions every other month in 1967. In 1977, the Conference board began monthly mailings of a five-question survey to 5,000 households. The Board conducts the survey during the first 18 days of each month, averaging 3,500 responses. Consumers are asked what they think about: (1) current business conditions, (2) business conditions six months in the future, (3) current employment conditions, (4) employment conditions six months in the future, and (5) their expectations of their total family income six months in the future.

The CCI is an average of the relative value of responses to all five questions. The relative value is the number of positive answers divided by the sum of positive and negative answers. Results are released on the last Tuesday of the month. In addition to the monthly national index, a confidence index is also calculated for each of the nine census regions.

The other consumer confidence index, the Index of Consumer Sentiment (ICS), is produced by the Survey Research Center at the University of Michigan. The center has been tracking consumer sentiment since 1946. At first the center produced an annual survey; in 1952 the survey became

See also:
Business Cycles; Recession.

The Conference Board's Consumer Confidence Index.

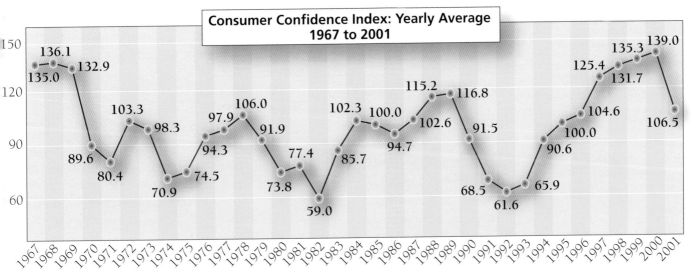

Consumer Confidence Index: Yearly Average 1967 to 2001

Source: © The Conference Board. Used with permission.

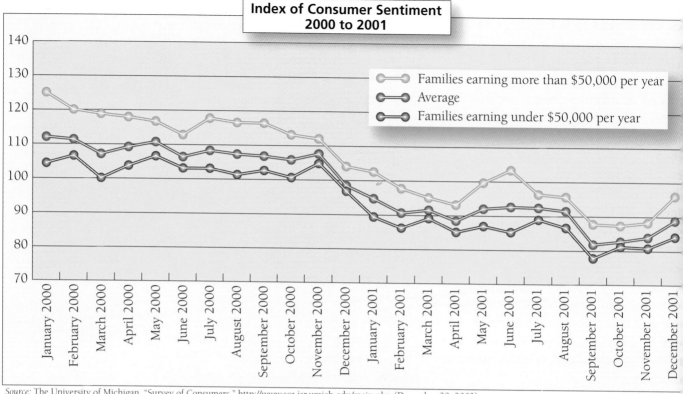

Index of Consumer Sentiment 2000 to 2001

- Families earning more than $50,000 per year
- Average
- Families earning under $50,000 per year

Source: The University of Michigan. "Survey of Consumers," http://www.sca.isr.umich.edu/main.php (December 30, 2002).

The Index of Consumer Sentiment is prepared by the Survey Research Center at the University of Michigan as a reflection of consumer confidence.

a quarterly; and in 1978 the survey became a monthly. The Survey Research Center asks about a longer time horizon: one to five years instead of six months. Unlike the Conference Board, the center does not compile regional indexes.

At the beginning of every month, the University of Michigan's Institute for Social Research polls 500 families by telephone. The survey asks 50 questions about personal finances, general business conditions, and household buying plans. The index is based on responses to five questions. Consumers are asked to: (1) compare their current financial situation to their situation a year earlier; (2) predict what their financial situation will be a year in the future; (3) predict business conditions in the country as a whole a year later; (4) predict business conditions during the next five years; and (5) say whether it is a good or bad time to buy major household items.

Like the Conference Board, the Survey Research Center calculates a relative score for each question. The details of the calculation, however, are different. A relative score is the percent of favorable responses minus

the percent of unfavorable responses, with the difference added to 100. The index is the total of all the relative scores divided by the base period value and added to a correction factor. This method "flattens out" the movement of the ICS compared to the CCI, as illustrated in the graph.

The ICS questions that involve making predictions are used to derive an Index of Consumer Expectations (ICE), which is part of the Leading Economic Indicator Index. Other components of the Leading Economic Indicators Index are manufacturing levels, interest rates, and employment. The Conference Board has compiled the Leading Economic Indicators Index since 1995; earlier it was done by the Commerce Department.

Movement of the indexes anticipates some changes in the business cycle and is therefore of great interest to businesspeople and policy makers. Movement that is not related to the business cycle, however, must be identified separately. Therefore, both indexes are adjusted seasonally for changes in consumer confidence that may be normal, annual occurrences. Without such djustment, the indexes might seem to suggest that confidence takes a huge leap every year in November and December, whereas data related to those months may merely reflect planned holiday spending.

Unlike other measures, an index is unitless; it is measured in points, not dollars or tons or inches. It has meaning only when compared with itself. Each measure sets a base year when the index equals 100. The CCI has a base year of 1985. The University of Michigan's base year is 1966. Monthly reports of an index will indicate its movement up or down, by how much in both absolute and percentage terms, and how the current month's index number compares with historical values. For both measures, what has happened on average over the previous six months is a better indicator of consumer opinion than one month's figure.

Which index is more useful depends on the question being asked. The Conference Board's focus on employment conditions provides good information about the labor market. If responses indicate positive feeling about the current and future job market, then consumers probably will be buying more than if they are unemployed or fear they will be laid off in the near future. Positive responses can also anticipate rising wages from a tighter labor market—that is, a market with more jobs than workers to fill them.

The University of Michigan's focus on the longer term and household goods provides slightly different information. Positive answers to the final question about purchase of household goods may result in more washing machines, refrigerators, and cars being bought in the near future. Positive answers to questions about future economic conditions may not result in higher spending today; they may indicate that consumers will wait until the economy is stronger before buying more.

Neither index by itself is a perfect predictor of recessions or recoveries. Both indexes provide a snapshot of consumers' opinions about the economy, based upon reactions to

Holiday shopping in Little Italy in New York City. Consumer confidence indexes are adjusted for normal increases in spending, like those that occur during the holiday season.

events, news, and commentary. One month's rise or fall in an index is not as significant as the direction the index has taken over the previous few months. Along with other leading indicators, however, consumer confidence indexes present a picture of general and household economic conditions.

Further Reading

The Conference Board. http://www.conference-board.org (December 30, 2002).

Danthine, Jean-Pierre, John B. Donaldson, and Thore Johnsen. *Productivity Growth, Consumer Confidence, and the Business Cycle.* New York: Columbia Business School, Columbia University, 1997.

Surveys of Consumers The University of Michigan. http://athena.sca.isr.umich.edu/ (December 30, 2002).

—Donna Miller

Consumerism

The consumer culture is largely a twentieth-century Western phenomenon that has since spread to most developed countries. Never before in human history have people purchased so much—goods, food, services, technology gadgets, homes—and this trend has significantly altered the physical and psychological landscape of the world.

The word *consumerism* has been loosely attached to late-twentieth-century consumption; however, its formal roots go back to the 1920s and 1930s movement in the United States to inform consumers about what they buy and why they buy, and to develop a more regulated marketplace.

Consumerists sought not only to understand the reasons for these new buying trends but also to monitor the policies driving them and the production, selling, and advertisement of products. The communications and manufacturing innovations of the twentieth century required a forum that would inspire America and other developed countries to receive a new message: Consumption is good, healthy, family-building, and moral. As a result, a consumer culture has developed in which individuals define themselves by what they eat, own, and wear.

Roots of American Consumer Culture

Scholars have identified a consumer culture in colonial America, but the emergence of

In 1909 passersby gaze into a window of the original Marshall Field's department store in Chicago.

industrialism made widespread consumption possible. An increase in the population
because of emigration from Europe combined with large-scale manufacturing, a
national transportation network (the railroads), and a national communication network (telegraph and later the telephone) to
improve producers' abilities to reach an
expanding market.

In the 1850s Marshall Field and
Company first opened its doors to the public in Chicago, introducing the world to the
first department store. The department
store concept caught on—the stores were
often called "palaces of consumption"—and
Field opened nearly 60 others throughout
the Midwest. These stores, as well as the
many competitors that sprang up in their
wake, were carefully constructed to make
shopping enjoyable and efficient—some
even boasted restaurants. By the early
twentieth century, Americans were no
longer going to department stores simply to
buy goods. They went to furnish their
houses, seek fashion advice, dine; the
department store came to represent a way of
life. Meanwhile, mail-order catalogs from
companies like Sears and Montgomery
Ward enticed rural inhabitants.

Advertising as a business appeared in the
early 1920s, boosted by the U.S. government's
success during World War I in conducting
nationwide bond drives. Manufacturers and
advertisers gradually convinced Americans
that going into debt to purchase consumer
goods was acceptable. Going into debt forced
the consumer to work to pay off debts; thus,
consumerism, which might seem antithetical
to the American work ethic, evolved into a
philosophy that encouraged the work ethic.

In 1924 radio broadcasting stations
were born, and the United States had, for

*The remarkable expansion
in U.S. consumer spending
over the course of the
twentieth century is shown in
the chart below.*

Personal Consumption Expenditures in the United States 1930 to 2000
(in billion dollars)

	1930	1935	1940	1945	1950	1955	1960	1965	1970	1975	1980	1985	1990	1995	2000
Durable goods															
Motor vehicles and parts	2.2	1.9	2.8	1.0	13.7	17.7	19.7	29.9	35.5	54.8	87.0	175.7	206.4	249.3	346.8
Furniture and household equipment	3.8	2.5	3.8	4.5	13.7	16.4	18.0	25.1	35.7	54.5	86.7	128.5	171.4	225.0	307.3
Durable goods total[1]	7.2	5.1	7.8	8.0	30.7	38.8	43.3	63.3	85.0	133.5	214.2	363.3	467.6	589.7	819.6
Nondurable goods															
Food	18.0	16.2	20.2	40.6	53.9	68.6	82.3	100.7	143.8	223.2	356.0	467.6	636.9	755.8	957.5
Clothing and shoes	8.0	6.0	7.5	16.5	19.6	23.3	27.0	34.1	47.8	70.8	107.3	152.1	204.1	247.8	319.1
Gasoline, fuel oil, and other energy goods	3.3	3.0	3.8	4.0	8.9	12.4	15.8	19.2	26.3	48.1	102.1	110.8	120.2	127.4	183.2
Nondurable goods total[1]	34.0	29.3	37.0	71.9	98.2	124.7	152.9	191.6	272.0	420.7	696.1	928.8	1,246.1	1,497.3	1,989.6
Services															
Housing	11.2	7.9	9.7	12.8	21.7	34.4	48.2	65.4	94.0	147.0	255.1	406.8	585.6	740.8	958.8
Household operation	3.9	3.2	4.0	6.4	9.5	14.2	20.3	26.5	37.9	64.3	114.2	182.2	227.6	298.1	385.7
Transportation	2.2	1.7	2.1	4.0	6.2	8.5	11.2	14.5	23.7	35.7	64.7	100.0	141.8	197.7	272.8
Medical care	2.3	1.8	2.3	3.7	7.2	11.3	17.6	27.9	50.4	93.4	181.2	322.5	540.6	780.7	996.5
Recreation	1.7	1.3	1.7	3.0	3.9	5.2	6.9	9.6	15.1	25.4	42.8	75.6	120.8	176.0	256.2
Services total[1]	29.0	21.5	26.4	40.0	63.7	95.4	136.1	189.5	292.0	476.1	852.7	1,420.6	2,117.8	2,882.0	3,919.2
Personal consumption expenditures total[1]	70.2	55.9	71.2	119.8	192.7	259.0	332.3	444.3	648.9	1,030.3	1,762.9	2,712.6	3,831.5	4,969.0	6,728.4

[1] Includes other expenditures not listed separately.

Source: U.S. Bureau of Economic Analysis.

An interior view of the Mall of America, located outside Minneapolis.

the first time, live broadcasts, full of news and music. The advertising on the air was highly profitable to the radio stations and helped establish commercial broadcasting as its own, legitimate industry. Radio became increasingly attractive as an advertising medium; by 1927 the United States had two major radio networks.

After World War II, wages increased, consumer credit expanded, and nearly every voice in America—corporate, governmental, familial—actively encouraged consumption, aligning consumerism with the American ideals of freedom and democracy. Advertisers sold consumer goods by claiming that they strengthened family ties. In the 1950s, consumerism became inextricably linked to the importance of family life.

Like its predecessor the radio, television, which was commercially available in

the 1940s and became wildly popular in the 1950s, was a boon to advertising and consumption. As with radio, families now had something around which they could center their free time, and both television shows and advertisements capitalized on this appealing to the emotional side of viewers who sought companionship and vicarious experience in television. Television swiftly evolved from technological marvel to defining cultural emblem. To be without a television was considered a deprivation.

The baby boom generation and television grew up together. Between 1946 and 1964, 76 million Americans were born. Thanks in large part to postwar prosperity and a bright economic forecast, many middle-class women abandoned their jobs and began producing families. Not only was this generation the largest ever, but its grea umbers contributed to an already strong attern of consumption. In 1953 alone, mericans bought 1.5 billion jars of baby od and seven million televisions.

Shopping malls first appeared in a inneapolis suburb in the late 1950s. hese concentrations of retail stores and ntertainment enterprises became wildly opular with Americans who built between) and 100 giant malls (at least 400,000 1. ft.) each year, for the next 30 years. The eight of shopping mall construction was eached in 1992 when America's largest all, the Mall of America, was built in loomington, Minnesota. At 4.2 million quare feet, if a shopper spent 10 minutes rowsing at every store, the shopper would eed more than 86 hours to complete a isit to Mall of America.

Shopping malls are dependent on georaphic location, but the most recent trend n consumerism effectively renders locaon irrelevant. The World Wide Web was orn in 1991; by 1996 nearly 10 million Veb shopping sites were available. Online hopping continues to become more reamlined, user-friendly, and a welcome ol for consumers, particularly in the nited States. The staggering number of nternet users (700 million in 2000) couled with the Internet's ever-expanding apabilities, is expected to usher in a diferent phase in the evolution of Western onsumer culture.

Consumption's Critics

Consumer advocacy is nothing new. The National Consumers League was formed round 1899 to raise awareness about food afety and labor conditions. In 1906 Jpton Sinclair published The Jungle, his ovel about injustices to the working class n Chicago; the novel offered a decidedly egative picture of capitalism and the merican consumer. By the 1920s the eague had focused on advertising and its npact on people, its false claims, and its ubious motives.

The consumer movement began in 936, when a group of labor leaders,

writers, professors, and engineers formed the Consumers Union, the publisher of *Consumer Reports,* to "maintain decent living standards for ultimate consumers." The union offered reports on products' false advertising and sought to educate the American consumer. Today, *Consumer Reports* has nearly four million subscribers.

During the 1950s, Americans bought with abandon. People bought houses, cars, appliances, anything and everything that made life easier and more glamorous. They were also buying books that warned against this new culture of consumption and its negative effects.

Vance Packard's 1957 book *Hidden Persuaders* called attention to what he saw as undercurrents in advertising and exposed the ability of some advertising campaigns to prey on alleged consumer vulnerability. In 1958, the economist John Kenneth Galbraith published *The Affluent Society,* an exploration of the divide between private wealth and public poverty and the effect that increased consumption had on both urban and uninhabited lands.

Reverend Billy and The Church of Stop Shopping

We are drowning in a sea of identical details . . .
Mickey Mouse is the Antichrist . . .
Times Square has been blown up by 10,000 smiling stuffed animals . . .
Don't shop, children, save your souls!

—Reverend Billy

The Reverend Billy, a.k.a. Bill Talen, is the charismatic leader of Reverend Billy and the Church of Stop Shopping, a grassroots team of activists based in New York City. The "minister" Billy and his expanding church blend activism with theater, targeting their Pentecostal-like crusade at consumerism, commercialism, and protecting public spaces.

Talen, a Minnesota native born in 1950, first donned his trademark clerical outfit and began "preach-ins" on Times Square sidewalks in 1997. His fire-and-brimstone sermons have been called entertaining, ridiculous, thought provoking, and some of the better theater in New York. He is often accompanied by the Stop Shopping Choir, a versatile singing team assembled to back up his protests with a repertoire of choruses like: "We come that you might not shop so abundantly!"

The Reverend Billy's disruptive and creative interventions are certainly attention-getting; past events have included preaching to shoppers at Disney's Times Square store, a week-long campaign against Starbucks, and 90-second lectures on National Public Radio's *Morning Edition* program. Talen is also a faculty member in the graduate media studies program at the New School for Social Research, in New York City. He runs a Web site (www.revbilly.com) devoted to his anticonsumption movement, replete with interviews, stories of past protests, and a calendar of future events.

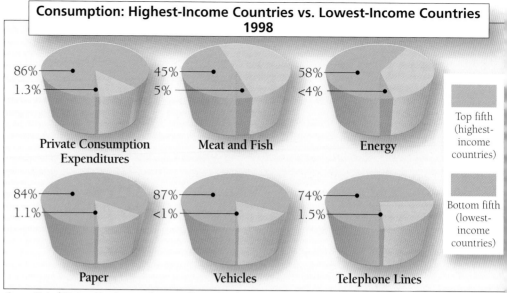

Consumption: Highest-Income Countries vs. Lowest-Income Countries 1998

Private Consumption Expenditures
86%
1.3%

Meat and Fish
45%
5%

Energy
58%
<4%

Paper
84%
1.1%

Vehicles
87%
<1%

Telephone Lines
74%
1.5%

Top fifth (highest-income countries)

Bottom fifth (lowest-income countries)

Source: United Nations Development Program, *Human Development Report,* 1998.

The 1962 book *Silent Spring*, by environmentalist Rachel Carson, gave impetus to the global environmental movement; some argue that it also brought into question America's devotion to industry, science, and, by extension, unbridled consumption.

In 1965, Ralph Nader exploded onto the scene when he published *Unsafe at Any Speed,* an account of the auto industry and its questionable safety standards. Nader's continued work would reinvigorate the consumer movement, and his efforts were crucial to the passing of the Freedom of Information Act (1966), the Wholesome Meat Act (1967), and the Clean Air Act (1970), and to the formation of the Consumer Protection Agency (1978). Nader remains at the center of the consumer movement; his name has become synonymous with consumer advocacy.

As globalization ties national economies ever closer, the world seems to be evolving into a giant consumer culture. People across the globe now have similar wants, and brands have proven to translate across borders. Although the United States—and indeed the world—seems largely pleased by the efficiencies afforded by new communication tools, growing numbers of people and organizations are dismayed by the negative effects of rampant materialism. These individuals and organizations, a new

facet of the consumerist movement, ofte[n] denounce the acquisitive nature of America[n] culture. These newer, more radical anticon[?]sumerists point to trophy homes, SUVs, an[d] lotteries as emblems of a culture with a con[?]sumption problem.

The consumer movement remains com[?]mitted to the same goal it has had since inception: to make producers of good[s] accountable to the public and to encoura[ge] more sustainable consumption pattern[s.] Consumerists believe the achievement [of] these goals will engender a culture that va[l]ues itself not for what it has but for what it i[s] and will exhaust fewer resources and pro[?]duce less waste.

Further Reading

Glickman Lawrence B., ed. *Consumer Society in American History: A Reader.* Ithaca, N.Y.: Cornell University Press, 1999.

Marchand, Roland. *Advertising the American Dream: Making Way for Modernity, 1920–1940.* Berkeley: University of California Press, 1985.

Robbins, Richard. *Global Problems and the Cultur[e] of Capitalism.* Boston: Allyn and Bacon, 2002.

Shiller, Robert J. *Irrational Exuberance.* Princeton N.J.: Princeton University Press, 2001.

Twitchell, James. *Lead Us into Temptation: The Triumph of American Materialism.* New York[:] Columbia University Press, 1999.

—*Richard McHu[gh]*

Consumer Price Index

The price of a good can go up for many reasons: an increase in production costs, an increase in demand, or inflation, among others. When the overall price level rises, then the economy has entered a period of inflation. The Consumer Price Index (CPI) measures the overall price level of goods. Specifically, the CPI reports a weighted average of the prices of a fixed set of goods and services over time. In addition to measuring inflation, the CPI is used to adjust prices for comparisons over time, change tax brackets, and determine cost-of-living adjustments to wages, pensions, and government payments like food stamps and Social Security.

Since 1913 the Bureau of Labor Statistics (BLS) in the Department of Labor has calculated the CPI. At the beginning of each month hundreds of BLS economic assistants collect prices in more than 80 urban areas. Their gathering of prices of the same goods and services is called a *market basket*. Items like pens, apples, computers, long distance telephone charges, postage stamps, dry cleaning, movie tickets, gasoline, rental fees—almost anything

consumers buy is in the basket. Having the market basket's contents and quantities fixed allows only the prices to change over time.

The national census and surveys of consumer spending patterns determine in what cities and stores BLS assistants shop, what they buy, and how important each item is to consumers. Individual items and services are put into 200 categories, for example, men's shirts, bedroom furniture, ice cream, and college tuition. Sales taxes and user fees such as water bills or car registration fees are the only taxes included. Items are added or dropped every two years based on survey results.

Categories are then sorted into eight major groups: food and beverages, housing (includes utilities and heat), apparel, transportation (includes gasoline), medical care, recreation, education, and communication, as well as other (for example, tobacco, funeral expenses, haircuts). Groups are weighted to reflect their proportion of household spending. This way a doubling in the price of gasoline will count more than the doubling of the price of salt because more of a consumer's budget goes to gasoline than salt. In 1999–2000, for example, housing weighed 40 percent and recreation 6 percent. Group weightings are adjusted every two years based on the survey data.

See also:
Cost of Living; Gross Domestic Product; Inflation.

Consumer Price Indexes by Selected Groups 1990 to 2000

- All items
- Medical care
- Shelter
- Apparel and upkeep
- Food

Note: baseline = 100.
Source: Bureau of Labor Statistics, *Monthly Labor Review and Handbook of Labor Statistics,* periodic.

U.S. Consumer Price Indexes for Selected Items and Groups 1990 to 2000

	1990	1995	1996	1997	1998	1999	2000
Household furnishings							
Bedroom furniture	118.5	136.4	139.3	141.5	141.3	141.0	138.4
Television	74.6	68.1	64.5	61.7	59.2	54.9	49.9
Video products other than television	91.5	70.3	66.3	63.4	NA	92.1	88.6
Audio products	93.2	92.1	90.7	88.9	85.2	81.7	80.2
Apparel							
Men's and boys'	120.4	126.2	127.7	130.1	131.8	131.1	129.7
Women's and girls'	122.6	126.9	124.7	126.1	126.0	123.3	121.5
Infants' and toddlers'	125.8	127.2	129.7	129.0	126.1	129.0	130.6
Footwear	117.4	125.4	126.6	127.6	128.0	125.7	123.8
Transportation							
New cars	121.0	139.0	141.4	141.7	140.7	139.6	139.6
Used cars	117.6	156.5	157.0	151.1	150.6	152.0	155.8
Airline fares	148.4	189.7	192.5	199.2	205.3	218.8	239.4
Medical Care							
Prescription drugs	181.7	235.0	242.9	249.3	258.6	273.4	285.4
Physicians' services	160.8	208.8	216.4	222.9	229.5	236.0	244.7
Dental services	155.8	206.8	216.5	226.6	236.2	247.2	258.5
Recreation							
Sporting goods, equipment	114.9	123.5	123.4	122.6	121.9	120.3	119.0
Sport vehicles, including bicycles	115.3	125.3	125.7	124.5	125.3	128.7	130.9
Pet supplies and expenses	124.6	132.3	139.0	142.7	143.5	144.5	144.3
Education							
School books and supplies	171.3	214.4	226.9	238.4	250.8	261.7	279.9
Elementary and high school tuition	182.8	259.2	272.8	288.1	307.9	327.3	349.9
College tuition	175.0	264.8	279.8	294.1	306.5	318.7	331.9

NA = Not available.
Note: baseline = 100.
Source: U.S. Bureau of Labor Statistics, *Monthly Labor Review* and *CPI Detailed Report,* 2001.

The CPI is calculated by computing a geometric mean within each category, like beef or men's athletic socks, and then a weighted average of the eight groups. As an index the CPI is unitless—it is measured in points, not dollars. The index has meaning only as compared with itself over time. The CPI was set to 100 in the base year of 1984. The month-to-month or year-to-year percentage change in the CPI is the inflation rate.

Estimate errors, called biases, occur in most economic measures. The CPI has three biases: substitution, quality, and outlet. The substitution bias is the result of the fixed content of the market basket; but shoppers' buying habits are flexible. When the price of a good rises, shoppers may buy less of it or substitute another, cheaper good for it.

Because consumers are not paying the highe price, they are not experiencing the inflatio measured by the CPI. Since 2002, the CF corrects for some substitution within cate gories. For example, if the price of Grann Smith apples increases, the BLS shopper will record the price of an apple that has no increased in price, like the Golden Delicious However, some consumers may buy pear instead. This sort of cross-category substitu tion was accounted for in a separate pric index beginning in 2002. Accounting for al possible substitutions shoppers may make would be impossible, thus the CPI overesti mates the actual inflation rate.

Quality bias occurs because some pric increases reflect product changes or th addition of new features, not just inflation

For example, cars today cost more than cars of 40 years ago. However, cars today are also safer and more fuel efficient and have more standard features. Although difficult, the BLS attempts to correct for this bias by subtracting the value of quality changes from prices. Nevertheless, this bias tends to overestimate inflation.

The outlet bias results from the location of BLS economic assistants in gathering their prices. More and more consumers use large food warehouses for grocery shopping. Prices at those stores are often lower than prices at grocery stores. Accordingly, the measured prices may be higher than what consumers actually are paying. Consumers find ways to avoid the higher prices used to compute the CPI. Overall, the biases in the CPI tend to overstate inflation.

Overestimates of inflation can mean overpayment by government and businesses. Changes in the CPI are used to adjust wages and payments in order to keep purchasing power constant. Purchasing power, or real income, decreases when prices go up and income stays the same. Government payments to more than 80 million people are adjusted every year for inflation. An additional two million worker paychecks covered by union contracts are also adjusted using the CPI. A 1 to 2 percent overadjustment of wages may not mean much for an individual retiree or worker but could mean millions of dollars to government and businesses.

The CPI does not work for all individuals or even all groups. If someone spends money differently from the group weightings, then that person's experienced inflation rate will differ from the overall rate. Social Security recipients, for example, have their checks adjusted for inflation, but they devote a higher proportion of their income to medical expenses. Medical prices are rising faster than other prices; thus even an adjustment for inflation will not allow the average Social Security recipient to buy the same amount of goods. The CPI is determined by prices in urban areas; thus a family living in a rural area may experience a different inflation rate. Each month the CPI is reported along with a breakdown for regions and urban areas in the

United States. Specific group increases are also announced, for example, indicating how important an increase in housing or fuel prices was in the total CPI change.

Other price indexes are available. The Producer Price Index includes wholesale and raw material prices. The GDP Deflator, which includes military and investment spending used to adjust the Gross Domestic Product (GDP) for inflation, is also available. Even with its biases, the CPI remains the best index for explaining how changes in price levels affect consumers.

Cars are more expensive than they were 40 years ago; however, thanks to developments such as the safety glass being tested here, cars are also safer. In calculating the CPI, analysts attempt to account for technological improvements that increase the value of goods.

Further Reading

Bryan, Michael F., and Stephen G. Cecchetti. *The Consumer Price Index as a Measure of Inflation.* Cambridge, Mass.: National Bureau of Economic Research, 1993.

Cagan, Phillip, and Geoffrey H. Moore. *The Consumer Price Index: Issues and Alternatives.* Washington, D.C.: American Enterprise Institute, 1981.

U.S. Department of Labor, Bureau of Labor Statistics. *The Consumer Price Index: Questions and Answers.* Washington, D.C., 1992.

—*Donna Miller*

See also:

Better Business Bureau;
Consumerism; Product
Liability; Regulation of
Business and Industry.

Consumer Protection

Everyone is a consumer. From food, medicine, and shelter to the latest gadgets and toys, the market economy of the United States revolves around the production, sale, and consumption of goods. The responsibility for protecting consumers from false advertising, unsafe products, and other marketplace dangers falls on numerous federal, state, and private organizations. Individuals have frequently played a role in shedding light on product shortfalls as well. The snake-oil salesmen of the 1800s may have vanished, but protecting the consumer remains an ongoing battle. Sometimes unwary and occasionally susceptible to telemarketing scams and pyramid schemes, consumers are, at least, not alone in their unceasing efforts to get what they paid for.

Who Protects the Consumer?

Many federal agencies and organizations have consumer protection duties in the United States, including the U.S. Consumer Product Safety Commission, the National Credit Union Administration, the Office of Thrift Supervision, and the Federal Reserve. Three others that directly address consumer issues and that have significant and far-reaching responsibilities are the Federal Trade Commission (FTC), the Food and Drug Administration (FDA), and the National Highway Traffic Safety Administration (NHTSA).

The Federal Trade Commission, an independent agency established in 1914, is responsible for keeping markets competitive. The FTC's Bureau of Consumer Protection oversees a variety of products and industries, and has several tools at its disposal. It issues consumer alerts warning potential buyers of possibly dangerous products and deceptive claims by manufacturers. Along with the Department of Justice, the FTC investigates business mergers to ensure that no single company gains a monopoly in its particular industry. Monopolies limit consumer choices. The FTC also looks into abusive lending practices, false advertising, and other issues that threaten to limit consumers' freedom of choice in the marketplace.

Another key federal consumer protection organization is the Food and Drug Administration. The FDA is charged with overseeing the food, medication, and cosmetics industries. The FDA regulates the food industry by making sure that all ingredients used are safe. When a food producer wants to introduce a new additive to a product, the additive must pass a series of safety tests before the product gains FDA approval for sale to consumers. The FDA covers most food products, but meat and poultry are under the jurisdiction of the United States Department of Agriculture (USDA). Medicines and medical products are regulated by the FDA and must be proven safe and effective before they can be used.

The FDA also approves the labeling of these products. For example, medical equipment must be labeled with clear instructions for its use. The FDA also handles cosmetics, but its regulation of cosmetics differs from that of food and drugs. The FDA monitors cosmetics to make sure they are safe and are properly labeled, but these products are not reviewed before they are placed on the market, and they do not

Lemon Laws

"Lemon laws" protect consumers who have bought vehicles that unexpectedly require significant repairs soon after purchase (in other words, from buying a real "lemon"). In 1982, Connecticut passed the first "lemon law"; now every state in the United States has some form of lemon law.

Although the specifics of these laws differ from state to state—some cover used cars and motorcycles, for example, while others do not—some basic features are common from state to state. Most establish a warranty period of one or two years during which the defects have to arise. Most define how significant the needed repairs must be and provide that the manufacturer, not the dealer, is responsible for them. Typically, after a number of unsuccessful attempts are made to repair a defect, the vehicle is considered a lemon and its owner is entitled to a refund or a replacement. In about half of the states, consumers may even recover attorneys' fees if they have had to take the manufacturer to court. While smart consumers will closely inspect any vehicle they are considering purchasing, lemon laws provide some protection against significant defects undisclosed and undiscovered at the time of purchase.

Key Consumer Protection Agencies

Federal Drug Administration
✓ Sets standards for drugs and cosmetics
✓ Ensures foods are safe, wholesome, and sanitary
✓ Forbids distribution of adulterated products
✓ Requires honest labeling

Federal Trade Commission
✓ Prohibits monopolistic practices
✓ Sets requirements for food, drug, clothing, and cosmetics labeling
✓ Requires advertisers to substantiate claims
✓ Issues consumer alerts on dangerous products or deceptive claims

National Credit Union Administration
✓ Supervises and insures 6,000 federal credit unions
✓ Cultivates the safety and soundness of federally insured credit unions
✓ Works to improve credit union service
✓ Encourages credit unions to extend credit to all Americans

National Highway Traffic Safety Administration
✓ Sets safety standards for motor vehicles and motor vehicle equipment
✓ Investigates safety defects in motor vehicles
✓ Sets and enforces fuel economy standards
✓ Provides grants to state and local government to conduct safety programs

U.S. Consumer Product Safety Commission
✓ Develops and enforces product safety standards
✓ Bans consumer products if no feasible standard can protect the public
✓ Initiates the recall of products
✓ Conducts research on potential product hazards

require safety testing. Part of the FDA's responsibility for products and ingredients it must approve prior to being placed on the market is to test and approve or disapprove them in a timely manner. The FDA, then, through its administrative rules, must balance the safety and effectiveness of products against the financial need for businesses to get new products out the door.

The National Highway Traffic Safety Administration is responsible for automobile safety. The Highway Safety Act of 1970 established the NHTSA. Its mission at that time was to carry out safety programs under federal legislation passed in the late 1960s. In 1972, the Motor Vehicle Information and Cost Savings Act was passed and charged the NHTSA with additional consumer protection duties. The agency is now responsible for reducing injuries, deaths, and financial losses caused by motor vehicle crashes. The NHTSA attempts to accomplish its mission by setting and enforcing safety performance standards for motor vehicles and motor vehicle equipment. The NHTSA also assists local and state governments by providing grants for highway safety programs and provides consumers with information on a wide range of vehicle safety topics including air bags and the proper use of child car seats and safety belts.

Augmenting these federal efforts, every state government in the United States has some form of consumer protection organization. The state of New York, for example, has a wide array of governmental agencies and departments responsible for protecting the consumer. They produce a consumer help

Thalidomide

Thalidomide is a sedative that was used to relieve morning sickness and nausea in pregnant women. Considered so safe that it was available over-the-counter in many countries, thalidomide was widely adopted for use around the world after its introduction in Germany in 1958. The application to market thalidomide in the United States arrived at the Food and Drug Administration in September 1960. FDA officer Dr. Frances Kelsey found troubling inconsistencies and incomplete data in the thalidomide application, and she delayed approval of the drug pending further review.

That decision saved thousands of American children. In November 1961 a German physician linked the use of thalidomide to an upswing in several rare birth defects, including facial abnormalities and the absence of arms and legs. Some 10,000 children would be born with birth defects caused by thalidomide before the drug was removed from most markets by the fall of 1962. In the United States, thanks to Dr. Kelsey, only 17 such children were born.

Inspired by the close call that averted an American thalidomide disaster, in the early 1960s Congress passed the Kefauver–Harris Bill, which lengthened the approval process for new drugs. Then hailed as a model of concern for consumer safety, the FDA would later come under fire from AIDS and cancer activists for delaying approvals and preventing patients from obtaining experimental drugs. In an ironic twist, one of the experimental drugs in demand by activists was thalidomide. Bowing to activist pressure, in 1998 the FDA approved thalidomide for use in AIDS, cancer, and leprosy patients.

—*Rebecca Sherman*

manual covering everything from state regulations on pawnbrokers to landlord–tenant relations. Consumers are told how to file utility complaints, what travel agent practices are prohibited, and informed about the various kinds of warranties that accompany products. New York handles consumer protection through agencies like the state attorney general, the Public Service Commission, the Banking Department, the Department of Health, the Governor's Office of Regulatory Reform, and the Empire State Development Corporation. Cities and counties in New York also host consumer affairs offices, like the Better Business Bureau.

Private citizens and organizations have played an important role in uncovering unsafe products and in bringing misleading marketing to light. Ralph Nader is perhaps the best-known consumer advocate of the twentieth century. He became famous in 1965 with his blistering critique of automobile safety in his book *Unsafe at Any Speed.* Nader argued that the automobile industry

was focused more on profits than on driv and passenger safety. The National Traffic an Motor Vehicle Safety Act of 1966 was at lea partly the result of the public outcry stem ming from Nader's accusations. The act estab lished important safety standards for ne cars. Nader later formed the consumer advo cacy organization Public Citizen, Inc. Sinc the 1960s he has addressed consumer protec tion issues in several other industries, includ ing health care and energy, as well as takin on tax and campaign reform.

Tools Used to Protect the Consumer

The tools used by those concerned with an responsible for consumer protection var widely. Individuals and private consume advocacy groups often use the media t expose marketplace dangers. They write arti cles and books, talk to community organiza tions, and attempt to influence legislators.

For government agencies and depart ments, the tools at their disposal depend i large part on the specific industry under the

In 1996 Consumer Reports *magazine urged manufacturers to stop selling 1996 Acura SLX sport utility vehicles because the cars could roll over during quick turns.*

Michigan attorney general Jennifer Granholm displays a mailing from Publisher's Clearinghouse that was judged deceptive to consumers. As a result of a lawsuit brought by Michigan and 25 other states, in June 2001, Publisher's Clearinghouse agreed to pay $19 million in restitution to customers and to stop using phrases like "guaranteed winner" in its mailings.

urisdiction. For example, the Food and Drug Act of 1906 laid the foundation for modern food and drug laws. The law was enhanced in 1938 with the Federal Food, Drug, and Cosmetic Act. The FTC also accomplishes its mission primarily through enforcement of federal statutes. Examples are the Fair Packaging and Labeling Act, the Consumer Leasing Act, and the Telemarketing and Consumer Fraud and Abuse Prevention Act.

In many nonfood and drug markets, industry standards offer what consumer protection exists. These nonstatutory standards do not have the force of law. Recommendations for industry standards, covering, for instance, the safety of electric kitchen appliances, are made with manufacturer input and even approval. A seal or symbol may be placed on the product alerting the consumer to the product's compliance with the industry safety standard. Whether these measures affect consumer choices is open to debate. Nor do the standards always address actual product effectiveness or ineffectiveness.

Complete protection of the consumer is not possible. The properly labeled medical device, for instance, must still be correctly operated by a trained professional, and the long-term effects of food additives are sometimes difficult to ascertain during a typical testing period. The American consumer receives a lot of attention, however. Agencies and offices at all levels of government, private organizations, and even dedicated individual advocates look out for their well-being. Consumer alerts notify potential buyers of faulty products and deceptive advertising. Significant federal statutes authorize government agencies to monitor and regulate whole industries, and industry standards offer some protection in areas that are difficult to address with legislation.

Further Reading

Asch, Peter. *Consumer Safety Regulation: Putting a Price on Life and Limb.* New York: Oxford University Press, 1988.

Bykerk, Loree, and Ardith Maney. *U.S. Consumer Interest Groups: Institutional Profiles.* New York: Greenwood Press, 1995.

Schor, Juliet B. *The Overspent American: Upscaling, Downshifting, and the New Consumer.* New York: Basic Books, 1988.

—*John Keckhaver*

Contracts and Contract Law

A contract is an agreement consisting of reciprocal promises that the law will enforce. Contract law is the body of law that oversees that enforcement. In a typical commercial contract, Party A promises to provide goods or services to Party B in exchange for a consideration, for example, a promise to pay a sum of money.

Contracts take many different forms: they can be as simple as verbal agreements between individuals and as complicated as 20-page signed documents. Written contracts between corporations, for instance, often involve detailed terms that account for the time and manner in which the goods or services will be delivered, the expected quality of the goods or services, and what happens if a breach of the contract occurs (expectations are not fulfilled). In this way, companies can set limits on their liability and come to an agreement about what remedies a party can expect if the contract's terms are not satisfied.

Contracts are used by everyone, not just businesspeople. Even the purchase of something as simple as a movie ticket creates contractual relationship with the movie theater, with the promise being that the purchaser will be allowed to enter the theater and watch the movie, and the consideration being the price paid for the ticket.

In the United States, contracts must meet a number of requirements to be considered legally binding. One requirement is legality of object: The purpose of a contract must not be against the law; a contract for drug deal, for example, would not be legally enforceable. Another requirement is consideration. Both parties must offer something; contract law does not enforce agreements where goods or services have been promised but no counter-promise has been made, as in the case of gifts or charitable donations. Contracts also require mutual agreement, often represented by the signature of both parties on a written contract. Finally, both parties must have contractual capacity—the legal ability to enter into a contract. A mentally ill person might be found by a judge to lack contractual capacity. Minors have limited capacity

Why Are Contracts Essential?

Consider the following: Company A agrees to supply Company B with 100 widgets, which Company B needs to build its product. Company A fails to provide the widgets, which results in the inability of Company B to complete production on time. Imagine, now, that Company B has no recourse because the law does not require Company A to pay damages for its failure. While over time Company A may gain a reputation for being untrustworthy and hence go out of business, Company B has still incurred a loss in the present. Because it cannot complete production in a timely manner, B's sales may suffer, and it may even be forced into bankruptcy. Nor does the tarnished reputation of Company A help Companies C, D, and so forth which in turn relied on Company B's product being completed by the projected time

Requirements for Legally Enforceable Contracts

Mutual assent

Consideration

Contract

Legality of object

Capacity

Considering all the many individuals, companies, governments, and countries that rely on each other's goods and services, imagine the chaos that would ensue if they could not trust that promises would be fulfilled—or that the law would intervene if the terms of their agreements were not satisfied. No market society could function smoothly without clear legal rules governing contracts. Accordingly, countries all over the world have created systems of contract law to facilitate trade within and between their borders.

Indeed, versions of contract law have existed for thousands of years, ever since early civilizations began to trade with one another. The ancient Romans had the principle *Consensus ad idem:* a meeting of the minds between parties where each understands the commitments made by the other—a basic principle in contract law even now. In the 1700s, as market societies emerged, England and France developed complex contract law systems that form the basis of the modern legal system.

Contracts are so essential to the smooth functioning of business that the founding fathers protected them in the U.S. Constitution. As Article 1, section 10 states, "No State shall . . . pass any . . . Law impairing the Obligation of Contracts." In other words, the government cannot create laws that void legal contracts or that render legal contracts illegal or unenforceable after the fact. Hence, in the United States, contracts are protected from the government as much as they are protected by it.

How Are Contracts Enforced?

Samuel Goldwyn, the Hollywood movie mogul, famously remarked that "A verbal contract is as worthless as the paper it's written on." This is not necessarily true: a verbal contract is just as enforceable under law as a written contract. A case like *Main Line Pictures v. Basinger* (1993) illustrates the validity of verbal contracts: in an infamous court decision, the actress Kim Basinger was ordered to pay $7 million in damages to Main Line Pictures because she was found to have breached a verbal agreement to star in the company's film *Boxing Helena*. Although this decision was ultimately overturned by an appellate court on

Written contracts are usually signed by both parties, showing mutual agreement to the terms listed.

Actress Kim Basinger was sued for breach of contract when she backed out of a verbal agreement to star in the film Boxing Helena. *The role was eventually played by Sherilyn Fenn, pictured here supine on the set.*

a technicality, it effectively changed the way Hollywood did business.

A verbal contract is never as reliable as a written contract because it depends on the contracting parties' memories and versions of events, which often differ. At their best, written contracts prevent misunderstandings about the terms of the agreement and leave very little open to interpretation. Some kinds of contracts must be in writing to be enforceable. These contracts are specified by an area of law called the statute of frauds, and include real estate and marriage contracts, contracts whose terms of performance extend for more than a year, and contracts involving sales of goods of $500 or more.

Even written contracts are subject to a court's interpretation, however. A court may find that the terms of the contract were unreasonable. For instance, sometimes a party will attempt to limit liability

for breach of contract by building in a contractual clause that protects against such a claim. The court, however, may still find the party liable. In other words, the court has the final say in interpreting the level of protection the contract offers and the fairness of the contract's terms.

Alternatively, a court may find that the purpose of the contract itself is illegal or otherwise against public policy. For instance, in the notorious "Baby M" case, Mary Beth Whitehead entered into contract with Richard Stern to carry his child to term and release the baby to him and his wife at birth; upon delivery of the baby, Whitehead was to receive $10,000 plus money for any extra medical costs incurred because of the pregnancy. When Whitehead changed her mind and refused to give up the baby, Stern filed suit in the state of New Jersey for breach of contract. Although New Jersey had no specific law governing surrogacy contracts, the appellate court of New Jersey ruled that the contract was against public policy because it amounted to an attempt to circumvent New Jersey's adoption laws, which do not allow payment for babies. Although the court decided to grant Stern custody of the baby, Whitehead was not held liable for breach of contract.

When a court finds that a breach of contract has occurred, the suffering party is often awarded remedies like the $7 million in compensatory damages awarded to Main Line in *Main Line Pictures v. Basinger.* Why $7 million? Because Main Line argued that the film would have been that much more profitable had Basinger starred in it.

An Ever-evolving System

In the Middle Ages, the sale of a property was conducted through a verbal contract. The sale was symbolically closed when a clump of dirt from the purchased land was delivered to the buyer. In the absence of a written contract, this delivery of dirt—called the *livery of seisin*—served as evidence of the transfer of property. As more and more people began to own property and a merchant class emerged, such transactions needed clearer guidelines and documentation. Such a transfer of property is now evidenced by written documents, facilitated by lawyers and real estate agents, and enforced by the courts if the agreement is disputed.

In the late twentieth century, as businesses crossed national borders to develop a global marketplace, new contract law questions emerged: Which nation's law would apply to the contract? Where would litigation take place in the case of a breach of contract? In recognition of these uncertainties, in 1980 the United Nations instituted the Convention on Contracts for the International Sale of Goods, which established a set of uniform rules governing commercial contracts between parties in participating countries.

New demands on contract law have since surfaced in response to the emergence of electronic business. The U.S. Uniform Computer Information Transactions Act, passed in 1999 and sent to the states for consideration, will allow states to adopt uniform laws that take into account the unique aspects of e-business. As of 2003, however, no clear international guidelines governing e-business exist. Organizations like the Business Software Alliance urge governments worldwide to develop a new set of guidelines to ensure the smooth functioning and development of this growing industry.

As much as contract law influences business and industry, business and industry influence contract law. Systems of contract law are always evolving to accommodate our ever-growing—and ever-more-complicated—global marketplace.

Further Reading

Australian National University Faculty of Law, Contract Law On-Line Information Network. http://law.anu.edu.au/colin (December 30, 2002).

Chesler, Phyllis. *Sacred Bond: The Legacy of Baby M.* New York: Times Books, 1988.

Frey, Martin A., and Phyllis Hurley Frey. *Essentials of Contract Law.* New York: Delmar Publishing, 2000.

Rohwer, Claude D., and Anthony M. Skrocki. *Contracts in a Nutshell.* Eagan, Minn.: West Information Publishing Group, 2000.

—*Andrea Troyer and John Troyer*

The Uniform Computer Information Transaction Act

Although the principles of contract law are old, debate still rages about how those principles should be applied in specific situations—especially regarding the information economy. In 1999 the Uniform Computer Information Transactions Act (UCITA) was designed to standardize contract law for products such as computer software, databases, and online and multimedia products. In particular, the law covers what are known as shrink-wrap licenses, the licenses that all users must accept before they are allowed to install software.

The UCITA was opposed by a wide variety of groups, including the American Library Association, the Association for Computing Machinery, and the attorneys general of 26 states. These groups felt that the UCITA was poor legislation for a number of reasons, including the fact that the UCITA permitted companies to change the terms of a license after the product has been purchased. As originally written, the UCITA allowed companies to deny responsibility for product shortcomings or damage their products might cause to users' computers. Furthermore, the UCITA permitted companies to prohibit users from publicly criticizing software they had bought. The UCITA was revised in 2002 to address some of the complaints. Opponents felt that the adjustments did not go far enough to protect consumers, however, and the law will be contested in the court system for some time.

Copyright

Copyright is an author's exclusive right to reproduce, publish, and sell works of literature, music, or art. Copyright is defined by law and protects both the content and the form of the work.

Knowledge before Copyright

Before the invention of copyright, knowledge was considered to be a general common good that belonged to anyone who could learn it. In a sense, knowledge belonged to the person who knew it. He or she could keep it, share it, sell it, or transmit it in any form at all. It was the form and not the content of knowledge that mattered.

The invention of the printing press led to the need for copyright laws. This illustration of an early printing press is from the title page of Hegesippus, *a book published in 1511.*

Once a manuscript or an idea left its author it was free for all to use.

Anyone who wished to profit from knowledge was required to protect it as proprietary information, much as trade secrets or proprietary processes are protected today. Material goods could be protected by walls and guards, but knowledge could be protected only by secrecy. The knowledge of the guilds, the arts, and sciences was jealously guarded. Manuscripts, maps, formulas, and other documents were protected as carefully as jewelry or coins. In many places, certain forms of protected knowledge were classified as state secrets. Sharing these forms of knowledge constituted an act of treason punishable by death.

The shift from feudal society to early modern society that gave rise to the new humanism and the birth of science also gave birth to new attitudes about knowledge. This change was connected to the invention of the printing press and to the growth and expansion of universities. With this shift came two forms of recognition about knowledge: first, knowledge is a common good that grows only through use and social interaction; second, individual knowledge creators require incentives to generate and share knowledge and they require the ability to protect the profits of their knowledge even while sharing it widely.

The Concept of Intellectual Property

While copyright laws were an innovation of the age of printing, they had three predecessor forms. One was the royal patent, or monopoly, over any useful trade, art, or practice. A second was the royal license of printing. The third was the early modern intellectual property law that began with the Venetian patent laws of 1474.

Property rights are the legal rights that govern the ownership and control of property. Intellectual property was an odd form of property in a world that looked on property as tangible goods. The appearance of books and the book trade played an important ole in shaping the idea of knowledge as a ood. In reality, knowledge cannot be separated from the active human knower. Once xternalized, it becomes information. When nowledge is externalized as information, it becomes tangible. This shift suddenly mphasized the role of knowledge and nformation as goods rather than as intangible human properties or attributes.

Before Johannes Gutenberg revolutionized book production, books were scarce, costly, and difficult to obtain. The birth of the printing press led to a dramatic increase in available books. In the 450s, Gutenberg launched his printing evolution. By the first decade of the 500s, more than eight million books had been printed—a greater number than all he handwritten manuscripts created in uman history.

In addition to the Bible and the classics, Europe saw the development of the first best-selling authors with the work of scholars like Erasmus. During this era, only authorized presses operating under royal icense legally produced books. The printing industry and the publishing industry were dentical, and printer–publishers controlled all rights in the new book trade. Before long, his monopoly created problems.

Information versus Knowledge

The solution was to switch ownership of he contents of a book to its author, granting control over content and control over he right to license production in any physical form. By granting an author complete control over the work for a limited period, an author could profit from writing. Authors thus had incentive to create new content for the growing book trade while helping to increase the stock of information that individuals could turn into knowledge as they read and retained the information that would lead to new learning and generate knowledge. Economist Adam Smith saw this as one of the few cases of monopoly that serves the public good.

The first copyright law was the Statute of Anne passed by the British Parliament in 1710. The purpose of copyright then, as now, was to serve the public good by protecting an author's interests in his or her work. The stated goal of copyright law was "the encouragement of learning." Granting copyright to authors gave authors an incentive to create knowledge.

U.S. copyright law is also based on that premise. Copyright was one of the first issues that the founders addressed when they framed the Constitution of the United States. In Article 1, section 8, Congress is charged with making laws "to promote the progress of science and useful arts, by securing for limited times to authors and inventors the exclusive right to their respective writings and discoveries."

Modern Copyright Law

The Statute of Anne was but a beginning. Today, three principles of intellectual property and common good form the public policy basis of copyright laws.

The first principle is that knowledge builds on prior knowledge. The second principle is that no one can finally own knowledge—it is a common property that grows through circulation while shrinking with disuse. The third principle is that knowledge grows incrementally. In science, literature, the arts, philosophy, and in every field of work, new knowledge must account for and embrace what is already known.

Before copyright protection, the ideas and words of an author could be used by

In 2002 a shop in Malaysia is decorated with antipiracy posters as part of a nationwide campaign to stamp out pirated software and DVDs.

anyone who gained access to them. While printing presses were controlled under license, any licensed printer could print any book for which he had a text. Anyone able to reach a market first gained the full benefit of an author's work while returning no profit to

the creator. Copyright laws secured the legitimate interests of creators in the fruits of their work. These laws now distinguish between legitimate and illegitimate uses of copyrighted material, and the law distinguishes between theft and proper acquisition.

Rights Granted by Copyright

- To **reproduce** the work;
- To prepare **derivative works** based upon the work;
- To **distribute copies** of the work to the public by sale or other transfer of ownership, or by rental, lease, or lending;
- To **perform the work publicly**, in the case of literary, musical, dramatic, and choreographic works, pantomimes, and motion pictures and other audiovisual works;
- To **display the copyrighted work publicly**, in the case of literary, musical, dramatic, and choreographic works, pantomimes, and pictorial, graphic, or sculptural works, including the individual images of a motion picture or other audiovisual work; and
- In the case of **sound recordings**, **to perform the work publicly** by means of a **digital audio transmission**.

Modern copyright laws cover all kinds of creations. Copyright covers the content of works and whatever forms they take or media they use. Copyright governs the literary, musical, and artistic content of works like books, magazines, Web sites, plays, films, and musical products, as well as artworks and architecture. Rights of performance, broadcast, and publication are linked to copyright control.

Copyright law is subject to specific constraints. For example, the contents of books can be copyrighted but book titles cannot. A title must be trademarked. Copyright covers the specific expression of an idea, but not the idea itself.

One of the interesting facts of copyright law is that the work of an author—however large or small—is automatically copyrighted and protected until it is published or made public. A grocery list, love letters, personal correspondence, and study notes are protected, along with any poem or drawing or manuscript an individual might create. They remain under the creator's control until he or she gives permission to publish them or transfers the rights to a publisher.

If a work protected under this form of copyright is released to the public—that is, published—without proper copyright notice, it falls into the public domain unless ownership of copyright is proclaimed. This is why it is important for an author, artist, or composer to place a copyright declaration on any work before it is released or shown in public. A copyright declaration takes the form of a statement of the author's name, claim of copyright, the copyright symbol, and the year of publication. If a work is illegally or inadvertently published, a creator must act swiftly to assert copyright to avoid the loss of copyright to the public domain.

The new information technologies like the World Wide Web, e-mail, and a world of new media developments place the concepts and functions of copyright in a new light. In the so-called knowledge economy, where so much business is based on the transaction and sale of information, copyright is more important than ever.

Digital technology makes easy the copying and redistributing of works without quality degradation. Previous copying technologies like photocopiers and tape recorders invariably diluted the quality of each copy. Napster, the online music-swapping service that made copies of music recordings available for free, is a key example. It came under fierce legal attack by the recording industry for copyright infringements and has been used to justify further strengthening of copyright protections in the digital age.

The 1998 Digital Millennium Copyright Act (DMCA) extended legal protections for software and content producers by forbidding unauthorized copying of digital works. In certain circumstances, making or selling devices that are capable of either copying or circumventing the protections of copyrighted works is also a crime under the DMCA. The law provides some exemptions for libraries, archival databases, and educational institutions.

Whatever its intent, the DMCA sparked controversy among civil liberties groups, digital-device manufacturers, and content users. Critics argue that the law does not merely extend previous copyright protection to digital media, but that

Copyright Registration[1] by Subject Matter 1990 to 2000
(in thousands)

Subject matter	1990	1995	2000
Monographs[2]	179.7	196.0	169.7
Semiconductor chip products	1.0	0.8	0.7
Serials	111.5	88.7	69.0
Sound recordings	37.5	34.0	34.2
Renewals	51.8	30.6	16.8
Musical and dramatic works	185.3	163.6	138.9
Visual arts[3]	76.7	95.5	85.8
Total	643.5	609.2	515.1

[1] Claims to copyrights registered with the U.S. Library of Congress for both U.S. and foreign works. [2] Includes software and machine-readable works. [3] Two-dimensional works of fine and graphic art, including prints and art reproductions; sculptural works; technical drawings and models; photographs; commercial prints and labels; works of applied arts, cartographic works, and multimedia works.
Source: The Library of Congress, Copyright Office, Annual Report, Washington, D.C.

Napster

The music file-sharing computer service Napster is universally recognized for launching peer-to-peer networking into the mainstream. While its foes argued that Napster facilitated copyright violations on a monumental scale, supporters call it a bellwether program that will be remembered as the beginning of a revolution.

College freshman Shawn Fanning began work on what would become the Napster program in his Northeastern University dorm room in January 1999. Fanning set about creating a system that would allow users to swap songs in the MP3 computer file format directly from one to another, without having to go through a Web site. Users who launched the program while connected to the Internet were plugged into Napster's central computer system, and the MP3 files they had designated to share were added to Napster's continuously updated index of files available at that moment. Napster did not store MP3s but only indexed files that were stored on its users' own computers. If users disconnected from Napster, their files were no longer available and were removed from the index. A user searching for a particular song typed the song title or artist's name into Napster's search engine, and a list of results would be returned from the index showing matching files held by other Napster users. By selecting one of the files, the user would begin downloading it directly from another user's computer.

Napster's ease of use, coupled with its outlaw status as a source of free music under fire, captured the popular imagination. The music industry, which had been steadily losing ground in its fight to halt unauthorized MP3 trading, saw Napster as a formidable threat. In December 1999, the Recording Industry Association of America, a trade group representing the major music companies, sued Napster, Inc., charging that the company facilitated piracy. Recording artists chose sides in the debate. Hard-rock band Metallica and rapper Dr. Dre filed their own piracy suits against the company, while rapper Chuck D defended Napster and rap-metal band Limp Bizkit embraced the company as a sponsor.

Computer programmers began developing other peer-to-peer networks, including Gnutella and Freenet. Unlike Napster, these systems are not owned by anyone, nor do they route files through a central server, which makes them nearly impossible to shut down. However, the systems tend to be less stable than Napster and require more computer experience from their users. By 2001 Napster had been driven out of business by legal problems, but its overwhelming popularity with users indicates that file-sharing could play a large role in the future of digital music.

—Kevin Featherly

it supersedes old copyright protections and, in some cases, cancels the public's traditionally guaranteed rights to fair use of copyrighted material. Fair use is a legal doctrine that allows individuals to duplicate copyrighted material without compensating the copyright holder if the copied material is used for education, research, criticism, or certain other purposes. The fair use doctrine suggests that such common acts as making copies of software programs to use on a second household computer or "ripping" tracks from CDs to make compilations for personal listening would be protected.

However, the legality of such behavior i[s] in fact, brought into question by prov[i-] sions of the DMCA. The DMCA provid[es] severe punishment: fines range as high [as] $500,000 and five years in prison for [a] first offense, up to $1 million and 10 yea[rs] in prison for subsequent offenses.

Not everyone is concerned about th[e] threat DMCA poses to civil libertie[s.] Analyst P. J. McNeely, for instance, has su[g-] gested that a free market will eventual[ly] determine the limits of the DMCA. If cop[y-] right protection and legal sanctions a[re] enforced beyond the public's toleranc[e,] McNeely told the Newsbytes New[s] Network in 2001, consumers will simp[ly] refuse to buy new digital media produc[ts] and continue buying older products—op[t-] ing to purchase paperbacks instead of [e-] books, for example. They will, in shor[t,] "vote with their wallets," McNeely says.

Another future battleground will like[ly] be the issue of copyright extension. I[n] 1998 Congress passed the Sonny Bon[o] Copyright Extension Act to extend th[e] terms of copyright protection, bringin[g] U.S. law into line with European law[s.] However, critics such as Lawrence Lessi[g] have argued that the law protects corporat[e] interests at the expense of individual user[s.]

Further Reading

Dyson, Esther. *Release 2.0: A Design for Living in the Digital Age.* New York: Broadway Books, 1997[.]

Febvre, Lucien, and Henri-Jean Martin. *The Coming of the Book: The Impact of Printing 1450–1800.* London: Verso, 1976.

Goldstein, Paul. *Copyright's Highway: From Gutenberg to the Celestial Jukebox.* New York: Hill and Wang, 1995.

Lessig, Lawrence. *Code and Other Laws of Cyberspace.* New York: Basic Books, 1999.

Samuels, Edward. *The Illustrated Story of Copyright.* New York: Thomas Dunne Books, 2000.

Stanford University Libraries: Copyright and Fair Use. http://fairuse.stanford.edu/ (December 30, 2002).

U.S. Copyright Office. "The Digital Millennium Copyright Act of 1998: U.S. Copyright Office Summary." December 1998. http://www.loc.gov/copyright/legislation/dmca.pdf (January 3, 2003).

—Ken Friedma[n]

Glossary

audit Review of the finances of publicly owned companies.

benefits Noncash items of value provided, in part, by employers to employees, including insurance, pension plans, and so on.

capacity Requirement that parties have the legal ability to enter into a contract and to be bound by the terms of the contract.

capitalism Economic and social system based on private ownership of the means of production. See encyclopedia entry.

certificate of deposit Receipt of money by a bank that the bank contracts to repay with interest after a specified period.

collective bargaining Negotiations between management and a union to establish a labor contract.

communism Economic and social system based on group ownership of the means of production. See encyclopedia entry.

comparative advantage One nation's ability to produce a good at a lower opportunity cost than can another nation. See encyclopedia entry.

compensation What a business gives employees in exchange for their labor.

compound interest The money earned on the original principal and on interest reinvested from prior periods. See encyclopedia entry, Interest.

consumer price index Measure of the overall price level of goods.

copyright Exclusive ownership rights of authors and artists to their works.

cost of living Index that reflects the average prices that consumers pay for common goods. See encyclopedia entry.

deregulation Process of removing government restrictions on business.

derivatives market Trading of financial assets based on other instruments; futures and options are derivatives with their values determined by the movement of stock and commodities prices.

downsizing Process of laying off employees and shrinking operations to cut business expenses.

e-commerce Conducting business transactions on the Internet.

exchange rates Price of one currency in terms of another.

franchise License to operate a business that is part of a larger chain. See encyclopedia entry.

futures Financial arrangement where those involved agree on a set price, quantity, and date for an exchange in the future.

globalization Process of world economic integration driven by a combination of free trade and information technology.

hedging Method by which individuals or businesses make financial transactions to protect against future price changes.

import substitution Encouraging economic development by limiting imports to encourage domestic production.

inflation Period of rising prices.

intellectual property Creations of the mind, for example, literary works and graphic designs. See encyclopedia entry.

interest Cost of borrowing money. See encyclopedia entry.

litigation Process of bringing a lawsuit.

macroeconomics Study of an economy as a whole. See encyclopedia entry.

monetary policy Government's use of its power over the money supply to influence economic growth and inflation.

monopoly A single company controlling an entire market.

negotiability Legal concept that requires an instrument (a check, for example) to be easily transferable without danger of being uncollectible.

negotiable instrument Signed document that contains a promise to pay an exact sum of money on demand on an exact future date.

networking Process of connecting computers to transfer data.

options Financial arrangement giving the owner the right to buy or sell a futures contract at a certain price for a limited time.

patent Legal instrument granting an inventor exclusive rights to his or her invention for a definite period of time. See encyclopedia entry.

price fixing One or more businesses colluding to charge prices higher than the normal market would determine. See encyclopedia entry.

privatization Sale of government providers of goods and services to the private sector.

procurement Process of businesses buying the materials they need.

productivity Amount of work accomplished in a given time.

profit sharing Annual or regular payment to employees based on the profitability of employer.

promissory note Written IOU.

protectionism Government action that protects domestic industries from foreign competition. See encyclopedia entry.

return on investment Percentage change in the value of an asset.

reverse discrimination Creating harm by favoring a minority or protected group in hiring, promotion, school admissions, and so on.

stock options Right of employees (granted by employer) to buy shares in a company at a certain price at some point in the future.

tort Broad area of law imposing liability for intentional and unintentional conduct. See encyclopedia entry, Liability.

uniform commercial code Set of same laws passed by all states except Louisiana that govern commercial transactions.

vertical integration Practice of combining all parts of the production process within a company.

Index

Page numbers in **boldface** type indicate article titles. Page numbers in *italic* type indicate illustrations or other graphics.